Heinrich Meinhard was born and raised in a wine-making region of Germany. A resident of Britain, he visited Germany every year at vintage time and laid down a cellar of over a thousand bottles of German wines in his home. A lifetime of knowledge and love of the subject is brought together in *The Wines of Germany*.

The International Wine and Food Society's Guide to

The WINES
of GERMANY

Herr: es ist Zeit.
Der Sommer war sehr gross.
Leg deinen Schatten auf die Sonnenuhren,
und auf den Fluren lass die Winde los.
Befiehl den letzten Früchten voll zu sein;
gib ihnen noch zwei südlichere Tage,
dränge sie zur Vollendung hin und jage
die letzte Süsse in den schweren Wein.

—Rainer Maria Rilke, *"Herbsttag"*

ᘒᕼᕼᘓ

The International Wine and Food Society's Guide to

The WINES
of GERMANY

HEINRICH MEINHARD

The International
Wine and Food Society's Publishing Company

STEIN AND DAY/*Publishers*/New York

A publication of
The International Wine and Food Society's
Publishing Company

First published in 1976
Copyright © 1976 by the estate of Heinrich Meinhard

Designed by Ed Kaplin
Printed in the United States of America
Stein and Day/*Publishers*/Scarborough House,
Briarcliff Manor, N. Y. 10510

Library of Congress Cataloging in Publication Data

Meinhard, Heinrich.
The International Wine and Food Society's guide
to the wines of Germany.

1. Wine and wine making—Germany, West.
I. International Wine and Food Society.   II.   Title.
III.   Title: The wines of Germany.
TP559.G3M45   641.2′2′0943   75-40474
ISBN 0-8128-1943-8

To my wife Alice, help and companion
in this present *Aeneid*—
"haec olim meminisse juvabit."

Contents

	Introduction	15
1.	The Natural Setting of German Viticulture	19
2.	Vines and Wines	27
3.	Grape Growing and Wine Making	61
4.	A Historical Outline	83
5.	Christianity and Wine	109
6.	Rheinpfalz (Rhenish Palatinate)	126
7.	Rheinhessen	136
8.	Mosel-Saar-Ruwer (Moselle-Saar-Ruwer)	149
9.	Baden	165
10.	Württemberg	188
11.	Nahe	201
12.	Rheingau	207
13.	Franken (Franconia)	220
14.	Mittelrhein	236
15.	Ahr	243
16.	Hessische Bergstrasse	248
	Appendix: The New German Wine Law	251
	Index	269

PALATINATE

Weinstrasse

Rhine

Albisheim ● ● Zell

Niefernheim ●

WORMS ◉

ODENWALD

Kindenheim ●
● Bockenheim

Grünstadt ●
Kircheim ●

● Freinsheim

Kallstadt ●
● Ungstein

MANNHEIM ▨

Bad Dürkheim ●

Forst ●
● Diedesheim

Neckar

Königsbach ●
● Ruppertsberg

Gimmeldingen ●
● Mussbach

Hambach ●
● Neustadt

St Martin ●
● Diedesfeld
Maikammer

Speyer

Speyer

PFÄLZERWALD

● Edenkoben

Rhodt ●

N

Anweiler ●
Siebeldingen ●

● Landau

Lainsweiler ●

Klingenmünster ●

● Harxheim

Weinstrasse

Bad Bergzabern

Wissembourg ●
● Schweigen

Scale

0   5   10 Miles

0   5   10   15 Kilometres

ALSACE

Rhine

WEST   EAST

GERMANY

● Frankfurt

● Stuttgart

MOSELLE-SAAR-RUWER

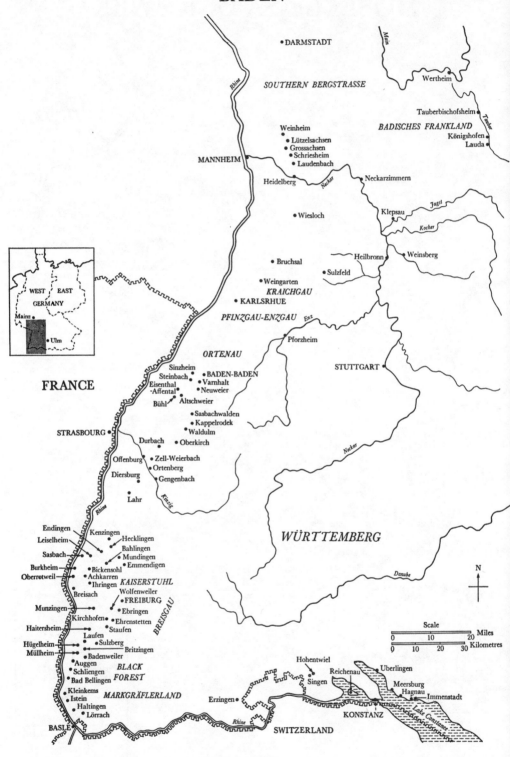

BADEN

WÜRTTEMBERG

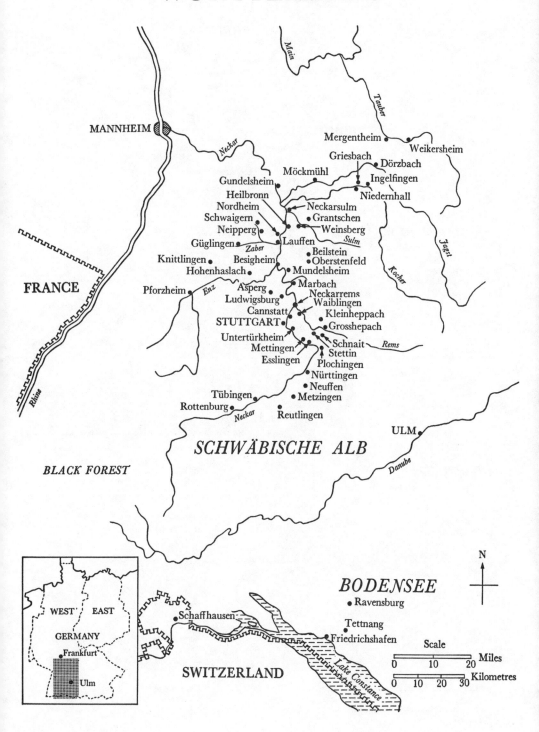

NAHE AND RHEINGAU

RHINE-HESSE

AHR AND MIDDLE RHINE

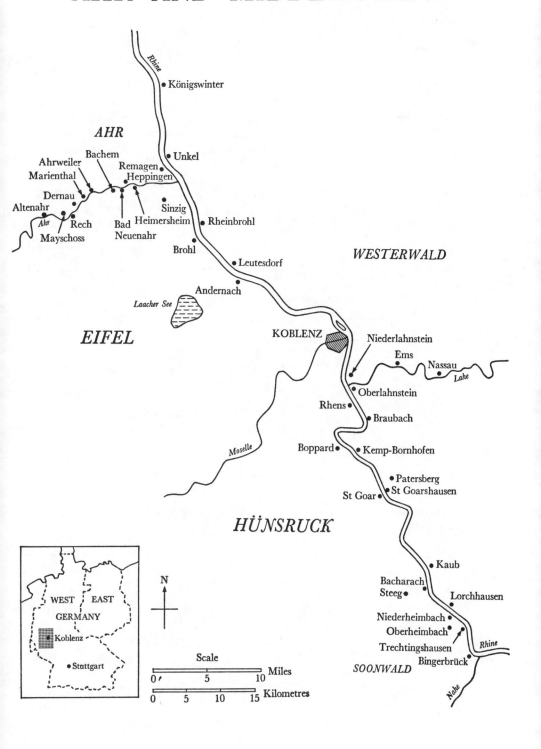

FRANCONIA

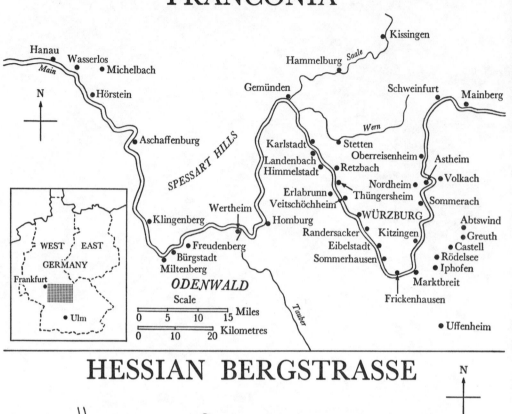

HESSIAN BERGSTRASSE

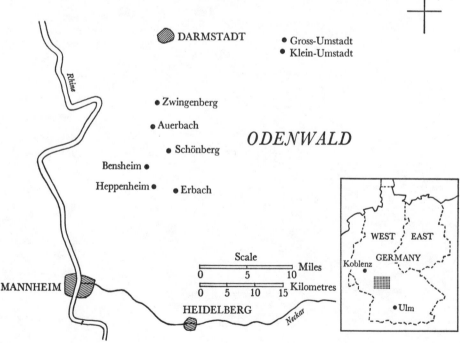

Introduction

WHAT IS generally understood by German wine comes, of course, from West Germany, the Federal Republic. All of it is grown within the basin of the Rhine. Father Rhine, as everyone knows from the unattractive epithets thrown at him, is a dirty old man these days, and most of his tributaries are not very salubrious, either. However, the wine lover may console himself with the thought that the vineyards, whether far away from the river banks or immediately bordering them, are not contaminated by industrial pollution.

Germany is the most northerly winegrowing country not only of Europe but of the world. To be more precise, vineyards in the Federal Republic stretch from about latitudes 47°30′, in the immediate neighborhood of Basel, to 50°40′, north of the Siebengebirge ("Seven Hills"), opposite Bonn. Viticulture in East Germany, the German Democratic Republic, extends even farther north, being situated between latitudes 51° and 51°30′ along parts of the Elbe River, its tributary the Thuringian Saale, and the latter's small tributary the Unstrut. Its total acreage is no more than about 350 hectares (about 865 acres), surpassing in extent only that of the smallest West German region, the Hessische Bergstrasse. However, if we exclude East German wine from consideration in a book on German wines, the main reason is that it is virtually unobtainable in West Germany, let alone the rest of the world outside the Iron Curtain.

Prewar Germany included a still more northerly winegrowing area, on the Fifty-second Parallel, amounting to scarcely 100 hectares (about 247 acres) in the neighborhood of the town of Grünberg, near the Oder River in Lower Silesia. As a well-established joke, the mere mention of its product sent shivers down the spines of West German wine drinkers. With the amputation of the lands to the east of the Oder–Neisse line, Grünberg and its wines are now Polish, and the town's name has been changed to Zielona Góra. If winegrowing were still going on around there, Poland would qualify for the distinction of being the most northerly winegrowing country.

Germany is a midget among winegrowing countries. Its vine-planted surface amounts to less than 1 percent of that of the rest of the world, a mere 84,000 hectares (207,480 acres) out of an estimated global total of 10 million (25 million acres). To restrict our comparison to the great wine-producing countries of Western Europe, the French vine-planted surface is about eighteen times that of Germany, the Italian about twenty-four times, the Spanish about twenty-three times, the Portuguese about five times. The difference is, however, marginally made up for by the fact that the average German acre is far more densely planted with vines and produces a correspondingly higher yield than that of any other country. For example, according to official statistics dating from the late 1960s, Italy produced 37 hectoliters (814 gallons) per hectare (1 hectare equals 2.47 acres); France, 40.8 hectoliters (897 gallons); and Germany, 80 hectoliters (1,760 gallons). Notwithstanding its limited production, there is an ever-growing demand for German wines. They are exported to many countries, the bulk going to Britain, the United States, and Japan, followed by the Netherlands and the Scandinavian countries.

German wines are widely appreciated as a singular specialty. They are for the most part white wines of a kind virtually nonexistent elsewhere. They are characterized by their diversity, freshness, fruity and spicy taste. They are well-balanced, relatively rich in acidity, and with an unobtrusive sweetness. They are wholesome, having a relatively low alcohol content; indeed, the alcoholic effect is only a small part of the enjoyment of

German wine. Most of them leave a delicate lingering after-taste, or "tail," as it is called, and some of them are remarkable for their distinctive subtle fragrance, the "bouquet," one of those "ultimate facts of nature" that are beyond scientific analysis.

German wines owe their reputation to a unique interplay of climate and soil. Under the warmer sun of Southern Europe the grapes ripen early, being harvested as early as in September or sometimes even before, lest they burst from their abundance of sugar. Consequently, they produce wines that are both sweeter and heavier. North of the Alps the vines obviously do not as a rule receive as much sunlight as in the warmer countries, but in return the more temperate climate allows the grapes a far longer growing and ripening period. Grape gathering extends into November, and occasionally even into early December, on an average lasting for two months longer than in Southern European countries. Thus, the vines of Germany are given a much longer time to nourish the grapes with the minerals of the soil and to develop taste and flavor substances more intensively. German soils vary in their composition, and climatic conditions also differ, resulting in wines of a very great range of diversity. Vines can be transplanted, but soil and climate are fixtures. The interaction of specific vine varieties, soil, and climate, produces wines that are unique and inimitable.

In addition to the diversities due to varieties of vines and different soils in specific regions and subregions, there is the diversity of climate over successive years. The weather forms the character and quality of a vintage. The table wines of southern countries often bear no indication of the vintage on the label. In Germany it is far more usually, if not invariably, shown, as it provides a distinctive mark of character. In southern countries the course of the weather tends to be more or less unvarying from one year to another; hence the wines of different vintages differ only slightly. North of the Alps the annual variations of climate may be considerable; hence the wines of different vintages are often widely different in general quality.

In Germany there are eleven designated winegrowing regions. They are Rheinpfalz (Rhenish Palatinate), Rheinhessen, Mosel-Saar-Ruwer (Moselle-Saar-Ruwer), Baden, Württemberg, Nahe, Rheingau, Franken (Franconia), Mittelrhein (Middle Rhine), Ahr, and Hessische Bergstrasse. Those regions which have a more familiar English name (Rhenish Palatinate, Moselle, Franconia, and Middle Rhine) will be called by the English name in this book.

English popular usage distinguishes only between "Hocks" and "Moselles." The former designation is unintelligible to the German who is not familiar with English, including most winegrowers and wine merchants. It is a corruption of the name of the little town of Hochheim, situated to the north of the Main River near its junction with the Rhine, and is regarded in the wine trade as indicating a wine from the Rhine Valley. Until fairly recently, few German wines other than 'Hocks and Moselles' were exported, but in fact wines from other tributaries of the Rhine are as distinctive in flavor and taste as are those of the Moselle, and even the wines from different stretches of the Rhine Valley itself are widely different in character. The object of this section of the book is to make known the high quality and wide variety of the whole range of German wines.

1. The Natural Setting of German Viticulture

THE CHARACTER and quality of a wine depend on the kind of vine from which it comes, the natural setting of the vineyards, and, of course, the human effort in the care of the vines in the vineyard and in the making of the wine in the cellar. The natural prerequisites for the vine to grow and thrive are the local climate, the location and topography of the vineyard sites, and the kind of soil—three interrelated elements that may be summed up as the natural setting of viticulture.

The climate, with its various elements—the temperature, duration of sunshine, humidity of the soil, atmospheric humidity, altitude, amount and distribution of precipitation over the year, and wind—is of obvious importance for the full maturing of the grape. In Germany the vine needs a mean annual temperature of at least 48.2°F (9°C), but one between 50°F (10°C) and 53.6°F (12°C) is the most favorable for producing the best wines. The most important viticultural regions of the country have a mean summer temperature of about 68°F (20°C) and a mean winter temperature not below the freezing point. Ideally, there should be an early beginning of spring weather; rare spring and autumn frosts; a long and predominantly warm summer containing at least thirty days with maximum temperatures above 77°F (25°C); a mild, sunny autumn; and, lastly, a winter temperature that only exceptionally drops below −4°F (-20°C). The overall temperature chiefly determines the duration of the vine's "vegetation," that is, the period from the sprouting to the shedding of its leaves, which should be as long as possible. In Germany this period lasts no longer than 190 days at best, while in southern France it amounts to as many as 245 days. Temperatures during the flowering time of the vine in June are also very significant. At temperatures below 59°F (15°C), fertilization remains deficient, and consequently the yield is irregular and generally inadequate. The temperature also sets limits to the vertical distribution of winegrowing. Above a certain altitude the vegetation period becomes too short. The bulk of German wines are grown up to an altitude of 1,000 feet; in exceptionally favorable circumstances, for example on the shore of Lake Constance, owing to the equalizing effect of a large sheet of water, they rise to 1,500 feet; in a very few special cases they reach even greater heights. By comparison, in especially sheltered Alpine valleys the upper limit is 2,700 feet in the South Tyrol; 3,300 feet in Piedmont; and 4,000 feet in the Valais.

During the vegetation period the vine requires a minimum of 1,300 hours of sunshine for the ripening of the grapes. Actually most regions have higher averages: The Moselle receives 1,375 hours of sunshine; Franconia, 1,660; and the Rhenish Palatinate, 1,870. The temperature of the soil largely depends on the amount of sunshine. The more sunshine the vine enjoys in summer and autumn, the better the quality of the wine. However, insufficient progress in maturation in damp and cold summer months with poor sunshine may to some extent be made up for by a long, mild, sunny autumn. The warming of the soil is the more intensive the longer and more vertically the rays of the sun hit it. Sites with a good southerly aspect are obviously most favorably situated for solar radiation and the warming of the soil and are therefore best suited to grape growing. However, for the quality of a wine the intensity of solar radiation by itself is not decisive. For the northern spheres of viticulture, frequent changes of individual climatic factors, for instance, cool and warm days, are characteristic. There, the grapes can ripen slowly; sugar and acidity, taste and aroma can develop more harmoniously.

Conditions of humidity and the amount and distribution of precipitation also influence the vine's growth. The vine contents itself with less soil humidity than most other cultivated plants, thriving on very dry hillsides that permit no other agricultural use. German viticultural regions are situated predominantly in dry zones with annual precipitations of between 500 and 600 millimeters (20 to 24 inches): the Middle Haardt in the Palatinate has 600 millimeters (24 inches), the Franconian region 525 (20.8 inches), Rheinhessen 520 (20.8 inches), and the Rheingau between 450 and 500 (18 to 20 inches). On the western slopes of the Odenwald and the Black Forest, rain is of course more plentiful: 710 millimeters (28.4 inches) in Hessische Bergstrasse, and up to 900 (36 inches) and more in the viticultural areas of Baden situated along the foothills of the Black Forest. Higher rainfall does not mean that the vine does not thrive well; unfavorable features may be largely canceled out by favorable ones. But it does make cultivation more difficult because it increases the occurrence of fungus diseases and the cost of controlling vine pests and often makes premature grape gathering inevitable. As a very rough generalization, dry areas yield better qualities, humid ones greater quantities. But in years with exceptionally low rainfall the vine may also suffer from the shortage of water.

The influence of atmospheric humidity on the vine is especially evident in river valleys and on lakeshores, where the evaporation of a large sheet of water brings about an equalization of temperature in the summer and autumn. In the autumn the formation of mists rising from the water prevents the occurrence of early frosts.

As to the seasonal distribution of precipitation, moderate rain is welcome in the early autumn before the beginning of grape ripening, and a good deal more of it after harvesting in the winter and early spring. Rain is harmful in the flowering time in June if accompanied by cold, when the tiny yellow-green blossoms trickle off from their panicles; on the other hand, some light, warm showers during flowering time may be more favorable for fertilization than dry, warm weather. Rain is harmful in the warmth of midsummer when it may promote mildew (*Peronospora*) blights, while incessant autumn rain is likely to cause grape rot. For grape picking, of course, a dry spell is needed. During late gatherings (Spätlese and Auslese) in November and later, rainy days are likely to be far more frequent than during the five-week period of the harvest from the end of September throughout October.

Wind, too, has an influence on winegrowing. The sensitive vine requires natural shelter from the hazards of cold north and east winds on the lee side of wooded hill ranges. Even warmer southwesterly winds can sometimes have a damaging effect. Hill crests on which the vines would be exposed to the inclemencies of the weather would obviously be out of the question for their planting. Where natural shelter is lacking, the vines have to be protected by artificial windbreaks in the form of stone walls, board fences, or hedges.

Within a fairly uniform climatic environment, the quality of a wine depends in particular on its local site; that is, its microclimate, made up of its altitude above sea level, the direction of the slope, and the angle of inclination of its vineyards. In Germany, wine grown on hillsides is almost always better than wine grown on level ground. Unlike France and the Mediterranean countries, in Germany larger complexes of vineyards on level ground are in an absolute minority, found only in the Palatinate and Rheinhessen. Flat sites, situated in a plain or at the bottom of a slope, are cheap to lay out and work, but warm up only moderately, tend to accumulate layers of cold air, and often suffer from winter and spring frosts, as well as from a greater infestation of fungus diseases.

Surfaces with a southerly slope having a gradient of between fifteen and thirty degrees prove to be the most favorable in northern winegrowing regions and produce the best qualities. At midday they are struck by the rays of the sun almost vertically, and therefore warm up best. Besides, they are relatively free from fungus diseases. Sites with a straight southerly direction are followed in quality by southwesterly and southeasterly ones. Next in quality, westerly slopes are generally preferable to easterly ones, although only early-ripening varieties can be grown on either. Slopes inclined northward cannot, as a rule, be utilized for winegrowing. They do not receive the necessary warmth and tend to be too damp. Warm sites may be recognized by the fact that they are the first to lose their cover of snow and therefore the soil can be worked earlier. Beyond a gradient of thirty degrees, the steeper a site, the more expensive winegrowing becomes. Costly supporting walls often have to be built to prevent landslides and soil erosion.

Incidentally, the terms "site" (in German, *Lage*; in Baden and Württemberg, also *Gewann*) and "vineyard" (*Weinberg*, *Weingarten*) are frequently confused. They are not synonymous, although they may occasionally coincide in meaning. A site is a named, demarcated unit of viticultural acreage formed by nature (however much improved by man), continuous in extent, relatively uniform in aspect and homogeneous in composition, from the produce of which wines of the same quality and taste and equal value can be gained. A vineyard is a piece of real property, a holding, whether owned individually or corporately. Generally, only a minority of sites are owned exclusively by one proprietor, or by a State Domain, in which case the wine list may contain the statement Lage im Alleinbesitz ("site in exclusive possession"). The great majority of sites are split up into a smaller number of larger, or a larger number of smaller, properties, the latter more frequent than the former. The fragmentation of sites into small vineyard plots is most extremely marked in Baden and Württemberg, where small holdings are the predominant feature of all agriculture.

Last but not least, the soil on which the vines are grown is an important factor determining the character and quality of a wine. As the soil can be adapted to the requirements of the vine only to a limited degree, the grower has to choose the kind of vine that is suitable for a particular kind of soil. The same kind of vine planted on different soils produces a wholly different wine; its bouquet particularly, that chemically indefinable substance, is derived not only from the kind of grape but also from certain vineyard soils.

The close relationship between the soil and the taste and fragrance of the wine grown on it is to be sought in the first place in the difference of the nutritive substances that even closely adjacent plots may often furnish. The vine is a deep-rooting plant with widely branching roots drawing up their water and nutritive supplies through thin fibrils often reaching a depth of up to twenty feet and more—at any rate, from a substratum upon which man can no longer exert a determining influence by soil cultivation and manuring. Vineyard soil must have a sufficiently loose and deep top layer to ensure satisfactory aeration, an easy filtering of precipitation into the substratum, and regular drainage. Furthermore, its color is significant. Dark rocks in the topsoil absorb the heat of the sun more easily, warm up more quickly, and have a better heat-retaining capacity than light-colored ones, which, to a large extent, reflect the rays of the sun. The grape hanging near dark, warm soil thus receives an extra supply of warmth radiating back from the surface after sunset.

Manuring with stable dung, compost, peat, and other organic substances is necessary to supply the soil with humus and thereby to preserve or increase its fertility. But while the addition of humus is a necessity, pure humus soils, albeit the richest in nutritive substances, ideal for water storage, and relatively easy to work, are nevertheless absolutely unsuitable for growing quality wine. The fat, fertile humus causes the vine to run to leaf too quickly and too easily, resulting in a massive production of flabby, characterless wines.

With the exception of pure humus, almost all kinds of soil are used for winegrowing, and they are all more or less suitable. The very best wines are almost always grown on stony, light, quickly warming and heat-retaining, permeable, dry soils; that is, on soils that would be of rather poor quality for all other forms of cultivation. These soils are rich in mineral content and voracious consumers of humus. The spectrum of such stony soils extends from well-weathered argillaceous slate, prophyry, volcanic rock, basalt, granite, gneiss, limestone, and variegated sandstone, down to moraine gravel, to mention only the most important kinds of rock. In some areas so-called stone manuring is practiced; at intervals of several years the vineyard soil is covered with a thick layer of broken local rock, especially in the case of argillaceous slate and basalt. The actual manuring value of this practice is usually slight, although it achieves a quicker warming and better loosening of the soil, apart from impeding the growth of weeds.

Sandy soils, too, are permeable, well-aerated, quickly warming, and dry, as well as being easy to work. Their fertility depends essentially on their content of clay particles. Pure sand soils are very poor in nutritive substances and have insufficient water-retaining capacity. In general they produce mild wines. Loam soils are a mixture of sand and clay. In accordance with the share of clay contained, they may be light, mild, or heavy. They are usually adequately aerated, though considerably damper and colder than either stone or sand soils. Nevertheless they are fertile, producing good quantities of vigorous wines of middling quality. Loess soils, originating in the dry, cold climate of the Ice Age from the fine, wind-blown dust of rock, lime, sand, mica, and loam particles, are similar to loam soils but drier and firmer, have great depth and provide good water storage, are rich in mineral substances and hence very fertile; they produce full-bodied wines, often with great bouquet, but somewhat deficient in acidity.

Lime and chalk soils are very variable. If they are sufficiently permeable and dry, the vines will thrive on them well enough. They need, however, a great deal of manure and water. Shell lime is limestone containing fossil shells and shell fragments; it is one of the best soils for growing hearty Silvaner wines. Marly soils consist of lime and clay. They often have characteristics similar to those of loam soils, are rich in nutritive substances, and if planted with suitable vines, produce good light table wines. There are, however, certain kinds of marl that are greatly superior to the ordinary ones. Keuper soils are red marl, mainly calcareous clay, a soil of many-sided suitability for light table wines, especially Müller-Thurgau. Pure clay soils have unfavorable characteristics. They are heavy, tightly packed, have a great water-holding capacity but poor drainage; they warm up slowly and retard the maturing of grapes. In droughts they tend to crack. On warm sites mildly clayey soils with a higher sand or stone content are not unfavorable for the vine, producing fruity wines with comparatively high acidity.

Unfavorable qualities of a soil, perhaps a too hard and heavy one, may be partly compensated by favorable features of topography and climate, for example, a higher situation on a south slope with long daily insolation, as well as by the amount and manner of manuring.

2. Vines and Wines

OF THE VARIOUS factors that determine the character of a wine, the foremost is, naturally, the kind of vine from whose grapes it is produced. In Germany nearly forty varieties of vine are planted; of these, 85 percent produce white and 15 percent red wines. Three varieties of vine, Riesling, Silvaner, and Müller-Thurgau, jointly occupy about three-quarters of the total vine-planted surface. The changes in their relative shares during the last decade are instructive as regards the adaptation of German wine policy to internal competition within the European Economic Community (E.E.C.).

	1962	1968	1971
Silvaner	35 percent	25 percent	21 percent
Riesling	26 percent	24 percent	23 percent
Müller-Thurgau	14 percent	24 percent	26 percent

Thus, Silvaner, the largest producer in the past, has come down by 14 percent, and Riesling by 3 percent, while Müller-Thurgau has gone up by 12 percent. However, we do not want to consider vines in the sequence of their productivity. The proper sequence would seem to be, first, the old-established natural varieties, white- and red-wine varieties, and second, the more recently developed crossbreeds, again white and red (Müller-Thurgau, now the predominant variety in quantity, is the oldest of the white crossbreeds). But at the same time we also want to keep an eye on ranking the vines according to the quality of their wines. And in this respect, Riesling takes the lead.

White-Wine Varieties

RIESLING

The international reputation of German wine is mainly based on Riesling, which is not only the indisputable queen of all German vines, but, other things being equal, produces a wine unsurpassed in quality by any other white wine anywhere. It is represented in all winegrowing regions of Germany, though in very different proportions, as the following percentages for the 1971 and 1964 vintages show:

	1971	1964		1971	1964
Palatinate	14	14	Rheingau	79	77
Rheinhessen	6	6	Franconia	4	4
Moselle-Saar-			Middle Rhine	84	88
Ruwer	71	79	Ahr	23	28
Baden	7	7	Hessische		
Württemberg	22	25	Bergstrasse	52	46
Nahe	27	29			

The genuine Riesling grown in Germany is known technically as White Riesling. The same vine is also grown in Alsace (which geographically is part of the Rhine basin), but not elsewhere in France. In Austria it is confined to the Wachau, the stretch of the Danube valley between Melk and Krems, and is known as Rheinriesling, an odd name for a vine that grows on the banks of the Danube. There are small quantities of so-called Rheinriesling grown also in northeastern Italy (Riesling Renano), Yugoslavia (Rajnski Rizling), Hungary (Rajnai Rizling), and other East European countries. But genuine Riesling is essentially a vine of the northern boundary of the winegrowing zone, requiring a long ripening period, often right into November. Attempts to plant it in more southern, warmer countries, where the ripening process naturally comes to an end much earlier, have been disappointing; southern White Riesling wines are lacking in the qualities that have brought fame to the northern ones.

The geographical origin of the Riesling vine cannot be ascertained with certainty, but it seems that the majority of ampelographers (vine experts) agree that it is a native of the Upper Rhine valley, a descendant of a wild Rhenish strain. It seems to have remained unsegregated and unrecognized for centuries in the "mixed settings" of the past; but its superior qualities seem to have been appreciated, at least locally, since the fifteenth century.

Riesling leaves have five serrated lobes; the grapes are of medium size; the berries are closely packed, round, small, and rather unimpressive to the eye, between a light greenish-yellow and yellow in color, and speckled with brown dots. The Riesling makes a poor table grape because of its big pips.

If Riesling is not planted more extensively, the reason is that it is among the most demanding of German vines in respect to soil, site, climate, and grower's care. On the whole, it prefers steepish hillsides with a southern aspect, and warm, stony, permeable soils; although hardier against frost, it is more sensitive to wind than other varieties; its grapes are among the last to ripen, exposing them to greater weather risks. Compared with other varieties, however, Riesling vines draw the most diverse extracts from the different soils on which they are planted, such as slate, volcanic rock, granite, basalt, loess, and loam, and consequently produce the most delicate differences of flavor and taste in their wines. High acidity and the most fragrant bouquet will be found in the wines grown on the argillaceous slate of the Middle Moselle, while those from vines planted on heavier soils are more full-bodied and broader in taste. Obviously, climatic differences also play a part in diversifying Riesling wines; for example, those grown in the warmer climate of Rheinhessen and the Palatinate have less fragrance and a higher alcohol content than Moselle Rieslings.

Although the life span of Riesling wines depends a great deal on the kind of soil on which they are grown, they will on an average last for six years in bottle storage before turning flat; and Rieslings from late harvests in good years can be relied upon to retain their freshness for many years longer. They mature in bottle storage mainly because of their fruity acidity. Indeed, it is often said with some justice that there are no "small" Rieslings, only too-young Rieslings. Riesling wine has been likened to a woman of the Nordic type, slow and late in maturing, but retaining her charm and attraction into old age.

PSEUDO-RIESLINGS

All local differences mentioned are physiological differences of a morphologically homogeneous variety—White Riesling. However—sorry to sadden some readers' hearts—there is one joker in the pack, the so-called Italian Riesling. In Germany, where it is not grown, and in Austria, where it is, this vine is known as "Welschriesling. The word *Welsch*, now obsolescent in ordinary German use, is, of course, etymologically identical with the English word *Welsh*, both having the primary meaning of "foreign," but in German use it denotes the Romance-language-speaking neighbors, both French and Italian. In this case, since the French do not grow the variety, Welschriesling becomes synonymous with Italian Riesling. Various local strains fall under that collective name. The official Italian designation is Riesling Italico; the Hungarian, Olasz Rizling; the Yugoslav, Italianski Rizling, Graševina, or Grašica. In Italy it is planted mainly in the northeastern provinces, including the German-speaking South Tyrol; in Austria, in Styria; in Yugoslavia, in Slovenia; in Hungary, around Lake Balaton, in the southern plains, the northern hills, and elsewhere. The variety is also grown in Czechoslovakia, Rumania, Bulgaria, and the Ukraine.

What prompted the choice of the name Riesling in the first place is not quite clear. A comparison of the ampelographical features shows that White Riesling and Italian Riesling are entirely different varieties. They are similar in that the leaf has five lobes, dissimilar in the serration of the leaf edge, which in the case of the Italian variety is much sharper, longer, and more pointed. The form of the grape is also different, that of the Italian variety being bigger and cone-shaped, the berries bigger and darker in color. Both types, however, require a long ripening period in warm locations on light and nutritive soils. The vine is very plentiful in yield, and in general produces good table wines, which, however, lack the fragrance and the fruity, spicy taste of genuine Riesling wines. They are at their best when they are drunk young, and preferably where they are grown. They do not stand up well to transport, nor do they keep long.

In Germany, Italian Riesling can only be imported with the name Welschriesling on its label. In Austria, whether for internal consumption or export, it must also be designated Welschriesling, while the genuine White Riesling is labeled Rheinriesling. However, there are no international agreements on names given to vines. In the rest of the countries producing Italian Riesling, no law requires the producer or merchant to distinguish the two varieties by a qualifying addition on the label. In the United Kingdom, with no White Riesling production of her own to protect, the wine trade need not enlighten the public that Italian Riesling is a different variety from White Riesling, because the law is indifferent to the question. Consequently Italian Riesling, or pseudo-Riesling, can freely cash in on the prestige of the name Riesling. The author, who tries everything more than once, has in the course of years bought and emptied many a bottle labeled Yugoslav (or Lutomer) Riesling, or Hungarian Riesling or Banat Riesling, or

South Tyrol Riesling. On none of these occasions has he felt that the contents had the remotest resemblance in flavor and taste to genuine Riesling.

TRAMINER

Traminer, with a variant called Gewürztraminer ("spicy" Traminer), is with Riesling in the top-quality class of German white wines, though entirely different from it in bouquet and taste. The Traminer bouquet is incomparable. Traminer also differs greatly from Riesling in quantity of production: While the latter vine produces about a quarter of the total of German wines, Traminer production amounts to no more than about 1 percent of the total. It figures neither in general nor in regional statistics. Like the Riesling, the Traminer vine is exacting with regard to climate and soil, demanding deep, warm, nutritious soils and good manuring, but thrives also on volcanic tuffs. Its leaves are broad, with three comparatively small indented lobes; the grapes are small to medium-size and densely clustered, maturing comparatively late, but earlier than those of Riesling. The berries are smallish and elongated, light red or flesh-colored, with very sweet and spicy juice. The vine is very sensitive to wind and rain in the flowering season, and consequently its yield is rather unreliable; indeed, two out of three vintages are said to be more or less a failure. This, of course, makes Traminer more expensive than other wines. It is low in acidity but high in alcohol content, full-bodied and velvety, and with a very fine aroma. It is, in fact, something of a connoisseur's wine, sometimes also described as a "ladies' wine" on the precarious assumption that its aromatic flavor is especially preferred by the female sex.

There is no genetic difference between Traminer and its more spicy variant, Gewürztraminer. Ampelographically, they are the same variety, having the same external features. Even the often repeated assertion that the latter is a mutation of the former goes too far. Either designation is chosen according to the degree of intensity of the wine's bouquet, which of course is determined by such external factors as situation, microclimate, soil, and so forth. The characteristic bouquet of Traminer is more strongly pronounced in that of Gewürztraminer, which is reminiscent of the fragrance of roses. Wines produced exclusively from grapes of the Gewürztraminer type exhibit an almost too obtrusive aroma; therefore they are often blended with wines of other valuable varieties, such as Riesling or Weissburgunder (see page 35). In bottle storage, Traminer keeps well for up to five years.

Because of its low acidity and high alcoholic strength, Traminer tends to be rather heavy in effect and a little less digestible than other wines. It is certainly no boozing wine; a hangover as an aftereffect is apt to be unpleasant. It is not even a wine to accompany a meal. It is, however, suitable as an appetizer before, or dessert wine after, dinner, or as a wine to be sipped in small quantities on special occasions. It should not be served too cold, which would "freeze" its fine aroma so that it would hardly be perceived, let alone properly appreciated.

The production of Traminer and Gewürztraminer is confined to the southern winegrowing regions of Germany. Most of it comes from Baden, probably more than 2 percent of its total production. Here its main centers of cultivation are the Ortenau hills opposite Strasbourg, and, farther south, the volcanic Kaiserstuhl hills northwest of Freiburg. It is also planted in smaller quantities elsewhere in Baden, but invariably on the best sites. Astonishingly, a very good Traminer is also grown on the moraine till of Meersburg on Lake Constance, more than 400 meters (1,300 feet) above sea level, and even on the steep, warm slope of the Hohentwiel, a phonolite cone near Singen, to the west of the lake, where it is grown at an altitude of 530 meters (over 1,700 feet), in the highest vineyard of the Federal Republic. Farther north, Traminer and Gewürztraminer are also grown in the Palatinate, mainly in the Middle Haardt subregion, but also even in the Upper Haardt (which does not cultivate Riesling), where the village of Rhodt enjoys the reputation of being the "Traminer village." Traminer is grown to a lesser extent in Rheinhessen and Württemberg, while in Franconia, with its generally somewhat less favorable climate and soils, Traminer is a rare specialty.

This vine is planted in far greater quantities in Alsace; indeed, the high reputation of Alsatian viticulture is largely based on its famous Traminer and Gewürztraminer wines.

The name Traminer is derived from the winegrowing village of Tramin (in Italian, Termeno) in the South Tyrol, south of Bozen (Bolzano). This derivation has been accepted with reservations, on the grounds that far more red than white wines are grown in the neighborhood of the village. However, Traminer and Gewürztraminer (Termeno Aromatico) have certainly been grown again near Tramin in the postwar period.

RULÄNDER

The vine known by this name in Germany covers 3 percent of the total German planted surface and 14 percent of that of the Baden region. Apart from its main Baden subregions, Kaiserstuhl, Ortenau, and Lake Constance, it is grown to a relatively large extent in the Middle Haardt subregion of the Palatinate and in Rheinhessen, in smaller quantities in Württemberg, and in minute ones in Franconia. Thus its distribution coincides roughly with that of Traminer.

It was named for Johann Seger Ruland, a merchant of the city of Speyer in the Palatinate, who introduced it from Burgundy in 1711. Its original French name is Pinot gris, a mutation of Pinot noir, the most valuable red-wine grape of Burgundy, which has an especially high rate of variability; in Germany it is also known as Grauer Burgunder ("Gray Burgundy").

The leaves of the Ruländer vine have between three and five lobes; the grapes are densely clustered, with berries of a peculiar grayish red-brown color. Not uncommonly, individual grapes reverting to the blue color of the original Pinot noir, or to the green-yellow one of the Pinot blanc mutation, can be observed on the same vine; occasionally the same grape may even be double- or tripled-colored, containing individual blue and/or green-yellow berries.

The vine is demanding, requiring deep, nourishing soils in favorable locations, preferring loess or volcanic rock. The wine is of a deep golden-yellow color. Everywhere, Ruländer wines are vigorous and full-bodied, high in alcoholic strength and low in acidity, with a typical bouquet of their own. They reach their highest quality in the powerful fiery and heady wines grown on the deep loess soil and partly on the naked black lava rock of the Kaiserstuhl, while those grown in Ortenau, the Palatinate, and Rheinhessen tend to be softer and to have a more delicate bouquet. At their best, Ruländer wines are equal in quality to Riesling and Traminer wines, however different in character.

WEISSBURGUNDER

Weissburgunder (White Burgundy, Pinot blanc) is a comparative newcomer to Germany, at present still little grown, but increasing fairly steadily. So far it has not appeared under its own name in the statistics of the German Winegrowers' Association, where it is still an anonymous item in the category "Other Varieties," which constitutes 12 percent of the total, including also Traminer and the great majority of the new crossbreeds. However, other regional statistics for the 1969 vintage indicate 3 percent for Baden (mainly Kaiserstuhl and Ortenau), 1 percent for the Palatinate, and somewhat less for Rheinhessen.

Pinot blanc (Weissburgunder) appears to be a grandchild, as it were, of Pinot noir (Blauer Burgunder), with Pinot gris (Grauer Burgunder, or Ruländer) as its parent. This means that Pinot gris seems to be a discolored natural mutation of Pinot noir; and Pinot blanc, a further discolored natural mutation of Pinot gris.

The vine prefers deep, chalky soils and a good location in warm climates. It has big, triple-lobed leaves, and grapes with densely clustering yellowish-green berries containing an intensely sweet juice of low acidity. The wine is a light golden-yellow in color, very well balanced, with a fine aromatic yet unobtrusive bouquet and very smooth taste. It is rich in alcohol and low in acidity, but ages quite well. In good years it is a very distinguished wine of the highest quality, though not so fragrant and stimulating as Riesling.

The main distribution of Pinot blanc is in Burgundy, where Chablis, Meursault, and Montrachet are its most famous local representatives. A variant is Chardonnay, grown both in Burgundy and the Champagne. Ordinary White Burgundy is also well represented and very popular in Alsace, where its official designation is Pinot blanc ou Clevner.

AUXERROIS

Auxerrois is a variant, or mutation, of Pinot blanc (White Burgundy), or, at any rate, closely related to it. In France, Auxerrois is grown in Burgundy as well as in the Champagne and Alsace. It is only of local significance in France, and in Germany it occurs only in very small quantities in Baden and the Palatinate. To judge from its rare German representatives, it is somewhat less full bodied and juicy than Weissburgunder, but surpasses it with its more vivid and very distinguished bouquet.

MUSKATELLER

The Muscatel vine, which appears in many variants in Mediterranean countries, in Austria and Hungary, in the Italian South Tyrol, in Switzerland (especially near Lakes Neuchâtel and Biel), as well as in Alsace, is very rarely found in Germany and does not appear in regional statistics. It does, however, have some local significance in Baden, especially in the Kaiserstuhl hills and in the Markgräflerland, as well as in the Upper Haardt section of the Palatinate. It has big, densely berried grapes, the berries having a pronounced muscat taste. The neighboring Muscatel wines of Austria have a good reputation, but for some reason those of southern Germany are a little disappointing. They do, indeed, have the characteristic, unmistakable aroma that reflects the taste of the berries, but they frequently tend to be somewhat thin in body.

MUSKAT OTTONEL

Muskat Ottonel is a Central European mutation of Muscatel, closely connected with it in bouquet and taste. It produces its best wines in Austria, but is also grown in Alsace. In Germany, it is found sporadically from southern Baden up to Rheinhessen. Its big-berried and very sweet grapes are, because of their strong muscat taste, often fermented together with those of varieties of slight bouquet, such as Gutedel, Silvaner, and even Weissburgunder. Like those of Muscatel, its quantities are too small to figure in statistics.

SILVANER

The Silvaner (also spelled Sylvaner) vine, the undisputed great staple of many past generations, has been dealt hard knocks by the new viticultural policy. As indicated at the beginning of this chapter, its overall contribution went from 35 to 21 percent between 1962 and 1971. It has, indeed, retained its traditional highest proportion in most regions where it was always most strongly represented—the Palatinate, the Nahe, and Franconia—and has been slightly surpassed only in Rheinhessen. The accompanying table shows its regional percentages, comparing the 1971 vintage with that of 1964:

	1971	1964		1971	1964
Palatinate	29	40	Rheingau	6	8
Rheinhessen	36	47	Franconia	43	55
Baden	6	8	Middle Rhine	4	4
Württemberg	10	13	Hessische		
Nahe	32	40	Bergstrasse	20	29

The Moselle-Saar-Ruwer region and the Ahr region do not grow any Silvaner.

The name is variously derived from the Latin *silva* ("wood," "forest") and from Transylvania; at any rate, older names such as "Österreicher ("Austrian") and Franke or Frankentraube ("Franconian," "Franconian grape") suggest its expansion in an east–west direction; indeed, there is evidence that it arrived on the Main River in the mid-seventeenth century.

The reasons why this vine was, and to a reduced extent still is, planted so widely are that it is less choosy in its demands on soil than other varieties; it is more fertile, with a higher yield to the acre; it is generally more reliable; and its grapes ripen earlier. On the other hand, it is more sensitive to a cold winter and to spring frosts than, for example, Riesling; and it is allergic to strong rainfall during the ripening season, when the grapes tend to contract chlorosis. Late gatherings of Silvaner grapes are more risky for the grower than are late gatherings of Riesling grapes.

If one asks what kind of soil the Silvaner vine prefers, one is likely to get rather varying answers from ampelographers, which, however, may be at least partly due to the varying character of local soils and also to the high variability of the vine itself. The most frequent answer is that it thrives best on warm, loose, deep loam soils, or on loamy sand soils, but that it is apt to become chlorotic on heavy, damp, calcareous, or marly ones. Others assert that it produces excellent quality precisely on heavy calcareous soils. Both these contrasting opinions come from the same region, the Palatinate. In Franconia, it is said that Silvaner produces generally better wines on shell-lime than on Keuper (red marl) soils, that red sandstone soils are much less suitable, and that primary rock is absolutely unsuitable. (As one can see, ampelography, like meteorology, is not yet one of the exact sciences.) However, all agree that Silvaner demands good manuring. The virtual nonexistence of Silvaner in the Moselle-Saar-Ruwer and Ahr regions is sometimes said to be due to the fact that as the northernmost regions they are not warm enough for the vine; on the other hand, one might argue that their salty soils are unsuitable for it. But neither opinion is entirely satisfying.

The leaves of the vine are triple-lobed, the grapes densely clustered with round, greenish berries that turn yellow in the autumn. Its wine is usually mild and harmonious, perhaps a little broad and soft, with a neutral bouquet and slight acidity. After all, not every wine drinker favors a wine with a very distinctive bouquet like Riesling or Traminer; some, perhaps even most, are happier with a mellow one. In good years and on favorable sites, Silvaner does indeed produce mellow, pleasantly fruity and juicy wines with a gentle bouquet; and, in the best years, even full-bodied, vigorous, pithy ones of excellent quality and fine bouquet. In middling vintages and on average sites it will still produce an agreeable table wine, while on unfavorable soils and level ground its wines stay small and thin.

The Silvaner vine is capable of great variability. Many natural mutations have brought about a number of local variants with grapes ranging in color from the usual light greenish-yellow to something nearer to red or even blue. The variability and adaptability of the vine have lent to several successful crossings with other varieties.

GUTEDEL

This variety is virtually confined to Baden, where between 1964 and 1971 its production went down from 16 to 11 percent of the total. Its main center, with 90 percent of the total production, is the Markgräflerland, the foothills of the southern Black Forest between Freiburg and Basel, where it was introduced by the margrave Karl Friedrich of Baden from Vevy on Lake Geneva about 1780.

Gutedel occurs in a white and a light-red form, differing only in the color of the grapes, not in that of the wine. The vine prefers deep, nourishing, moist soils of chalk, marl, or loess in warm locations, and in normal years is very productive. The leaves have three to five lobes. The big, somewhat loosely clustering grapes have round berries, light yellow-green, more rarely light-red in color, with a pleasantly sweet juice. Indeed, Gutedel grapes make excellent table grapes. The wine is light, fresh, and pleasant, with slight bouquet, low in acidity and alcohol content; it is a wholesome table and tippling wine. In most years it may remain in its natural condition, not requiring "improvement" (that is, additional sugaring). However, it does not, as a rule, keep long in bottle storage.

The wine has been criticized by some writers as no more than a good tippling companion, not a noble growth exciting the mind, or a suitable aid in amorous adventures. No one in his senses would claim Gutedel to be in the same class as Riesling, or Traminer, or Weissburgunder, or Ruländer. It is also true that if you drink it with the small, part-time producer who grows it only for family consumption, and has his supplies of one vintage running out by the time the wine of the next year's vintage is in fermentation, it is likely to be poor stuff. And naturally there are many poor sites with indifferent exposures, often, but not invariably, where the hill country flattens out into the Rhine plain. Nevertheless, wines from good Markgräfler sites deserve better than being rated as second-class table wines or boozing wines. They are light and delicate, and often delicious. They are by no means all consumed locally, but have found an increasing circle of adherents elsewhere in southern Germany; for instance, throughout wine-thirsty Württemberg, and in the towns and villages fringing the shores of Lake Constance.

ELBLING AND RÄUSCHLING

Elbling and Räuschling are varieties about which German viticulture is not overenthusiastic. Their significance is more historical than savory or commercial. In current regional statistics, Elbling appears with 11 percent of the Moselle-Saar-Ruwer production; the closely related Räuschling, not at all.

Elbling (also known as Alben or Kleinberger; dialectically and affectionately also called Klemperich on the Moselle) is believed to have been grown in the Roman period.

The Elbling vine has retained its hold on two stretches of the Moselle valley. One is the Upper Moselle above Trier and along the Luxembourg border, where the soil is composed not of slate, as in the rest of the Moselle valley, but of rather impermeable shell lime. Another refuge of the vine is on the Lower Moselle, especially in the Cochemer Krampen (literally "staple"), the bulge of the river above the town of Cochem, about twelve miles in length, where natural conditions for Riesling are equally unfavorable. The little town of Bremm, for instance, situated at the upper end of the Krampen, unashamedly admits to growing 30 percent of "Klemperich" within its boundaries. However, there will be hardly any bottles labeled with the name Elbling or any of its synonyms. The inquisitive but uninured visitor who is rash enough to ask for a sample straight from the barrel, and unsugared, will take a draft so acid that it will make his teeth ache and his taste buds wince. Insofar as the stuff is not drunk by hardy local adherents, open in quart (one-quarter-liter) glass goblets, it goes into blends.

The Elbling vine makes no great demands with regard to soils and sites, but at the same time is very prolific in yield. It has big, triple-lobed leaves and densely clustered grapes with yellow-green berries. In poor and even average vintages, the grape juice is very low in natural sugar and high in acidity. This natural shortcoming is aggravated by the grapes' vulnerability to grape rot, which causes their skin to burst open, with the result that they often have to be picked before they are fully mature. The wine is usually low in natural sugar, high in acidity, thin in body, and without bouquet. At the same time, local people appreciate it as being prickly and refreshing. However, it is used mainly for blends with wines of low acidity, or sold as a basis for cheaper Sparkling Moselles or Sekt.

The distribution of Räuschling is, or was, confined to the Alemannic dialect region, mostly between the northwestern part of the Kaiserstuhl, through the Breisgau, and as far as the southern limit of the Ortenau. In the early 1950s it was still lurking in some corners of these parts of Baden, but at the present time it seems to be virtually eradicated in Germany, although it is said still to be grown in Switzerland around Lake Zürich. Like Elbling, the Räuschling variety is very prolific. Although the vine is rather different in appearance from the Elbling, its wine is essentially similar.

It is likely that these prolific but inferior vines, together with long-dead worse ones, were the mainstay of the mass production of past centuries. Today, Elbling and Räuschling wines no longer satisfy the more sophisticated and exacting taste of wine drinkers, and are marketable only with difficulty. Even the Sekt cellarages have begun to look down their noses at them as basic ingredients of their products. So it seems that their days are numbered. They are nowadays increasingly supplanted by the Müller-Thurgau vine (see page 50). However, not a few local people mourn their disappearance; they were used to the acidity and refreshing natural prickliness of the much-maligned Elblings and Räuschlings.

Red-Wine Varieties

It seems that the bulk of the grapes grown (in the area that is today Germany) in Roman times, and for centuries thereafter, were red-wine grapes. Nowadays the Moselle is, indeed, an exclusively white-wine region. But in between Roman times and the present, a good deal of red wine was grown. At the end of the sixth century, Venantius Fortunatus, describing the Moselle vineyards, spoke of a *vinea purpurea* ("purple-colored vineyard") and of *uvae coloratae* ("colored grapes"). And as late as 1836, an ampelographer asserted that "at Cochem and within its environment chiefly red wine is grown from the Klebrot vine".

BLAUER SPÄTBURGUNDER (BLUE LATE BURGUNDY)

Klebrot, Klävner, and Clevner are antiquated synonyms of the present name Blauer Spätburgunder, the German equivalent of the French Pinot noir, the name of the vine predominantly grown on the Côte d'Or. In Germany, where the Spätburgunder vine produces 4 percent of the total yield, it is especially represented in Baden, with 21 percent—mainly in the Kaiserstuhl and Ortenau hills, on Lake Constance and the Hohentwiel, in the Glottertal of the Breisgau area, and in the Markgräflerland; in the valley of the Ahr River, with 24 percent; in the Rheingau, with 1.5 percent—mainly at Assmannshausen; in Franconia, with 1 percent—mainly at Klingenberg; and in small quantities in Rheinhessen—mainly at Ingelheim—in a small area to the south of Weinheim, in the Baden half of the Hessische Bergstrasse, and sporadically in the Palatinate and Württemberg.

Württemberg has two closely related, though perhaps slightly inferior, mutations. One is the misnamed Schwarzriesling (although this is the official designation, it has absolutely nothing to do with Riesling, and should be called, rather, by its local name, Müllerrebe, or by that of its French equivalent, Pinot meunier). The Müllerrebe, then, reaches as much as 10 percent of Württemberg's production.

The country's second Pinot noir mutation, St. Laurent, is grown sporadically and in too small quantities to appear in regional statistics. Its name is supposed to be derived from that of St. Lawrence, whose feast day is August 10, and to have been chosen because of the early maturing of its grapes.

A further mutation of the Müllerrebe is the Samtrot (velvet-red); but this is not a mutation in the usual sense—that is, a change brought about by a natural process—but a change caused by an ampelographical operation, in this case at the Weinsberg Viticultural Research Institute in Württemberg. It is no doubt an improvement on its parent variety, the Müllerrebe, but so far has been grown only in minute quantities.

Leaving the best claret aside, Pinot noir is unequaled among French red wines; and similarly, Spätburgunder is as much the undisputed aristocrat among German red wines as Riesling is among the whites. For obvious reasons of climate, the German Spätburgunder cannot, on the whole, be expected to match the quality of the French original; however, in really good years it may be equal to a good average of the latter. Wherever it is found in Germany, it is grown on the best sites available.

The vine requires warm sites and deep, loose, nutritive, calcareous, and moderately humid soils. A requirement or preference occasionally alleged—namely, level sites or level hill sites—need not to be taken too seriously; Spätburgunder is successfully grown on slopes that are among the steepest in Germany—for example, on the Ahr River, at Assmannshausen in the Rheingau, at Meersburg on Lake Constance, and on the Hohentwiel cone nearby—although, of course, such sloping sites need terracing. As its roots reach very far down into the ground, the vine does not suffer very much from drought in hot, dry summers. In geological composition the soils where this vine is grown are very variable. They are slaty in the Ahr valley and at Assmannshausen; loose, sandy soils at Ingelheim, loess and loam, limestone, volcanic rock, and basalt in the Middle Haardt of the Palatinate; crumbling granite in the Ortenau; loess and volcanic rock in the Kaiserstuhl; loam in the Markgräflerland; volcanic rock on the Hohentwiel; moraine till at Meersburg; red sandstone in the southern Baden half of the Hessische Bergstrasse and at Klingenberg in Franconia.

The leaves of the vine are medium-sized, with three or five lobes, turning ruby-colored in the autumn. The grapes are thick-set and densely berried; the berries are small, between round and oval, and dark blue; the pulp is very juicy, sweet, and aromatic; the skin contains a high content of pigment, giving the wine a ruby- to dark-red color. The wines develop slowly; when young they are apt to be a little rough and dry. Two years at least in the cask allow them to mature, but they require another three to five years in the bottle to reach perfection. When fully mature they become soft and full-bodied, rich in alcoholic strength, with a velvety taste sometimes reminiscent of almonds, and with an incomparably fine bouquet. When properly stored, their quality may remain undiminished for many years.

Weissherbst (literally, "white harvest") wines, better known in the United States under their French name Rosé, and in Germany now officially designated as Rosee by the new wine law, may be made from other kinds of blue grape, but its best qualities are invariably derived from that of Spätburgunder. Its difference from the red wine is caused by a different method of preparation. In the making of red wine, the blue grapes are crushed into a "mash" that is left to ferment for several days in an open vat before being pressed. During this process of mash fermentation, the juice of the blue grapes, which is naturally as colorless as that of the light-skinned ones, assumes its color from the tannic acid contained in the red pigment of the grape skins. On the other hand, the light-skinned grapes for making white wine go more or less straight through the press after being gathered. In the case of the blue grapes for making Weissherbst, or Rosé, the same method is followed; that is, they are pressed immediately after gathering, exactly as are white-wine grapes, and in this way they can, in fermentation, absorb only a limited amount of the tannic acid from the pigment of their skins.

In color, Weissherbst varies between peach and pale red. In taste, it is fresh and hearty. It is served cool, as are white wines (not at room temperature, as are red wines), and is suitable for drinking before, during, or after any kind of meal.

The reasons for making Weissherbst vary. There may have been a year with little sunshine, so that there may be an insufficiency of red pigment in the skins of the berries even when the grapes have reached maturity. On the other hand, in a good year the red pigment has been, or is in danger of being, damaged by an attack of the *Botrytis* fungus, which would make the grapes useless for making red wine (see page 70). Or it may be produced because the simpler method of making it involves a less complicated cellar process. Or, lastly, simply because there is a greater demand for it. By contrast with red Spätburgunder, Weissherbst is very short-lived. It is usually drunk open, from a quarter-liter glass, or served in a carafe. Only the best of it has sufficient stability to be worth bottling; even so, it should be drunk within about two years.

FRÜHBURGUNDER (EARLY BURGUNDY)

This is a variant of the Spätburgunder vine, ripening as early as the end of August, but slighter and less reliable in yield. The wine is lighter in color, a vivid garnet-ruby red. Although of typical Burgundy taste and quite distinguished in good vintages, it generally falls short of the quality of Spätburgunder in fullness, alcoholic strength, and bouquet. It is grown only sporadically and in small quantities in Franconia, northern Baden, Rheinhessen, and the Palatinate, never appearing in any statistics.

TROLLINGER

The name suggests the Tyrol, and in this case, unlike that of Traminer (see page 32), the authenticity of its derivation admits of no doubt. In the South Tyrol, the same variety goes by the name of Gross-Vernatsch, with a number of other synonyms. Trollinger and Gross-Vernatsch produce not only a good grape for wine making but also an excellent table grape, which in the South Tyrol is known as Meraner Kurtraube ("Meran cure-grape"), and which turns up again in the Brussels Conservatory Grape and the English Black Hamburgh. German synonyms of the name Trollinger are Frankentaler and Blauer Malvasier (Blue Malmsey).

Trollinger covers 2 percent of the total German vine-planted surface and is virtually confined to the Württemberg region, where its share is 25 percent. It is rather demanding as to sites and soils; it loves warm, well-protected, not-too-steep hill sites with a southern exposure, and deep, warm, stony shell-lime and Keuper (red marl) soils with a good humus cover. Its fertility is great and constant, but it is not very resistant to blights and cold. The leaves are very big, with three to five lobes; the grapes are also very big and heavy, with dark-blue berries containing a spicy-sweet pulp. They are comparatively late in ripening. The grape skins contain less pigment than those of other red varieties; consequently, the color of the wine is of a lighter red. It is a fresh, light, hearty, pithy wine, with a relatively high acidity for a red variety. It is generally of medium quality, a pleasant table wine of limited life span. However, in good years its color becomes darker, and it may gain greatly in quality, even have a pleasant bouquet, and attain a considerably longer staying power.

Owing to the virtual concentration of its cultivation in Württemberg and its great popularity in that area, it is almost entirely consumed locally. Consequently, Trollinger is very hard to come by elsewhere, and is more expensive than its general quality would seem to warrant. Like Spätburgunder, it is also used for Weissherbst (or Rosé), but must, in that case, be designated as Trollinger Weissherbst or Trollinger Rosee.

LEMBERGER

This variety, known in Austria as Blaufränkischer (Blue Franconian), is grown in Germany only in Württemberg, where its share of the total production is 6 percent, and sporadically in adjoining northern Baden. It prefers warm southern sites sheltered from the wind, but seems to be less demanding with regard to soils than Trollinger, thriving also in heavier Keuper (red marl) soils. The leaves of the Lemberger vine are triple-lobed and turn reddish in autumn; the grapes ripen late, but are very productive; the berries are small and dark blue, containing a pleasant, sweet-dry juice. The wine has a good red color, is full-bodied and with great character, fruity-dry, pithy, and spicy, with a bouquet approaching that of Spätburgunder, although Lemberger is unrelated to that vine. It has greater staying power than Trollinger, with an optimal maturity in bottle storage of between four and six years. By contrast with most other red wines, it has a stimulating effect. Lemberger is often blended with Trollinger to give it better color and more roundness, and with the milder and somewhat insipid Portugieser (see below) to improve it generally.

PORTUGIESER

This is a Central European variety that came to Germany from Austria. It is entirely unknown in Portugal, and nobody seems to know how it came to be labeled as "Portuguese." It occupies 6 percent of the total German vine-planted surface; represents 14 percent of the vines of the Palatinate (mainly Bad Dürkheim and Ungsteim), 6 percent of those of Rheinhessen (mainly Ingelheim, where there is a good deal more of it than of Spätburgunder), 30 percent of those of the Ahr region (on the less favored sites), an unrecorded share in Franconia (perhaps less than 2 percent; mainly in its western part), as well as an unrecorded percentage in Baden (in the northeast, where the Neckar River flows from Württemberg into Baden). As in the case of Silvaner, the cultivation of Portugieser is decreasing everywhere.

The vine can be planted on almost any kind of soil, though it prefers deep, loose, dry ones. It is sensitive to frost. Its leaves have five lobes, changing to red in autumn. It has biggish, densely berried, dark-blue grapes, and is very prolific, with regular good yields. Portugieser is an early ripening variety, usually initiating the grape harvest. The wine is lighter in color than that of Spätburgunder, owing to the lesser pigment content of the grape skins. It is an unassuming country wine, the cheapest German red wine, mild, low in acidity and alcoholic strength, with practically no bouquet, and aging early.

It is used a great deal for undeclared blends with better red wines, as, for example, Spätburgunder; and the cautious purchaser of the latter wine might find it worth his while to try to find out, if he can, exactly how much Portugieser has joined his Spätburgunder in the bottle. However, State Domains, which have to keep an eye on their reputation as model viticulturists, can usually be relied upon to sell an unblended Spätburgunder. Red wines without special designation are, as a rule, Portugieser wines. Weissherbst (or Rosé) wines made from Portugieser grapes have to be designated Portugieser Weissherbst or Portugieser Rosee.

New Crossbreeds

In constrast to mutations, the creation of new varieties by a natural process changing some of the hereditary factors of a vine (for example, Pinot gris, Pinot blanc, etc., as mutations of Pinot noir), crossbreeds are new varieties developed by the intervention of man applying a process of selective breeding. In their ampelographical features, new crossbreeds differ considerably from their parent varieties. By means of crossbreeding, new varieties can be developed, combining features that previously appeared only separately in different varieties, and that achieve better results of one kind or another—for instance, ripening earlier than their parent varieties, producing bigger yields or better qualities, possessing a more distinguished bouquet, being more modest in their claims on soils, and having greater resistance against cold or against blights and parasites. The development of new varieties has been one of the main preoccupations and activities of ampelography for nearly a century.

In naming the parent varieties of a crossbreed, joined by the letter x, the maternal variety is given first, and the paternal one, second. For example, Riesling x Silvaner is an entirely different new variety from Silvaner x Riesling. Even two crossings made from the identical maternal and paternal varieties—for example,

Riesling x Silvaner and Riesling x Silvaner—may result in different varieties.

White Crossbreeds

MÜLLER-THURGAU (RIESLING X SILVANER)

As the table on page 27 shows, Müller-Thurgau is now the predominant German variety, covering 26 percent of the total vine-planted surface. It is the oldest German crossbreed, developed in 1882 by the Swiss ampelographer Hermann Müller (who added the name of his home canton to his family name) at the State Teaching and Research Institute at Geisenheim in the Rheingau.

The steady increase in the cultivation of this vine is accounted for by its many advantages. It is content with almost any kind of soil—thought of course it has its preferences—often being planted on very slightly sloping or even flat and heavy ground just above the valley bottom; it is modest in its claims on climate, hardy against winter cold and spring frosts, rich in yield, and early in maturing. A normal grape harvest begins with the picking of Müller-Thurgau and Portugieser.

Its preferences with regard to soil vary to some extent with the regions. It is said mostly to prefer deep loam or loess soils, but also heavy lime and marl soils. In the climatically rather more difficult Franconian region, it produces its best results on the Keuper (red marl) soils of the Steigerwald slopes, the eastern boundary of the region, but is also quite successful on the lighter shell-lime soils of its middle portion.

The leaves of the vine have five lobes; the grapes are big and heavy; the berries are oval in form and yellow-green in color, and their pulp has a light muscat aroma. The wines are light, fresh, mild, and pleasant, low in acidity, and with a distinct Muscatel bouquet. Its acidity being low, Müller-Thurgau wine rarely requires additional sugaring and may almost always be left in its natural condition. However, it is limited in staying power and should, therefore, be drunk young, not beyond two years after fermentation. On the other hand, it is very suitable for blends with Riesling and Silvaner wines, and especially qualified in supplanting inferior old varieties such as Elbling and Räuschling.

Thus it is, no doubt, an eminently successful crossing. But is it a crossing between Riesling and Silvaner, as the labels say? Ampelographers have doubted this for quite a while, and more recently seem to have been able to prove that Silvaner, at least, can be ruled out as the male parent of Müller-Thurgau. They now tend to assume that the variety represents a crossing and recrossing between Rieslings of different viticultural regions. But its exact recipe remains a puzzle. The secretive professor has taken it to his grave.

MORIO-MUSKAT

This is a Silvaner x Weissburgunder crossing, and the only crossbreed besides Müller-Thurgau that has so far appeared in official statistics. It occupies 3 percent of the total vine-covered surface. It does not show up in regional statistics, but is said to be the most widespread crossing in the Palatinate (with about 4 percent of the vine-planted surface), probably also in Rheinhessen, and it is also found in Baden. The first half of the hyphenated name is that of its breeder, who developed it in 1916 at the Federal Research Institute at Geilweilerhof, near Siebeldingen, in the Palatinate; the second half of its name refers to the wine's muscat bouquet. The vine requires deep, humid loam soils and good sites; it is very prolific, with regular high yields. The wine is of medium alcoholic strength and moderate acidity. Although Muscatel does not come into the crossing, its bouquet has a rather intense, often obtrusive muscat scent, much more strongly marked than that of Müller-Thurgau.

SCHEUREBE

This is a Silvaner x Riesling crossing, named after its breeder, who developed it at the State Research Institute at Alzey, in Rheinhessen, in 1916. The vine makes no strong demands as far as soils are concerned, marl and clay, but demands very good sites, well sheltered against wind and frost. It is prolific but somewhat late in ripening. It is grown mostly in the Palatinate and Rheinhessen; and, in smaller quantities, in the Nahe and Franconian regions, as well. Its wines are harmonious, more full-bodied than Riesling, but with a pleasant, Riesling-like acidity and a charming, fruity bouquet.

FREISAMER

Freisamer is a Silvaner x Ruländer crossing, developed at the State Viticultural Institute, Freiburg im Breisgau, as the third crossing of the year 1916. The name seems to be a cross between that of the town where it was developed and that of the little Dreisam River which runs through it. The vine, cultivated predominantly in Baden and the Palatinate, requires nutritive soils and medium-to-good sites. It is hardy against frost, and it combines the advantages of the parent varieties—the high quality of Ruländer and the good, regular yields and relatively early ripening of Silvaner. Its wines are full-bodied and harmonious, fresher than Ruländer and with a delicate bouquet. In unfavorable years and sites, they are more like Silvaner; in favorable ones, more like Ruländer.

RIESLANER

This is a Silvaner x Riesling crossing, developed at the State Viticultural Institute, Würzburg-Veitshöchheim in 1921 and formerly (wrongly) named Mainriesling. Its cultivation is confined to Franconia, where it provides 3 percent of the yield. It is a very successful crossing, thriving on less favorable soils and on sites where Riesling would not fully ripen, although it is at its best on shell lime. Its wines are juicy and pithy, rich in alcohol content, with a Riesling-like acidity and a fruity, Riesling-like bouquet, although this does not quite match that of Riesling itself. The wine matures slowly in bottle storage, reaching its best quality in between four and six years, and with a very good keeping capacity beyond that time.

PERLE

Perle is a Gewürztraminer x Müller-Thurgau crossing, developed jointly by the Alzey and Würzburg institutes, but cultivated apparently only in Franconia, where its share of the vine-planted surface is between 4 and 5 percent. It ripens early, like Müller-Thurgau, and makes no great demands concerning soil and site, though it is at its best on shell lime. Of all the new varieties, it is the hardiest against cold; indeed, it is planted mostly on sites open to wind and frost. The color of the grape is similar to that of Traminer. The wine is light, dry, and mellow, with a delicate, flowery bouquet, which is, however, inferior to that of Traminer.

The following more recent, and so far less widely cultivated, crossings may best be noted in relation to the viticultural institutes where they have been developed.

State Research Institute, Alzey

SIEGERREBE

A Madeleine angevine (table grape) x Gewürztraminer crossing, developed in 1929. It requires noncalcareous soils that are not too heavy. Its grapes ripen at the end of August. The wine has little acidity but a rather obtrusive bouquet, which makes it almost impossible as an independent, separate wine, though suitable for blends.

HUXELREBE

A Gutedel x Courtillier musqué crossing, developed in 1927 and named after a Westhofen grower who especially promoted its planting. Grown mainly in Rheinhessen, the Palatinate, and the Nahe, it demands warm, loose, noncalcerous soils, and warm sites safe from frosts. The grapes ripen together with those of Müller-Thurgau. The muscat-like bouquet of the wine tends to be obtrusive.

KANZLER

A Müller-Thurgau x Silvaner crossing, developed in 1927. The name ("Chancellor," in the German sense of "prime minister") is meant to underline the high quality of its wine. It prefers medium-heavy soils, thrives on calcareous ones also, but demands climatically favored sites. Its grapes ripen before those of Müller-Thurgau. Its disadvantages are sensitivity to frost, susceptibility to vine diseases, and variability of yields; its advantages, a "must" gravity far higher than that of its parent varieties, fullness, fruitiness, and fine bouquet.

FABER

A Weissburgunder x Müller-Thurgau crossing, developed in 1929. The name is taken from the Latin translation of Schmied (which means "blacksmith" in German), the name of a viticulturist who successfully experimented with the crossing. Its claims to soil are modest, like those of Müller-Thurgau, but it is hardier against frost and ripens even earlier. The wine is vigorous, fresh, and fruity.

REGNER

A Luglienca bianca (table grape) x early Gamay crossing, developed in 1929, whose name was chosen in honor of a member of the institute's staff. The vine is similar in yield to that of Müller-Thurgau, and the quality of the wine is rather better.

WÜRZER

A Gewürztraminer x Müller-Thurgau crossing, developed in 1932. The name refers to the spicy (würzig) taste of the wine. The vine produces a good yield, with a high "must" gravity and an intense bouquet.

SEPTIMER

Another Gewürztraminer x Müller-Thurgau crossing, developed in 1927, whose name derives from the Latin septimus (meaning "seventh," that is, the seventh new variety bred by Georg Scheu, the head of the institute). The wine has only slight acidity and is therefore mild and soft, but with a very strong, sometimes harsh, bouquet reminiscent of both Traminer and Scheurebe.

Federal Research Institute, Geilweilerhof

BACCHUS

A crossing of (Silvaner x Riesling) x Müller-Thurgau, whose name, of course, was taken from that of the Roman god of wine. It is similar to Müller-Thurgau, but more fertile and superior in quality.

OPTIMA

Another (Silvaner x Riesling) x Müller-Thurgau crossing. It is a high-quality variety with limited yield; early ripening; and a high "must" gravity, with harmonious acidity and fragrant bouquet.

FORTA

A recent Madeleine angevine x Silvaner crossing; agreeably fruity, reminiscent of Riesling, and resembling Optima somewhat; superior in quality to Bacchus.

GLORIA

A recent Silvaner x Müller-Thurgau crossing; full-bodied with slight bouquet, neutral in taste, similar to Silvaner, but with higher "must" gravity and less acidity.

NOBLESSA

Another recent Madeleine angevine x Silvaner crossing; early ripening and with a high "must" gravity; a high-quality variety with limited yield.

ARIS

A recent crossing of (Riparia x Gamay) x Riesling. The name Aris is said to be a contraction of Riparia and Riesling. (*Vitis riparia* is the name of a wild vine growing along wooded river banks in North America.) A high-quality variety with limited yield.

State Viticultural Institute, Freiburg im Breisgau

NOBLING

A Silvaner x Gutedel crossing, developed in 1939. High and regular yield; a fruity, full-bodied wine with a Silvaner-like but finer bouquet.

State Teaching and Research Institute, Weinsberg

KERNER

A Trollinger x Riesling crossing. The name is said to refer to the pithy, robust (*kernig*) character of the vine, with its good resistance to frost and diseases. (But it may also have been chosen to honor Justinus Kerner, a physician and celebrated poet who spent most of his life in Weinsberg, and died there in 1862.) The variety is one of the best new crossings, producing a very pleasing, fresh wine, similar to Riesling but with slight muscat bouquet.

State Teaching and Research Institute, Geisenheim

EHRENFELSER

A Riesling x Silvaner crossing, developed in 1929. Its name is taken from Ehrenfels, a ruined castle near Rüdesheim. It is a fruity wine of the Riesling type, with fine acidity.

MULTANER

This is also a Riesling x Silvaner crossing, but less satisfactory than Ehrenfelser.

REICHENSTEINER

A Müller-Thurgau x (Madeleine angevine x a Calabria vine) crossing. Its name is taken from Reichenstein Castle near Trechtingshausen, Middle Rhine. The wine has the character of Müller-Thurgau, but is more neutral and with little bouquet.

RABANER

A crossing between two different Riesling clones. The name commemorates the scholastic theologian Hrabanus Maurus, archbishop of Mainz from 847 to 856. A vine of limited yield, its wine is similar to Riesling but more neutral, less fruity, and mild, with little acidity.

SCHÖNBURGER

A crossing between Spätburgunder and the vine of an Italian table grape. The name is taken from Schönburg, a ruined castle at Oberwesel, Middle Rhine. A high-quality wine with a fine bouquet similar to that of Traminer.

GUTENBORNER

A Müller-Thurgau x Chasselas Napoléon crossing, it has the character of Müller-Thurgau and is juicy and neutral.

State Viticultural Institute, Würzburg-Veitshöchheim

ORTEGA

A Müller-Thurgau x Siegerrebe crossing, named in honor of the Spanish philosopher José Ortega y Gasset. The grape ripens early and has a high "must" gravity; the wine is full-bodied, with a fine bouquet, and requires long maturing in the bottle.

MARIENSTEINER

A Silvaner x Rieslaner crossing. The vine has a good yield, ripens relatively late, and has a high "must" gravity; the wine is fruity and full-bodied, with rather high acidity.

OSIRIS

A Riesling x Rieslaner crossing, named after the ancient Egyptian deity who, among other functions, presided over the growing of wine. The grapes ripen early; the wine is similar to Riesling, with a fine bouquet.

ALBALONGA

A Rieslaner x Silvaner crossing. Its name was taken from Alba Longa, the oldest town of Latium and mother city of Rome. The vine has a good yield, with high "must" gravity; the wine is fruity and of a high quality.

Red Crossbreeds

Federal Research Institute, Geilweilerhof

DOMINA

A Portugieser x Spätburgunder crossing. Early ripening; a pleasant, full-bodied wine.

CAMINA

This is also a Portugieser x Spätburgunder crossing; slightly more acid than Domina.

State Viticultural Institute, Freiburg im Breisgau

DECKROT

This is a Ruländer x Färbertraube crossing; a good cover wine for blendings, not an independent red wine. (European vines with strongly colored grape juice, which have, presumably, descended from wild vines and which yield inferior wines are known as Färbertraube—"coloring grapes." They are used only for crossings, to obtain a cover wine of intense color.)

KOLOR

A Spätburgunder x Färbertraube crossing. Similar to Deckrot.

State Teaching and Research Institute, Weinsberg

HEROLDREBE

A Portugieser x Lemberger crossing, named for its breeder. Its cultivation is limited to Württemberg.

HELFENSTEINER

A Frühburgunder x Trollinger crossing; limited to Württemberg.

State Teaching and Research Institute, Geisenheim

ROTBERGER

A Trollinger x Riesling crossing; light-red in color, like Trollinger; full-bodied and fruity.

3. Grape Growing and Wine Making

THERE CAN be little doubt that viticulture is the most demanding form of cultivation. No farmer has to carry out so many, so varied, and such constant tasks as the winegrower. This remains true even in our time, when a good deal of the old backbreaking toil on steep hillsides and with primitive tools—like the two-pronged hoe used in antiquity—has largely been eased by mechanization. Not only modern technology but also chemistry has made an appreciable difference. However, there has never been a remedy for the hazards of the weather. The grower's success depends on innumerable and imponderable external influences, and on his constant care and labor in the vineyard and cellar throughout the entire year.

Two main methods of training, or supporting, vines are practiced in Germany. The first is the traditional one introduced by the Romans of tying them to fairly high single stakes. This method is used on the Moselle and its tributaries as well as in parts of the Middle Rhine and the Ahr, Franconia, and Württemberg—wherever the terrain is very steep and terraced. The other method of training, predominant nowadays, is to attach the vines to frames consisting of shorter stakes connected by wires. The protagonists of the former method claim the advantages of a closer spacing of vines, better exposure to sun and air, and the opportunity to cover slaty topsoil with fresh slate, which is necessary at intervals of a few years, and which would be more difficult with the wire-frame method—although they have to admit this method requires more labor in the summer. However, when the advantages and disadvantages of the two methods are compared, the advantages of the wire-frame system outweigh those of the single-stake one, particularly because a somewhat wider spacing of vines in straight rows assures a more even exposure to the sunlight and facilitates mechanical working.

The first of the vineyard labors begins in late winter, between the end of January and the middle of March. The many dead woody shoots have to be cut off with vine shears. This is the first pruning of the vines, one of the most important cultivation measures. It gives the vine shape and form, adapts it to its support, rejuvenates it, preserving its growing power, and determines the quality and quantity of its yield. Of the many shoots of the vine, only a few are left, with a small number of buds remaining, from which the new green shoots will grow.

The exact manner of pruning differs somewhat according to the different manner of training. Good pruning requires considerable expert knowledge and is anything but pleasant work in raw winter weather or in the cold and damp of early spring. After pruning, every single vine has to be bent, in the majority of cases by fastening to the wire frame. The bending causes an accumulation of sap in the wood that furthers fructification. The green runners issuing out of the buds climb into the frame, clasping to it firmly.

In the spring, foliage work begins, the breaking off of useless sprouts and the shortening of healthy young ones. After the main pruning between January and March, there still remains a great deal of pruning to be done in the summer.

After the foliage work in spring, the soil has to be loosened by hoeing or plowing, cleared of weeds, and manured. These labors, toilsome anyway, become still more arduous on steep and stony ground. On steep sites, the requisite humus in the form of stable dung and compost has to be carried into the vineyard in heavy baskets on the worker's back, whereas on more level sites it can be pulled on sledges or moved on special carts. Besides organic manure, chemical fertilizers are, of course, also spread. As to the loosening of the ground, on not-too-steep surfaces it is broken up and turned over by motorized plows, but there are slopes on steep hillsides that cannot be worked either with ordinary motorized plows or with draft animals. In the past, all work on such difficult slopes had, of course, to be carried out manually; nowadays there are motorized winches fastened with their cables to the upper ends of the narrow lanes between the vine rows that haul up the plow. Here the plowman has only to steer the machine.

There are various measures employed to protect the vines. By means of coverings, fumigation, or even heating with special vineyard ovens, the vines are sheltered against the notorious mid-May frosts. Even more than frost, the grower dreads blights and pests affecting his vines. In the spring he has to begin the work of spraying or dusting the vineyard, and this has to be repeated regularly until a few weeks before the grape harvest. Chemical protection of the vines by means of fungicides and insecticides, preventing the disastrous ravages that were common enough hazards in the past, is not much more than a hundred years old. One of the most dreaded fungus diseases is the *Peronospora* mildew. An old-fashioned spray, copper-lime wash, also known as "Bordeaux solution" from its origin and first application, is still occasionally used today. Spraying and dusting techniques have been greatly improved. Since the turn of the present century a manually operated piston sprayer carried on the worker's back has been in use; with one hand he manipulates the piston pump, and with the other he holds the spraying tube. When filled, the sprayer has a weight of about fifty-five pounds, which makes the work arduous enough, especially in the heat of a summer's day and on a steep slope.

A spraying apparatus mounted on a special vineyard tractor permits reliable plant protection, provided the treatment is kept within the proper time limits. At the present state of mechanization, this is likely to be the most widely used method.

The most modern and most efficacious, but also the most expensive, method of diffusing fungicides and pesticides is by means of a very-low-flying helicopter. Because of the dangers involved, this is, of course, confined largely to level or only moderately inclined surfaces. Furthermore, in Germany, viticultural acreages belonging to a single owner are rarely of very large dimensions, and so the use of airborne treatment is still at a somewhat experimental stage.

Turning to a different field of modernization, there is a trend toward restructuring, repartitioning, and reconsolidating the entire viticultural acreage of a locality or larger area, referred to by the terms *Flurbereinigung* or *Umlegung*. In general this does not apply to the larger properties, which are mostly continuous wholes to begin with. But most of the smaller holdings are, traditionally, by way of inheritance through generations, fragmented into a number of often widely scattered patches, often difficult of access, and interspersed with similar parcels of other holdings—a situation that contradicts economic sense. The remedy consists in drastic restructuring, exchange of plots, and merging of several adjacent plots into new units, with the result that the individual small holder gains an undivided, larger piece of land, that narrow, steep, and often impassable field paths can be replaced with suitably graded vineyard roads flanked by drainage channels, and that cultivation can be intensified by mechanization. Naturally, since plots not only are unequal in productive value but also often have a sentimental value for their owners, the process requires a good deal of patience and more than simple persuasion, involving payments or other compensation and, above all, government aid.

However, difficulties may also arise even where the growers themselves are well satisfied with the change and the expectation of the resulting greater profitability. An example is the low volcanic Kaiserstuhl hills in Baden, Germany's warmest corner, where *Flurbereinigung* was begun in 1973–74. Here howls of dismay and despair reverberate through the land from conservationists and vacationers, who see a formerly idyllic and beloved countryside suddenly made ugly by endless gray concrete walls, huge, sharp-edged loess heaps piled up by gigantic excavators, and a unique subtropical flora and fauna threatened with extinction. However, while *Flurbereinigung* is perfectly possible technically in the not overly steep Kaiserstuhl hills, there are topographical limits to it elsewhere, especially as regards the use of machinery, as everybody can see who looks at the steep slopes of the Middle Rhine region, the lower Moselle, the Ahr, the Main, and parts of Württemberg. At any rate, the process of an economically viable redivision and reallocation of vineyard sites has only been going on since World War II and is as yet far from completion.

To return to the description of the viticultural year, June brings the flowering time of the vine, a little marvel of nature but also a time of anxiety for the grower. The vine is a self-fructifying plant, requiring no bees for pollination. The slightest puff of air sprinkles the buds with pollen. These insignificant-looking tiny single buds are tightly packed in a cluster, or inflorescence, called a panicle. The winegrower calls this cluster *Geschein*, a word that Germans living outside winegrowing regions are unlikely to understand, but which may be derived from the verb *scheinen* ("to shine" or "to gleam"). An individual shoot usually forms between one and three, more rarely four or more, clusters, each having, according to the variety, up to 80 or 120 buds.

Flowering does not take place all at once, but usually starts at the top of the plant and continues cluster by cluster. While it lasts, it fills the air with an intense, mignonette-like fragrance. Duration of flowering depends on the variety, but still more on the weather. In warm, calm weather it runs its course quickly, within ten days or two weeks; in damp, cold weather it may last for three weeks. Cold rain may also cause the blooming to remain incomplete and the tiny seed vessels to drop off. The grower refers to this contingency with an expression meaning "trickling through." If all goes well, the buds begin to grow immediately after flowering. After about three weeks they are as large and hard as peas, and because of the increasing weight, the panicle, which thus far has been standing in an upright position, is tilted over to droop downward. In another few weeks the young grapes, beginning to ripen, become translucent.

When the grapes ripen in autumn, the grower's greatest enemies are the starlings, which invade the vineyards in vast swarms and sometimes manage to strip them of grapes in a matter of minutes. Simple deterrents like scarecrows and a selection of other silly contrivances are of no use whatsoever. To frighten them off, the old-time field guard, patrolling the vineyards untiringly, fired alarm shots from time to time; nowadays automatic firecracker devices are being set up that bang away from morning to night. The most effective protection is the covering of at least part of the vineyard with a fine-meshed network of nylon thread. Unfortunately, it is also the most expensive method, almost impossible to use for larger surfaces. Less serious grape pilferers are the blackbirds, which do not appear in large flocks, and voles, rabbits, and hares.

Whether foxes are habitual grape eaters, as the Aesop's fable about the sour grapes implies, does not seem to be zoologically established, but certainly their favorite provender, the pheasants, occasionally attract the winegrower's ire. Standing on the ground, the pheasants nibble at the lower-hanging grapes from below. This problem is especially acute in some places because these birds have greatly increased as a consequence of the systematic gassing in their holes of their archenemies, the foxes, in order to combat the spread of rabies. Blood-sport enthusiasts, who consider this method of eradicating foxes ungentlemanly, may console themselves with the thought that vineyards are not ideal fox-hunting country, anyway. Deer, red deer, and boar, coming out of the woods above the vineyards, are rather more of a nuisance because of their habit of defoliating the vines.

The ripening of the grapes occurs between mid-September and the end of October, depending on local climatic conditions and the kind of vine. Only after attaining full maturity may grapes be cut from the vine; at this time their sugar content has reached its highest concentration. No grower anywhere is allowed to begin his grape picking whenever he thinks fit. The time to begin the harvest is determined by a local committee, sanctioned by state authorities, whose decision is binding on all growers. During the last two or three weeks before the official beginning, vineyards are closed, and signs are posted warning the public to keep out. People entering vineyard paths at this time are liable to police prosecution. The worst offenders are often weekend drivers who stuff the trunks of their cars with loads of grapes under cover of dark. The closure applies not only to outsiders but, occasionally and perhaps less strictly, also to the owners themselves. In this case the idea is to prevent a premature harvest that might lower the quality of a whole area. Strictly speaking, only the field guards and starling shooters are allowed free access.

When the vineyards are opened again for the beginning of the harvest, everybody feels tense and full of expectation. The anxious question is whether the good weather will last. When it rains, grape picking is out of the question. In the process of harvesting, speed and precision are essential. Weather permitting, the harvesting team works flat-out, with only a short picnic break thrown in, and there are no who-does-what disputes. The only division of labor is a natural one. The cutting is done with pruning shears, mainly by women. Strong men collect the grapes from the women's buckets into large containers that they carry on their backs, often bearing loads of more than a hundredweight through long rows between the vines, up or down to the path where a trailer is waiting; then they climb up a ladder and dump the loads over their shoulders into large tubs—a procedure, incidentally, which is not quite so easy as it might appear.

When the weather is fine and the grapes are good, everybody is in high spirits. But October and November are not always a golden Indian summer, and the grape harvest is not always the happy labor that romantic poetry suggests. Often enough the harvesters have to labor for long hours in cold, damp weather, with icy hands, dripping noses, cold feet slithering on sludgy ground, and the warmest clothing penetrated by a clammy fog. Grapes picked in the course of the day have to be taken to the cellar before evening to be pressed as quickly as possible.

In traditional practice, collected grapes were, often still in the vineyard, crushed into a "mash" by means of a portable grape mill mounted on a tub. This is still often done, at least with less valuable grapes, although owners of large estates as well as cooperatives may object to it. At any rate, better-quality grapes should be delivered straight to the cellar in, if possible, undamaged condition, to go first into a machine that strips them of stalks, skins, and pips, and at the same time crushes them before they are pressed. Increasingly, the practice is to give the grape "mash," or the "must" (grape juice), a preliminary sulfurization by the use of sulfites immediately after pressing. This has a favorable effect on the future development of the young wine by preventing its turning brown and by counteracting the growth of harmful microorganisms because the emerging sulfurous acid absorbs and binds the oxygen necessary for the microorganisms to survive.

The term "Spätlese" means "late gathering"; it may be applied only to natural wine, not to additionally sugared wines made from fully ripened grapes gathered after the end of the official harvest period. While the beginning of the general harvesting is decided officially and is obligatory for all growers, everyone is free to gamble on the weather, leaving at least part of his grapes for further ripening and picking a shorter or longer while after the end of the general harvest. The grower may feel that the reward is commensurate with the risk. He has, however, to have the fact recorded at the local mayor's office. "Auslese" means "a gathering of selected grapes," describing wines produced exclusively from carefully selected, fully ripe or overripe— at any rate, entirely unblemished—grapes after eliminating all unripe, damaged, or diseased ones. "Beerenauslese" goes a step farther in demanding a stricter standard of selection; that is, overripe berries picked individually from the best grape bunches of especially favored sites and covered with *Edelfäule* ("noble mold" or "noble rot"; in French, *noble pourriture*). The discovery of the beneficial effect of the "noble mold" fungus in the vineyards of the Benedictine Abbey of Johannisberg in 1775 is described in the chapter on the Rheingau region (see page 211). *Edelfäule* designates the beneficial action of a fungus, *Botrytis cinerea*, on fully ripened grapes; it covers the grape with a gray coating, rotting the skin, extracting the watery and acid content of the berries, and concentrating the juice and sugar. The highest quality is indicated by the term "Trocken-beerenauslese" ("selection of dry berries"). This means the individual picking of overripe berries that, in addition to being daubed with "noble mold," have shriveled on the vine to a raisin-like condition.

The two highest degrees of quality are attainable only under the very best weather conditions. They require a warm, dry late summer with an early autumn to match, and a warm but humid October and November, the humidity caused by morning mists followed by warm sunshine in the afternoons. Again, the autumn mists should not arrive too early, so that the *Botrytis* mold settles only on fully ripened grapes. If it settles on unripe ones—for instance, in a rainy September—it is anything but noble and beneficial, and is very destructive. But even supposing that, in ideal weather conditions, it has done its work really nobly, it is obvious that an increase in quality can be achieved only at the expense of quantity, even though the grower does not have to throw away all the grapes that do not come up to the desired standard.

It is possible, though rare, to buy a bottle of Auslese in the cellar of a growers' cooperative. It is only the large producer who can afford to go in for any quantities of Beerenauslese or Trockenbeerenauslese, and in spite of the high prices that these wines fetch, he does it not for gain but for reasons of prestige.

And, another fly in the ointment, the mold of *Botrytis cinerea* can be beneficial, under the most favorable conditions, only to white-wine grapes, and especially to those of the late-ripening Riesling; if it befalls red-wine grapes, it destroys the pigment and is absolutely ruinous. A last observation about these peak wines that may surprise the novice: They are not more, but rather less, alcoholic than lesser wines. A Trockenbeerenauslese contains less alcohol than an ordinary table wine. It seems that Spätlese wines are highest in alcoholic content, but that the highest-quality grades are characterized mainly by their content of residual sugar, producing a refined and highly aromatic sweetness that is very different from the coarse sweetness of some southern wines.

On labels of pre–1971 vintage bottles, especially in the case of Rheingau Rieslings, the designation "Kabinett" may be found, either by itself or in conjunctoin with those of Spätlese or Auslese. The history of the former term is also mentioned in the Rheingau chapter (see pages 218 and 219). In any case, it served as an assurance of a naturally pure wine. The new wine law, which came into force in 1971, prohibits its use in conjunction with other quality designations, and assigns it to the bottom of the list of specially graded quality wines, to be followed in official valuation by Spätlese, and so forth. (See Appendix.)

There are three more names in this little maze of quality designations. The harvest may occasionally extend into early December, when the grapes may be picked on December 6, St. Nicholas day, in which case the grower will be entitled to decorate the bottles with the name St. Nikolauswein. Very exceptionally, a grower may decide to leave some of his grapes on the vine until January 6, the feast of Epiphany, called in German *Dreikönigstag* ("Three Kings' Day"), whence the wine will be named a Dreikönigswein. These two designations, although permitted on the label, are not, however, part of the officially recognized category of quality terms because they do not necessarily comply with the conditions officially laid down for specially graded quality wines.

However, the third of these wines—"the wine that came out of the cold"—has its place within that category. It is "Eiswein" ("ice wine"), a rarity produced only by occasional vintages. It can be given that designation only if at the picking of fully ripe grapes temperatures were at least between 14°F (−8°C) and 18°F (−10°C) below zero. The berries are then coated with a film of ice and are as hard as glass globules. They must be taken to the press in this frozen condition, where only the highly concentrated aromatic sugar juice is pressed out, the frozen water remaining in the press. According to quality, Eiswein may be graded Eiswein-Kabinett, Eiswein-Spätlese, or Eiswein-Auslese. Depending on the temperature prevailing at this time, a Dreikönigswein, or even a St. Nikolauswein, may actually be an Eiswein, but in that case the producers will presumably choose the latter name as the more prestigious and financially more promising one. Or he may combine the two designations. The highest-priced Eiswein to date seems to have been one that went by the name 1970–71er Hochheimer Domdechaney Riesling Heilig-Dreikönigs-Eiswein-Auslese, quite a mouthful. It fetched 206 Deutsche marks per bottle at the 1971 spring auction at Eberbach Monastery. Chancellor Willy Brandt shared one with his official visitor, the late French President Georges Pompidou, on a Rhine trip from Mainz to Koblenz in September of the same year.

The natural sugar and potential alcohol content of a "must" are ascertained from its specific gravity, before the pressing, from a sample of grape "mash." This is done by means of the so-called Öchsle "must" scale, a thermometer-like hydrometer consisting of a glass tube containing a calibrated glass float. It is named after its inventor Ferdinand Öchsle (1774-1852), goldsmith, pharmacist, and physicist of the town of Pforzheim in Baden, who developed it early in the nineteenth century. The device is based on the fact that sugar is heavier than water, and indicates the specific gravity of the "must"; that is, the number of grams by which 1 liter of "must" is heavier than 1 liter of water—which weighs 1,000 grams. For example, if the specific gravity of the "must" is 1070, it represents 70 Öchsle degrees.

The "must" of a normal harvest of a middling-quality vintage has a specific gravity of between 70 and 80 Öchsle degrees.

German viticulture is always subject to the unpredictabilities of a northern climate. There are good, bad, and indifferent years. Of the postwar years, the best vintages were 1945 (the smallest in quantity and brought in almost entirely by women), 1947, 1949, 1953, 1959, 1964, and, the greatest of them all, 1971. The vintages of 1965 and 1968 were, on the whole, duds. In a year with poor sunshine and too much rain, when the grapes do not mature fully, some or most "musts" do not reach the natural content of glucose necessary for the yeast to convert into an adequate alcohol content, or they may suffer from an excess of acidity. Such "musts" have to be artificially sweetened to produce a potable wine. In Germany, this practice is known by the terms *verbessern* ("to improve") or, more occasionally, *anreichern* ("to enrich"); both, of course, euphemisms for sugaring. However, to translate the terms by such words as "adulterating" or "doctoring," with their implications of falsification and dishonesty, would not only be altogether unfair but also reveal gross ignorance. There is absolutely no jiggery-pokery about *verbessern* or *anreichern*. Indeed, it would be quite wrong to speak of such wines in condescending terms at all. The practice is permitted within strict limits by the law, which lays down not only the maximum amount of additional sugar but also the span of time within which it is allowed.

The process consists of adding dry sugar, or a sugar solution, not to the wine, but to the "must" before fermentation. The extraneous sugar combines with the grape sugar, and this, as an entity, is split up into alcohol and carbon dioxide by the process of fermentation. In this way, a wine can be produced that in alcohol, sugar, and acid content more or less equals a natural wine produced from the same site in a better vintage. The basic objective of the addition of extraneous sugar is not to make the wine sweeter, but to raise its alcoholic content, which in turn will enhance its roundness and fruitiness and, above all, increase its stability. It takes an exceptional palate to tell a properly improved wine developed in a good cellar from a natural one. Sugaring within legally permitted limits makes no difference to taste. Nor can it be detected by chemical analysis.

The practice of additional sugaring is by no means confined to Germany. The French had started it before the Germans even thought of it. They have a more elegant word for it, preferring *chaptalisation* to plain *sucrage*, the former word having the advantage of being understood by only a few people outside France.

The sweetness of a wine may be increased without the addition of extraneous sugar. Natural wines contain a certain proportion of unfermented sugar. They may—or may not—be *durchgegoren* ("fermented right through"), a very important difference. In the case of a very good "must," the natural sugar content is so high that it cannot ferment into alcohol without leaving a considerable amount of residual sugar in the wine, as the yeast producing fermentation stops acting when a certain level of alcohol has been reached. In this case, the process of fermentation is terminated naturally; the wine is fermented right through and still retains a high degree of natural sugar. This is the *Restsüsse* ("residual sweetness"), welcome to the majority of German drinkers.

On the other hand, the cellar master may have in his casks a still fermenting "must," promising a wine with a good natural-sugar content and corresponding moderate acidity. He may consider that if he were to allow fermentation to go through, he would get a wine of high alcohol content but a little deficient in sweetness, whereas if he stopped it he would get a sweeter yet still sufficiently alcoholic wine. If he interrupts fermentation prematurely before it stops by itself, he artificially interferes with a natural process; the wine is not fermented right through, and purists might object.

The quality of a wine may also be heightened by blending in order to obtain a more palatable product. There is a good deal of ignorance about this. Many people who accept the blending of teas, coffees, tobaccos, or other stimulants as a matter of course, shrink back from the very idea of blending wines. There are, of course, a great many fine wines from various winegrowing regions and particular sites within them that are so independent and so unmistakable in quality that in their case a blending could not result in an enhancement of quality; on the contrary, they would lose the charming differences of taste and bouquet that characterize them. On the other hand, the word *blending* is often misunderstood. It has nothing to do with the admixture of any undefinable ingredients, as is often assumed. The consumer is protected against this by strict provisions of the law.

Wine is allowed to be blended exclusively with wine. Moreover, the blend must be superior in quality and balance to the wines of which it is composed. Unfavorable weather conditions may produce a wine that by itself does not have a satisfactory taste and bouquet. One wine may lack spiciness; another, sweetness; a third, a fruity acidity. These disadvantages are skillfully balanced in the cellar by a harmonious blending, so that the compounded wine makes up the deficiencies in taste of its parts. The simplest case would be to blend two wines from the same site but of different vintages; for instance, one from a hot, dry year that has abundant alcoholic and sugar content but insufficient acidity with another from a poor year that is somewhat lacking in alcohol and sugar but has plenty of acidity. However, a blend may contain more than two parts, from different localities—even from different regions—as long as all are German wines. Before the new wine law came into force in 1971, the name of the blend was determined by that of the locality that had contributed at least two-thirds of the total, leaving its predominant stamp on the general character of the product. It could also be described as a natural wine if none of its parts had been artificially sugared; and it could even be described as a Spätlese or Auslese, provided that all of its parts had a claim to these special quality designations.

The proportions of blends of wines of different names have been drastically narrowed down and precisely limited by the new wine law. It provides that a narrower geographical designation than Deutsch can be given only when at least three-quarters of the total amount comes from the locality or area whose name it bears, and that the rest must be of equal value and must be derived from the same viticultural region. The only exceptions to this rule are wines belonging to the Tafelwein (Table Wine) category, which are allowed to contain portions coming from two or more different regions. Thus the new law has regulated blending in such a way that the consumer can recognize from the label whether the wine comes from a definitely limited site, or is a blend of produce from within a larger area within the same region—or, generally, from one and the same region—or from two or more regions. The label also indicates whether the wine has been made from a single grape variety or from a blend of two or more varieties. As an example, a Gewürztraminer, whose bouquet is often found to be too obtrusive and in need of toning down, may be blended with a Riesling or Weissburgunder of equal quality. What remains disallowed is a blending of red and white wines. (See Appendix for a fuller explanation of the new wine law.)

Having discussed the special needs and tasks of cellar technique, we may now concentrate on an account of the ordinary processes of cellar treatment.

Wine making, or vinification, denotes the conversion of grape juice, or "must," into alcoholic wine by fermentation. It is a comprehensive term, including the whole of the cellar treatment from the delivery of the harvested grapes to the storage of the bottled wine. The technology of cellar work is an applied science in its own right, and can be touched upon here only in broad outline. The traditional huge and often picturesquely carved wooden winepresses of the past, which were worked by manual labor, have been museum pieces for a long time. They are now generally replaced by mechanical presses of various systems and designs. There are comparatively small vertical hydraulic presses consisting of wooden slats joined together cylindrically—already old-fashioned but still widely used, especially by small producers—much larger horizontal hydraulic presses of stainless steel, and the increasingly popular pneumatic horizontal press. The latter consists of a large thick-walled rubber hose placed inside the contrivance and inflated with compressed air so that the surrounding grape mash is squeezed outward against the stainless-steel wall of a revolving cylinder perforated by a multiplicity of slits.

On the other hand, oaken wine casks, used for both fermentation and storage, in larger or smaller sizes, slightly varying in shape from one region to another and often beautifully carved, are still very much in evidence. In larger cellarage works with their multifarious gadgetry, huge cylindrical glass- or enamel-lined metal tanks with much higher capacities than the oaken casks, as well as rectangular concrete containers, are the dominant features of the scene. The fermentation cellar, storage cellar, and bottle cellar are always separate.

The "must" is drawn off from the winepress into the fermentation casks—or, nowadays, more frequently into tanks—where after a few days a noisy bubbling and rumbling indicates the beginning of fermentation. The process of fermentation was known to the ancient world, but its true nature was revealed only as late as 1860, by the fundamental research carried out by Louis Pasteur. He proved that fermentation does not take place if the ferments already present are killed off by heating (pasteurizing) and the access of new fermenting agents to the "must" is prevented by secure, sterilized plugging. Fermentation is caused by microscopically small unicellular yeast fungi that are supplied by nature, deposited on the grape berries by wind and insects. As soon as they come into contact with the sugar contained in the "must," they set to work splitting it into alcohol and carbon dioxide.

Fermentation receptacles are not tightly closed. At the top of a cask is a funnel-shaped spout filled with water and covered with a cap, allowing the carbon dioxide gases to escape and preventing the access of additional oxygen to the "must."

Without an outlet of this kind the cask would burst. In high-pressure tanks carbon dioxide cannot, of course, freely escape in the same manner; here the cellar master has to regulate the pressure, intensity, and duration of fermentation as well as the unfermented sugar content of the young wine.

The quality of the wine and its alcoholic content depend, of course, on the degree of ripeness of the grapes. The riper they are, the higher their content of grape sugar. And when the yeast fungi have more grape sugar to play with, they can produce correspondingly more alcohol. After having reached a certain level of alcohol, a volume ratio of between 12 and, at the most, 15 percent, fermentation comes to a standstill. When the yeast fungi have finished their work, they drop to the bottom of the cask to form a lees. Sugar still present in the turbid liquid remains unfermented, as a residual sweetness. The warmer the contents of the receptacle during fermentation, the more uncontrolled and impetuous the fermenting process will be—"stormy" fermentation, as it is called. Therefore, the process has to be restrained by a low cooling of the "must" in order to delay complete fermentation to up to three or four weeks. At low temperatures bouquet substances and carbonic acid remain better preserved, and the wine will be fresher, more lively, and more resistant to aging. The young wine emerging when fermentation has reached its highest point—usually four days after its beginning—is known as Federweisser ("feather-white"), or Sauser ("rusher" or "whizzer"—if such words may be coined), or by some other local name. The stuff is still muddy with yeast and fizzy with carbonic acid, but nevertheless is a highly popular beverage in most winegrowing parts.

A good deal still remains to be done before the just-fermented turbid liquid turns into a clear wine. As described above, when the yeast fungi have finished converting the grape sugar into alcohol, they precipitate to the bottom of the cask as a lees. A few weeks after the beginning of fermentation, the upper and larger part of the cask is filled with the still-muddy young wine, while the greater part of the no longer active yeast forms a thick sediment below. Thus, sometime after fermentation has ceased, the young wine has to be "racked off," that is, drawn from the lees by transferring it to a second cask. A cask has a bunghole at least six inches from the bottom, high enough to be above the yeasty sediment. The young wine is pumped through this hole into the top opening of the other cask, leaving the greater part of the lees behind in the original fermentation cask. Racking may take place in late November or early December. But the wine is still not entirely clarified; remains of yeast and other turbid particles—*Trübstoffe*, as the cellarman calls them—have again settled down or are still floating within it. These impurities remaining during the winter months require a second racking to follow in the early spring.

For the elimination of these impurities, there exist old household remedies and modern procedures referred to as "fining" and "blue fining," terms meaning simply the clearing of the wine by the application of one or another chemical method. An old-fashioned means is isinglass, a semitransparent, gelatinous substance, which is shredded and strewn on top of the wine in the cask. Here it forms a kind of film, which, being heavier than the wine, slowly sinks to the bottom, taking the impurities with it. Other means of fining are absorptive kaolin clay or ground charcoal, which combine with the impurities and draw them to the bottom. After their application the wine, of course, has to be racked again. These more or less time-honored procedures of chemical fining are, unfortunately, also very time-consuming, often involving repeated rackings until all impurities have been eliminated. Many cellars of the larger wine-making enterprises therefore employ such physical means of clarifying wine as powerful sterilized filtration or centrifuging apparatuses or special separators that fling out all ingredients heavier than the wine itself.

Modern cellar techniques make it possible to bottle a germ-proofed wine that has a long storing stability. To do this, bottles and corks have to be sterilized. Since, however, the cork is not absolutely impermeable to air—and thus to germs—the cellar master adds a minimal dosage of sulfurous acid to the wine—a precaution that has been practiced since antiquity. This addition, owing to the reductive effect of sulfur, serves to keep the wine healthy, fresh, and light-colored. Unsulfurized wines tend to have a stale, insipid taste, and to age and change color prematurely. The amount of sulfur permitted by the wine law is so slight that it can neither be perceived by taste and smell nor affect the human organism injuriously. Sulfurization is also used for empty casks, which are kept hygienically clean by burning sulfured wicks in them; and the same is done in the case of only partly filled casks, for the purpose of using up any oxygen left in the empty space above the liquid.

When the wine is left to itself in the storage cask or tank, natural changes take place within it, the sum of which is usually called its *Ausbau,* meaning its maturing or gradual completion to its optimal condition. How long a wine is left in the storage cask depends on a series of factors. Generally speaking, wines are bottled much earlier nowadays than they were in the past, when they were customarily kept in the cask for years. Compared with a metal tank, a wooden cask is, of course, not absolutely airtight. *Ausbau* takes place more quickly in the wooden cask because it can take up oxygen through the pores of the wood. The metal tank is preferred for longer storing because it preserves the wine better, keeping it fresher and more sparkling. Table wines may never see a cask from the inside. They tend to be kept in the tank for only half a year or a little more, better-quality wines for a year or more, while the more valuable ones may have a year or two of cask storage after previous tank storage.

Modern cellar techniques ensure that bottled wine keeps in good condition for years, does not become turbid, remains free of flocculence, and does not start a secondary fermentation. Nevertheless, the bottled wine remains alive—indeed, improves—at least for a number of years. It is the tail end of maturing that takes place in the bottle. The wine becomes more harmonious in the course of time and gradually assumes a certain *Firne*—meaning a peak condition of aging—which tends to be especially appreciated by the older age groups of wine connoisseurs. At the same time its color becomes somewhat darker. This is a sign of slow oxydizing; that is, certain minerals in it combine with the oxygen, which penetrates through the cork in minute quantities. Another reason why the wine tastes more rounded and balanced after a certain period of bottle storage is that its acidity content has shifted chemically. This may go so far that wine stones, that is, potassium salt crystals of tartaric acid, are deposited on the lower end of the cork and/or the bottom of the bottle. They are absolutely neutral in taste and harmless to health. Far from being a sign of deterioration, they are rather one of quality, revealing that it is a good old wine that has matured slowly and has been treated with care in the cellar.

What is the best age for wine to be drunk? As a rough simplification, a Spätlese or Auslese keeps longer than an ordinary wine made from grapes picked at the normal harvesting time, and a good Beerenauslese or Trockenbeerenauslese may, with luck, even become a centenarian before deteriorating. Every wine has its successive phases of life—youth, maturity, and age. Light table and ordinary quality wines without much body should be drunk when young and should not be stored for more than two or at most three years. Quality wines such as Kabinett are good for between two and eight years, Spätlese can be relied upon to keep in the best condition for up to ten years, Auslese for up to fifty, Beerenauslese and Trockenbeerenauslese for up to a hundred and more.

Of course, their optimal condition is largely dependent on such factors as vintage year, viticultural region, vine variety, and cellar treatment, but in general it may be said that full, sweet maturity and high fruity acidity are the best prerequisites for long durability. If you should be fortunate enough to be able to purchase some bottles of Rheingau Riesling Beerenauslese or Trockenbeerenauslese of a really first-class vintage, the best thing to do with them would be to bequeath them to your grandchildren, with the proviso that they enjoy them in their old age, preferably on the day of their golden wedding anniversary.

German white wine is normally found in long-necked, flute-shaped brown bottles containing 0.7 liter; only the wines of the Moselle-Saar-Ruwer region appear in green bottles of the same shape and size. The bulgy "Bocksbeutel" bottle is considered a privilege of Franconian wines, but may also be used, as a special concession, for those from a few places in northern Baden. The "open" wines retailed in restaurants or hotels come in 1-liter bottles. Red wines nowadays are found mostly in brown bottles indistinguishable from those used for white wines. The cylindrical, short-necked Bordeaux bottle in which red wines appeared in the past has become rare, as has the more bulgy Burgundy bottle.

In addition to the ordinary label, bottles may also have special seals attesting to the quality of the wine. The most usual one is the Deutsches Weinsiegel in red and black, showing the figure of Bacchus holding a thyrsus staff. The Diabetiker Weinsiegel (for wines containing less than 8 grams of sugar per liter) is similar, but is yellow instead of red. Both are awarded by the Deutsche Landwirtschafts-Gesellschaft, or DLG (German Agricultural Society), which has the wines tested appropriately. The Deutsches Weinsiegel can be applied for by producers of any German wine, and does not exclude "improved" wines as long as they conform to the general conditions. There are further regional quality signs, which are more exacting in their stipulations, for instance, in demanding a really above-average quality and excluding "improved" wines. The best-known example is the Gütezeichen ("Quality sign") awarded by the Baden Winegrowers' Association.

However, while such seals are certainly meant to, and generally do, protect the purchaser, one may find that State Domains, large private producers, and even growers' cooperatives apparently do not bother to apply for such awards. They seem to think, often quite rightly, that their products have no need for any additional paper decoration stuck on the bottle. Moreover, the new German wine law with its stringent conditions demanding that the consumer receive a perfect impression of the quality of the wine straight from the label makes any additional assurances of quality increasingly superfluous.

At home, white wine is best stored in a dark, cool room— best of all, of course, in a proper wine cellar—with, if possible, a more or less constant temperature of between 46°F (8°C) and 53.6°F (12°C). Red wines may also be stored in a dark place at ordinary room temperature. But whether white or red, wine likes light as little as, or even less than, it does neighboring perishable victuals or any objects emitting a sharp, penetrating smell. The wine inhales through the cork and may take on extraneous and unpleasant smells. And the most important point: Bottles should never be kept standing up, but always in a horizontal or slightly reclining position—best of all, in proper wine bins—so that the bottom end of the cork remains immersed in and kept moist and resilient by the liquid.

When putting the bottle upon the table, the temperature should be treated delicately. White wine should be drunk at the recommended storage temperature; on a very warm day, half an hour or a little more in the refrigerator may be permissible, but to keep it there for hours or even days is rank barbarism, as is the use of an ice bucket at the table, because if served too cold, the wine loses its bouquet. If the storage temperature should be too low for red wine, it should on no account be brought up too suddenly, for instance, by putting the bottles in hot water, in front of an open fire, or too near a radiator. It should be drunk at ordinary room temperature, 60.8°F (16°C) to 64.4°F (18°C), or even a little higher. This is best achieved by placing the bottle in the room several hours before opening it.

4. A Historical Outline

IT IS a time-honored commonplace that the Romans were the tutors of the Germans in the cultivation of the vine. This is true in the general sense that it was predominantly the Romans who transmitted viticulture to the transalpine countries; not in the literal sense that from the beginning of their contact the ancient Germans were the viticultural pupils of Roman colonists directly. It was no doubt largely from adjacent, later subjected and eventually absorbed, more or less Romanized Celts as mediators that the Germans learned the skills of grape growing.

A divergent view held by some authors assumes that viticulture spread through Gaul and eventually reached the left bank of the Rhine without the intervention of the Romans; indeed, long before their appearance in Gaul. This view is based on the colonizing activities of the Phocaean Greeks who settled on the coast of southern Gaul and founded Massilia (Marseilles) about 600 B.C. However, there is no evidence whatever of viticulture in the northern half of Gaul before Caesar's time. In whichever direction Greek viticulture may have spread from the Marseilles neighborhood, it does not seem to have advanced northward to any great extent during the centuries preceding the Roman conquest.

In earlier times itinerant tradesmen from Italy bartered their homegrown produce to the Celtic and Germanic barbarians, thereby also spreading its Latin name. As an early loanword, the Latin *vinum* passed into all Romance, Germanic,

Baltic, and Slavonic languages. How great the demand for wine seems to have been becomes evident from a possibly somewhat exaggerated comment that has reached us at secondhand from the writings of Posidonius (c. 100 B.C.), telling us that "many Italian traders carry the wine on ships over navigable rivers or on wagons through the plains, bartering a jar of wine for a slave." Two centuries later, Tacitus tells us that the Germanic tribes on the right bank of the Rhine bartered for wine with foreign traders. This was probably a luxury that only wealthy chiefs could afford. The ordinary heathen Germans, like their Celtic neighbors, used to cheer or fuddle their brains with mead—grain fermented with honey. The Celtic Nervii and the Germanic Suevi, according to Caesar, prohibited the importation of wine altogether on the grounds that it was a means of sapping their manliness and undermining their warlike strength. They may also have found the price—a slave for a jar of wine—a trifle steep.

For most of the nearly five centuries of Roman rule, the Rhine was the frontier of the empire, and the Rhine was also, broadly speaking, the border between Germanic and Celtic populations, though along its upper reaches the latter extended far to the east of the river. In the turbulent conditions before and during Caesar's time, when many Germanic peoples moved, in intermittent and slow migrations, westward and southward in search of new land, agriculture was more or less itinerant and probably confined to the growing of summer corn; the tribes generally cultivated the land during intervals between expansionist movements. In 58 B.C., Caesar defeated a large invading German army under Ariovistus in Alsace and threw most of it back over the Rhine. The writer Varro, in a treatise on agriculture, records the observations of a senior officer in Caesar's army, who, on approaching the Rhine with his unit, found himself in parts "where neither vines nor olive trees nor fruit trees were grown." Tacitus, writing about 150 years later, when the German tribes had already become a good deal more stable, confirms Caesar's opinion that the mainstay of Germanic economy was cattle husbandry, that free men had no taste for agriculture, which they left to women, oldsters, and slaves, and that fruit trees, and horticulture generally, were conspicuous by their absence. Now, it is obvious that this pattern of life, with its rudimentary agriculture, migratory tendencies, or at least restlessness, is wholly incompatible with the cultivation of the vine, which demands an absolutely sedentary way of life and involves the utmost care for the future with the planting of the vines and their nurture over the years until they bear their first grapes.

From Rome, provincial viticulture was discouraged as far as possible, obviously in the interest of Italian landowners and exporters. Cicero, about the middle of the first century B.C., refers to an old decree prohibiting the cultivation of olive trees and vines by the transalpine peoples. This decree did not, however, apply to the immediate environment of Massilia. Nor could it be enforced elsewhere. This can best be seen from the writers Pliny and Columella, according to whom Gaul, in the first century A.D., was self-sufficient in wine production, planting its own varieties of vine, competing with and even exporting to Italy. Among the wines of Gaul, Pliny mentions the Allobrogian, named after the Allobroges, the tribe occupying what later became known as Burgundy. Another famous wine of that time was the Biturigian, named after the Bituriges, who lived in the vicinity of the present Bordeaux. Toward the end of the first century, winegrowing appears to have increased so much at the expense of corngrowing that the emperor Domitian ordered the destruction of the greater part of the vineyards outside Italy, a decree that again proved ineffectual. It was much later, under the emperor Probus (A.D. 276–282), that prohibitions were officially repealed; according to his biographer, he "from now on permitted all the Gauls and the Spaniards as well as the Britons to have vines and to prepare wine." To permit officially what had been practiced more or less freely for more than two hundred years may seem a little superfluous, though, of course, making it legal is likely to have given viticulture further encouragement. It also seems that the new edict promoted the settlement of army veterans who had viticultural experience on vineyards in the Rhine and Moselle valleys as well as elsewhere.

It was in the first century A.D. that vine cultivation reached the left bank of the Rhine and the Moselle—at the time, of course, still part of Gaul and inhabited by people of Celtic stock. The archaeological evidence for this dating is a grave at Kobern on the Lower Moselle, presumably that of a wine-grower, containing two pruning knives, several pieces of earthen-ware vessels, and Roman coins, all of these grave gifts datable to the first century A.D.; further, a tombstone found at Dienheim, near Oppenheim, Rheinhesse, datable about 80 A.D. Viticulture may have reached these parts by either of two ways—or by both, more or less independently. It may have spread to the Upper Rhine via the gap between the Vosges and the Jura mountains, the "Burgundian Gate" (more popularly called "la Trouée de Belfort" by the French and "Mülhauser Loch" by the Germans), to what is now Alsace, the Palatinate, and Rheinhessen. Or it may be that the Moselle valley was the gate through which it reached the Rhine.

The latter route is marked most distinctly by archaeological and literary evidence. Trier, Germany's oldest city, was founded under Augustus, about 15 B.C., named Augusta Treverorum after a local tribe, the Treveri, and soon became the capital of the Provincia Belgica. Owing to its strategic situation, it also soon became the most important rear base and provisioning center for the Rhine armies. A vigorous indigenous economy with a flourishing trade developed in the Moselle valley from the second century A.D. No other part of the Rhine basin has yielded such a wealth of Roman remains as the Moselle region: stone monuments decorated with illustrations of viticultural scenery, earthenware and glass receptacles for storing and drinking wine, vineyard tools, etc.—most of them now in the Landesmuseum in Trier. Most of the stone sculptures, the most instructive evidence of the prosperity of the valley, are known as the "Neumagen finds" and date from the late second and early third century. The complete Neumagen collections of the museum can now be seen in a new hall that was opened on June 15, 1974. They are grave monuments illustrating scenes of the ordinary daily life of obviously wealthy people; indeed, their main purpose seems to have been to advertise the importance of the families and business houses of the dead. Paradoxically, the sculptures, mostly in relief, owe their preservation to the fact that under Constantine the Great (314–37) the Romans found it necessary to erect a fort as a bulwark against German raiders. This was placed at Noviomagus ("New Field," the Celtic *magos* being the equivalent of the Latin *campus*), the present Neumagen, about twenty miles down the river from Trier. The stronghold's builders strengthened it by enclosing the local grave monuments within its walls. The largest of them is, presumably, that of a wealthy wine merchant; it is in the shape of a galley sculptured in the round, stem and stern drawn up in the form of doglike monsters, laden with a cargo of large wine casks, rowed by twelve oarsmen, with a helmsman at the stern and another man at the bow. Replicas of this sculpture and of some reliefs that could be restored may be found in the village itself. There are two more grave monuments in the form of wine galleys in the museum, but both are fragmentary; one of them is especially notable for the happy expression of its helmsman's slightly befuddled grin. The overland transportation of a large barrel on a four-wheeled wagon is also represented on one of the stone reliefs.

Another relief, showing a group of tenants paying their rent, in coin, to the landowner's stewards, tells a different story. The tenants are native small holders, in hooded cloaks and with gaunt, tired faces. There are also fragments of similar reliefs, one showing a bookkeeper, a wizened old man with a bleak look about the eyes, the other a tenant with a brooding face dulled by hopeless poverty.

There is a Latin poem entitled "Mosella," dated 371, which pays tribute to the beauty of the river's countryside. At the time, Treveris (as Trier was then, for a short time, called) was, for a few decades, the imperial residence of the Western Empire. The author of the poem, Ausonius, a learned rhetor from Burdigala (Bordeaux), had been invited by the emperor Valentinian to be the tutor of his son Gratianus, and he continued to stay at the court under the latter's reign. The "Mosella" describes his journey from Bingen through the woods of the Hunsrück hills to Neumagen, which he greets as "the divine Constantine's glorious fortress," and thence by boat to Trier. The river scenery reminds him of that of his native Garonne, where his own vineyard is mirrored in the water's surface. Like the Garonne, the Moselle is bordered by green vineyards climbing up the steep slopes in neatly planted rows of vine stakes. Vineyard workers are busy on the slopes, hailing the passing boatmen; the pillared halls of country mansions are reflected in the river; and so forth. The "Mosella" may not be rated among the gems of Latin poetry, but it has its merits as the oldest literary evidence in praise of a charming and peaceful river valley in the last century of provincial Roman civilization.

The Rhine Valley cannot boast any mention of viticulture by Roman authors. However, there is, in the Palatinate and Rheinhessen, ample archaeological evidence in the form of Roman vineyard tools, especially two-pronged hoes, sickle-shaped billhooks, and pruning and reaping knives of varying sizes. There are also large quantities of Roman earthenware and glass vessels of various shapes for preserving and drinking wine (similar to those found in the Moselle valley), goblets, urns, jugs, pitchers and amphorae, and pottery vessels in the shape of miniature wine casks with spouts. Some were containers of funerary offerings in Roman graves. Many of them have Latin inscriptions expressing toasts to the health of the drinker. Most of this evidence is to be found in the museums of Speyer, Worms, Mainz, and other cities. A special attraction of the Speyer museum is a glass amphora discovered in the stone sarcophagus of a Roman landowner of the third century, still containing a remnant of transparent pinkish wine, covered by a layer of olive oil turned into a dark-brown resin.

Larger stone and metal sculptures are a good deal less frequent than those of the Moselle—for example, in the Palatinate, a bronze figure of Bacchus with a bunch of grapes, and a large cylindrical stone column with a grape-harvesting relief, showing a naked boy wielding a vine dresser's bill with an ax-shaped appendage at the back; in Rheinhessen, a stone altar dedicated to Bacchus in honor of the imperial house, a grave monument of (presumably) a wine merchant, showing two men rolling barrels on board ship over a gangplank, and a tombstone of a certain Silius, son of Atto, a trooper. He is represented in a form called by archaeologists a "funerary banquet," resting on a sofa and holding a drinking vessel in his right hand, a boy standing in front of him and two wine vessels placed on a stool. This monument has been found at Dienheim, near Oppenheim, and dated to about 80 A.D.

There is one kind of discovery in which the Palatinate and Rheinhessen are unique; namely, several specimens of original wooden wine barrels, or what remains of them. From the Moselle we know them only from representations in sculpture. Incidentally, wooden wine barrels are not a Roman invention, but were devised by the Gauls, from whom the Romans adopted them. The Romans transferred the word *cupa*, originally used for an open vat, to the closed barrel. The traditional Roman receptacle for fermentation and storage was a large bell-mouthed earthenware vessel lined with a coating of pitch and known as a *dolium*. *Dolia* were kept in a special wine cellar, partly sunk in cavities in the floor.

The existence of Roman viticulture in the Ahr valley, near the northern end of the winegrowing area, appear to be a little controversial. About the middle of the nineteenth century, drainage works carried out at the Apollinaris spring are said to have uncovered, at a depth of fourteen feet, a Roman vineyard, with vine stakes set in regular rows, and with shards of earthenware and glass vessels and finds of coins of the emperor Valerian (253–260) and Gallienus (260–268). A later report claimed the chance discovery, on the occasion of excavation for new buildings in the same neighborhood, and at the same depth belowground, of more Roman pottery and glass remains and coins of the same period. However, it seems that no further discoveries have been made; at any rate, a more recent local writer on the history of viticulture in the Ahr valley does not even mention these earlier claims.

The question of Roman viticulture to the east of the Rhine, especially in what are now the Baden and Württemberg regions, is still more doubtful. Between the end of the first and the middle of the second century the Romans completed the Limes, a defense line running from the Middle Rhine to the Upper Danube, which in time became a series of permanently garrisoned forts connected partly by stone walls and partly by steep earthworks crowned by stockades. The new appendage to the empire, the land between the Rhine and the Limes, a narrow strip in the north but widening to a broad chunk of country toward the south, where it enclosed the Odenwald hills and the Black Forest, is referred to as the *Decumates agri* by Tacitus. It had a predominantly Gaulish population, immigrants from the left bank, of whom Tacitus speaks in most uncomplimentary terms, but also included fragments of Germanic tribes. Besides, there were Roman garrisons, farmsteads, small townships, and such famous spas as Wiesbaden, Baden-Baden, and Badenweiler. Natural conditions being, by and large, as favorable to the east of the Rhine as they are to the west of it, it seems surprising that the spread of viticulture should have bypassed the eastern side altogether. Yet there does not appear to be a scrap of archaeological evidence of viticulture in the area during the period of Roman occupation.

Shortly before the year 260 the Alemannians succeeded in breaching the Limes defenses, overrunning the country enclosed by it, and, together with bands of Frankish warriors, launching their invasion of Gaul, sacking Trier in 275–76. This and following incursions each ended in defeat, the Romans following up their victories by thrusts into enemy-held territory east of the Rhine. But these operations did not succeed in dislodging the Alemannians definitely from the country that they had conquered after breaching the Limes. In fact there seem to have been no serious attempts on the part of the Romans to reconquer the territory that they had had to evacuate about 260, or indeed to rebuild the Limes. For nearly a century and a half, the Rhine again formed the frontier of the empire.

The names *Franci* and *Alemanni*, not known to the earlier Roman authors, appear for the first time in the third century. They refer to large tribal aggregates, probably formed by the need for greater solidarity in the face of the Roman military presence on the Rhine front. The Franks occupied the country to the north of the Main River, while the Alemannians extended southward as far as Lake Constance.

It seems that the Alemannic incursions into Roman Gaul were nothing like the old-style tribal migrations in search of new land, as at Caesar's time and before, but raids in search of adventure and plunder carried out by bands of young warriors while the rest of the people stayed at home tilling the land. Hostile relations with the Romans prevailed only for a smaller part of the period in question, between about 260 and the beginning of the fifth century. Moreover, they did not usually involve all the Alemannians; some of their chiefs remained at peace with the empire. It is also safe to assume that after a considerable period of culture contact with Romans and Gauls, the agricultural methods of the Alemannians were far superior to those described for the Germans of earlier centuries. They had taken over the indigenous rural economy of the Gauls whom they had replaced, and had themselves at last struck deep roots into the soil. Furthermore, the archaeological evidence reveals that not all of the previous inhabitants disappeared from the country after its conquest by the Alemannians. Some Gauls, no doubt, became agricultural bondsmen of the victors, but a sizable number of Romans and Gauls remained as craftsmen and traders living in townships surrounded by Alemannic farms. There is also evidence that in times of peace these Roman and Romanized elements living under the rule of Alemannic chiefs traded with their compatriots on the other side of the Rhine, thus playing the role of mediators between Roman civilization and Germanic peasant economy. Under these conditions it would be conceivable that Alemannians, on their home ground, became familiar with viticulture about the turn of the fourth century.

If viticulture in present-day Baden and Württemberg during the Roman period is possible but not demonstrable archaeologically, its apparent absence in Alsace is a real conundrum. Assuming that one stream of viticultural expansion reached the Rhine valley through the Burgundian Gate, and considering the well-documented Roman viticulture in the Palatinate and Rheinhessen, the lack of archaeological evidence for it in the intervening region is very surprising. The first evidence of Alsatian viticulture appears to be the mention of vineyards in the neighborhood of Saverne (Zabern) in 589 by Gregory of Tours in his *History of the Franks.*

Finally, another remarkable lacuna in archaeological evidence. The famous decree of the emperor Probus (276–82) permitting winegrowing to "all the Gauls and the Spaniards as well as the Britons" has already been mentioned. Yet there appears to be no conclusive evidence of viticulture in Roman Britain, though of course there is any amount of evidence for the consumption of imported wines. The first explicit evidence for vineyards in England, in about 700, is provided by the Venerable Bede in his *Ecclesiastical History of the English People.* His near-contemporary, St. Boniface, the Anglo-Saxon "Apostle of the Germans" and martyr, seems to have been either unaware or skeptical of indigenous English wine, for toward the end of his life, when he was archbishop of Mainz (747–54), he sent some of his Rhine wine to Archbishop Egbert of York, accompanied by a letter saying, "We are sending your Grace two little casks of wine, wishing that you may make yourself a happy day with your clergy." However, a law issued by Alfred the Great at the end of the ninth century, laying down a penalty for the offense of damaging another man's *wingeard* ("arable field"), seems to suggest, by naming the vineyard before the field, that at the time viticulture did indeed have a certain economic importance.

What, then, about the Germans, whom Probus significantly omits to mention in his edict? He certainly knew them well enough from his campaigns against them as commander in chief for his predecessor Aurelian. All we can say is that the Germans got involved in the cultivation of the vine anonymously. Before the consolidation of the Roman frontier, the Rhine never was a tight barrier between Germanic and Celtic peoples. As there were Gaulish immigrants on the east bank, especially in the areas of present-day Baden and Württemberg, Germanic tribes were intermingled with Gauls on the west bank. Caesar mentions three of them, the Vangiones (in present-day Rheinhessen), Nemetes (in the present Palatinate), and Triboci (in the present Alsace), who appear to have come over as tribal contingents with the army led by Ariovistus, and to have been allowed to remain as settlers after their leader's defeat in 59 B.C. Tacitus mentions them again explicitly as Germanic peoples occupying the left bank. Hence the official Latin name of Worms became Civitas Vangionum, and that of Speyer, Civitas Nemetum.

Most of the first and second centuries A.D. appears to have been a period of relative calm and security on the Rhine frontier, favoring a peaceful spread of Roman civilization. In 37 A.D. the Romans settled the Ubii on the left bank of the Middle Rhine, where they appear to have experienced a time of prosperity, the tribal center, Cologne, becoming a Roman provincial town in 50 A.D. Also, elsewhere, during the comparatively quiet period of the first two centuries, the Romans appear to have admitted small groups of Germans as soldiers and settlers into the empire. In conjunction with the presence of already established Germanic elements on the left bank, this immigration facilitated an intimate Roman-German cultural exchange, revealed especially by a considerable number of Latin loanwords in the German language.

Under Diocletian (285–305) the left bank of the Rhine was made secure by the forcible settlement of thousands of Germans. In northern Gaul, stretches deserted by the suppression of a peasant revolt were repopulated with Frankish and Saxon prisoners of war. Thus there was an influx, in ever-increasing numbers after the end of the third century, of Germanic elements into the Roman military service and agricultural labor force in Gaul. The semiservile Germanic peasant communities, partly prisoners of war or their descendants, seem to have made up a sizable proportion of the population of Gaul. One may reasonably speculate that not a few of them must have been vineyard laborers or otherwise become familiar with the production of wine.

Post-Roman Period

In the early years of the fifth century, Roman rule on the Rhine came to an end; the legions guarding the frontier had to be withdrawn to meet the threat of the Visigothic invasion of Italy. At this time Alemannians and Ripuarian Franks (that is, riverain Franks, from the Latin *ripa* ["river bank"], meaning the Franks of the Middle Rhine), with the newly arrived Burgundians settling between them, occupied the left bank for good, though at first still nominally recognizing Roman sovereignty. At the same time, they failed to stem the flood of Vandals and a medley of other barbarian tribes surging across the frontier. In 435 the Burgundians, in and about Worms, came close to being utterly destroyed by the Huns. The Romans, who still held onto parts of Gaul, offered them a refuge in Savoy, whence within a few decades they established a new kingdom covering most of the Rhone and Upper Loire valleys. After this resettlement, their former Rhenish kingdom was again occupied by the Alemannians.

From about the middle of the fifth century, when the last of Roman rule in Gaul was crumbling, Salian Franks from the Lower Rhine occupied the northern part of the country as far as the Somme, the first step in their gradual conquest of virtually the whole; the Ripuarian Franks occupied the country to the west of the Middle Rhine, seizing Trier in 460; at about the same time, the Alemannians completed the occupation of the left bank of the Upper Rhine—the present-day Rheinhessen, Palatinate, Alsace, and northern Switzerland—while retaining their older seats on the eastern side of the Rhine, from the Main River southward. A few decades later, they clashed with their Frankish neighbors, who in the meantime had become more strongly united under Clovis (Chlodovech), the founder of the Merovingian dynasty, and suffered a decisive defeat at Tolpiacum (Zülpich in the Eifel hills) in 496. As a result, the Alemannians had to evacuate their northern territories: the present Rheinhessen and Palatinate, the northern parts of Alsace, Baden, and Württemberg, as well as the lands along the Main, which were now occupied by Frankish settlers. Furthermore, they had to recognize the suzerainty of the Frankish kings, though remaining under their own dukes.

Gregory of Tours records that when the battle seemed lost to the Franks, Clovis appealed to Christ, vowing that if he gave him victory, Clovis and his people would adopt Christianity. It is likely that the conversion of the Franks was followed by that of the defeated Alemannians; however, the southern Alemannians, who appear to have kept out of the war against the Franks, remained pagan for nearly another two centuries. In southern Baden, for example, archaeological evidence of Christian burials dates back only to about the year 700. The Christianization of the southern Alemannians appears to be due mainly to the preaching of the Irish hermit St. Gallus, in the first half of the seventh century, and to that of his disciples.

The long and violent period of Germanic migrations and territorial annexations does not seem to have been as destructive to viticulture as might be expected. However much wreckage the barbarian hordes left in their trail, there is little evidence that they willfully devastated vineyards or other cultivable land; in other words, they generally did not destroy an economic base from which they could draw advantage for themselves. The Merovingian law books, the *Lex Salica* (c. 500), and the *Lex Ripuaria* (from about the end of the sixth century) take a familiarity with an old-established viticulture for granted and bear witness to its peaceful continuation under Frankish rule. The former reveals its regard for the cultivation of the vine by raising the social status of the grower—though he was still not free—above that of the ordinary plowman, and consequently by fixing the blood compensation payable for the slaying of a vineyard laborer considerably above that laid down for the slaying of a mere agricultural serf. (The vinegrower shared his higher rating with other skilled members of the servile class—the blacksmith, the goldsmith, and, oddly enough, the swineherd.) The law of the Ripuarians, in a paragraph indicating the formalities attending conveyances, suggests by the wording "a country estate, or a vineyard, or any small piece of land" that vineyards were a common form of immovable property.

Evidence of a more or less undisturbed transition from the Roman to the Frankish period is also provided by a second poetic description of the Moselle scenery, as well as of a short stretch of the Rhine valley, two centuries after Ausonius's "Mosella," showing that vine cultivation was again flourishing as vigorously as it had been under Roman rule. It is a poetic itinerary of a boat trip, composed by Venantius Fortunatus, a scholarly cleric and the last Latin poet of his time. Though Italian-born, he spent most of his life in Merovingian Gaul, where he died as bishop of Poitiers. For some time he lived at the Austrasian court in Metz under the rule of Sigibert and his successor Childebert. The poem, written to commemorate an enjoyable excursion in 588 in the company of Childebert, has an additional significance in not only praising the vine-clad hillsides of the Moselle, but also mentioning extensive vineyards near Antunnacum (Andernach, about ten miles down the Rhine from Koblenz).

The Roman influence on German vine cultivation is immediately evident from a substantial number of Latin loanwords in its nomenclature. The German *Wein* is, of course, derived from the Latin *vinum;* this word, picked up from the early Italian wine peddlers, percolated as a loanword even into all the Baltic and Slavonic languages. The Latin word for the peddler himself, *caupo,* meaning both an innkeeper and a petty tradesman or hawker, is the ancestor of the respectable German *Kaufmann* ("merchant") and the somewhat less respectable English *chapman.* The word *Most* ("must") is derived from *mustum* ("unfermented grape juice"); *Keller* ("cellar") from post-classical *cellarium; Kufe* ("vat," "cask") from *cupa; Küfer* ("cooper") from *cuparius; Kelch* ("cup," "goblet," "chalice") from *calix.*

Of special interest are some loanwords peculiar to German, which are not, or at any rate no longer, used in French, and therefore also absent in English. There are three older words for *wine press,* two of Latin and one of German origin. The most widespread is *Kelter,* with the verb *keltern* used all over the Frankish northern half of the winegrowing regions, including Thuringia and Saxony (now in East Germany), and used also by the German minority of Transylvania, twelfth-century immigrants from the Moselle. It is derived from *calcatorium,* a derivative of the verb *calcare* ("to tread upon or underfoot"). The application of the loanword *Kelter* (Old High German *kelketra*) to a press is based on a misunderstanding. The Latin word *calcatura* denotes an action, and *calcatorium* means nothing more than a raised platform on which the treaders (*calcatores*) crushed the grapes with their bare feet (*calcare uvas*). It was only after the treading that the mash was put through the wine presses (such presses are known from descriptions by Roman writers and from wall paintings at Pompeii and Herculaneum). The most primitive contraption consisted of a heavy stone block lifted by a long wooden lever and slammed down on a basket containing the grape mash. More developed types operated by the pressure of a heavy beam. They, in turn, were replaced by the invention of a screw press, a smaller machine that could be operated without the inconvenience of a long lever press-beam. It is this last type that has survived the centuries and come down, with some modifications, to our time, although the great majority of the surviving specimens are now museum pieces.

The second term, *Torkel* (Old High German *torkula*) is restricted to a smaller area in the southeast, from Lake Constance to the Tyrol. This is derived from the Latin *torcular* or *torculum*, which actually denotes a press—to be precise, the later Roman screw press, since the noun is connected with the verb *torquere* ("to turn about or twist"). *Torcular* is also used to denote the wine press in the Vulgate, and survives in Italian as *torchio*.

In between *Kelter* and *Torkel*, the Alemannic region—that is, the greater part of Baden and Württemberg, Alsace, and Switzerland—uses the Germanic word *Trotte* (Old High German *trota* or *trotta*), derived from the verb *trotton* ("to tread"). Semantically, *Trotte* is the same kind of misnomer as *Kelter*, in that it properly refers, not to an actual press, but to the place where the grapes are crushed by treading.

There is another Latin word for *wine press—prelum* (from the verb *premere*, "to press")—that appears to have had little influence on the older German wine vocabulary. Unlike French, which uses *pressoir* (from the Latin *pressura*, "a pressing"), the German word *Presse* is rarely used in connection with traditional wine making, although it is, of course, used for modern machinery.

Like *Trotte*, the word *Rebe* ("vine") is a notable exception from the vocabulary of loanwords, but in this peculiarity it has a Latin parallel. The Latin *vinea*, derived from *vinum*, is ambiguous in that it means both vine and (together with *vinetum*) vineyard. In the first sense, it is synonymous with *vitis*. In English, the words *viniculture* (from *vinum*) and *viticulture* (from *vitis*) are synonymous. But semantics is one thing, etymology another. *Vitis* is synonymous with *vinum* only by chance; etymologically, the two words are unrelated. The basic meaning of *vitis* is "something that winds about," a pliant, flexible plant, a creeper. The German word *Rebe* (Old High

German *repa)* has the same meaning; it may have been applied to other kinds of winding plants before it was reserved for the grapevine.

To return to the viticultural expressions derived from Latin, perhaps the most important is *Winzer* (Old High German *winzuril)*, derived from *vinitor* ("winegrower"). The German word is more often than not restricted to the small holder, while its Latin prototype denotes, more specifically, a vineyard slave. It is only in Württemberg that the toiler in the vineyard is known as a *Weingärtner* ("wine gardener"); in Franconia, where no Roman ever set foot, he is called a *Häcker* ("one who hoes"). It is curious that in English books and articles on German wine one finds the word *Winzer* so often rendered by the English *vintner;* occasionally the German winegrower is even apostrophized as a *vigneron.* What the German and the English words have in common is their connection with wine, and the fact that they are alliterative. They are different both in meaning and in derivation. A vintner is, as one can see in any English dictionary, a wine merchant, the word being derived from the Old French *vinetier,* now extinct, which goes back to late Latin *vinetarius,* which again has replaced the *vinarius* of classical Latin. The German *Winzer* is, of course, synonymous with the French *vigneron,* but the French word has a different etymology, being derived from *vigne,* which again goes back to the Latin *vinea* in the sense of *vine.* In a collection of essays entitled *Vineyards in England,* one of the collaborators has dreamed up the bizarre neologism *vinearcon,* an Anglicization of the French *vigneron,* a novelty of which the *Oxford English Dictionary* has taken no cognizance. A visitor to the Moselle may refresh himself with a bottle of "Wintricher Grosser Herrgott." The name of the site of a theological nature, meaning "the Almighty"; that of the village, Wintrich, is derived from the Celto-Roman *Vinitoriacum,* meaning "wine-growers' village." So what is wrong with translating the German word *Winzer* with "winegrower" (or perhaps "vine dresser")?

There is an English word *vintager,* meaning "grape

gatherer," which does not seem to crop up very often in either speech or print; but it means no more than a person who helps with the work in the vintage season. A *vintager*, or grape picker, may be an occasional laborer or perhaps a voluntary helper, but he is certainly not a *Winzer*, or grape grower, who toils in the vineyard all the year round.

It is likely that the word *Trichter* ("funnel"), derived from *trajectorium*, came into the German language as part of the imported Latin wine vocabulary. The German *Kammerbau*, referring to the training of vines on trelliswork, can only be derived from *vinea camerata* because by itself *Kammer* does not mean "trellis," but "chamber," or "small room." Other Latin loanwords have been forgotten because the tools which they denoted have long since been replaced by tools of a different type. An example is *Sesel*, a sickle-shaped pruning and reaping knife, which is derived from *sicilis*; since sickle-shaped knives have given way to shears and secateurs, it is understandable that their name has disappeared from memory. Again, other loanwords reached only an early stage in the development of the German language, to be discarded later in favour of a genuine German word. An example is the Old High German *windemon*, derived from *vindemia* ("grape harvest"), the Latin word that has also produced the French *vendange* and the English *vintage*. The early loanword has disappeared and been replaced in literary German by *Weinlese*, and in the wine-grower's language by *Herbst*. This latter word is, of course, etymologically cognate with the English *harvest*, but its ordinary German meaning is "autumn"; it is only in the winegrowing regions that its primary meaning is "grape harvest."

Again, some Latin expressions seem to survive, as obsolescent loanwords, in local dialects. Thus it has been suggested that the verb *wimmeln*, used in parts of Baden, and unknown elsewhere, meaning "to gather grapes," is another remnant of the Latin noun *vindemia* or verb *vindemiare*, and that the verb *sälen* (in the same local dialect), denoting the chore of tying up vines, is connected with the Lain noun *salix* ("willow branch").

Again, in the Frankish dialect of the Moselle, as well as in that of the Middle Rhine and the Rheingau, the verb *putzen*, which in literary German is near-synonymous with *schmücken* ("to adorn"), is used in the sense of "trimming or pruning vines," and is clearly derived from the Latin *putare*, which has that meaning. In an old saying, the local grower is admonished to run into the vineyard with his hooked knife to begin his work straight after Candlemas Day, February 2, the feast of the Virgin Mary's purification in the temple.

There is also a good deal of Latin debris surviving in names of vineyard sites, especially on the Moselle; for instance, Calmont probably from *calidus mons* ("hot hill") or possibly from *calvus mons* ("bald hill"); Cramunt from *gradalis mons* ("hill in the form of steps," "terraced hill"), Monteneubel from *mons nobilis* ("famous hill") or, more probably, from *mons novellus* ("new hill"), *Auerkump* from *aurea cupa* ("golden cup"), Plenetsch from *planities* ("vineyard on level ground"), Plantert from *plantarium* ("newly planted vineyard"), etc. Of names of inhabited localities, that of Wintrich, from Vinitoriacum, has already been mentioned. A few miles farther down the river, the village of Brauneberg adopted its present name only in 1925, discarding its old name of Dusemont. The derivation of this old name is controversial; some suggest a connection with *dulcis mons* ("sweet hill"), others explain it as referring to a situation on the brow *(dorsum)* of the hill, others derive it from a proper name, Amandus, the local name on record for the tenth century being Duos Amandos.

Charlemagne (742–814) is on record for his active encouragement of viticulture. His *Capitulare de villis* contains detailed regulations concerning the cultivation of vineyards and treatment of wine, even including directions of a hygienic nature— for instance, one forbidding the crushing of the grapes with the bare feet. This prohibition proved, indeed, to be a trifle premature. It took over a thousand years more to discontinue the time-honored custom, and no doubt it is still practiced in out-of-the-way places. The poet Stefan George, born in 1868, the son of a winegrower in Rheinhessen, remembered that as a little boy he had to help tread the grapes in the vat, "but the feet had to be washed first." A more somber picture emerges from a learned German book on the production of red wines, published in 1855. The author describes a grape-treading scene which he observed in a well-known red-wine area abroad. In very big and high vats, naked men pounded the grape mash with their feet. With their minds befogged by the rising mixture of carbon dioxide and alcoholic vapors generated by the onset of fermentation, their sweating heads and chests sloped limply and apathetically over the rim of the vats. The author wonders what might happen to them in this condition below the visible range, which leads him to musings on the alleged qualities, regional character, earthiness, and so on, likely to be ascribed to the resulting wines.

However, to return to the contribution of Charlemagne, he is credited with sending for vines from his Burgundian domains, having them planted on German soil, and setting up model estates, each of which had to have its own wineshop displaying a wreath of vine leaves—a custom still surviving in the *Strausswirtschaften* ("wreath inns") or *Heckenwirtschaften* ("hedge inns"), winegrowers' cottages marked in the same way, where the owner can legally sell his own produce. (A distant echo of this is the English saying, "A good wine needs no bush.") From Charlemagne's reign we have documentary proof of about 350 winegrowing localities in German-speaking areas, the names of which are known from the records of monasteries referring to new endowments and bequests. Some of the emperor's feats in promoting viticulture appear a little apocryphal. An old story, very dear to the people of the Rheingau, is that, from his palace in Ingelheim on the other side of the Rhine, Charlemagne noticed that the snow on the wooded slopes opposite melted much earlier than elsewhere; he concluded that they received an extra dose of sunshine and immediately ordered them to be cleared and planted with vines. There may well be some truth behind the legend, for the first historical document mentioning the existence of a vineyard in the Rheingau, issued by the emperor's son, Louis the Pious, is dated 817, three years after Charlemagne's death. This is indeed late in comparison with early medieval documentary evidence of viticulture in other parts of Germany, which goes back to the seventh century and becomes plentiful in the eighth. Although there are a few more isolated records dating from the tenth and eleventh centuries, Rheingau viticulture on any substantial scale can only be traced back to the twelfth century, being associated with the foundation of the Benedictine monastery of Johannisberg and the installation of the first batch of Cistercian monks in the Eberbach monastery by St. Bernard of Clairvaux.

There is another legend connected with Charlemagne, one that takes us right into the realms of fancy, but reveals how intimately, in people's belief, the emperor's person was associated with winegrowing. In June, the story goes, when the vines are in bloom, the emperor rises from his tomb at night, wanders along the Rhine, and blesses the vineyards.

In the ninth century, wine production on the right bank of the Rhine generally appears to have been less than satisfactory. At any rate, when, by the Treaty of Verdun in 843, the Carolingian empire was divided among the three grandsons of Charlemagne, the situation seems to have been considered a political issue of some importance. Louis the German received the eastern portion of the empire, the lands to the east of the Rhine, but in addition claimed and received also the ecclesiastical territories of Mainz, Worms, and Speyer, that is, the present Rheinhessen and Palatinate. The chronicler to whom we owe this piece of information, the abbot Regino of the Benedictine Abbey of Prüm in the Eifel hills, tells us that the reason for the additional allocation of this chunk of west-bank land was its abundance of wine (*propter vini copiam*). The abbot himself does not seem to have been allergic to Rhenish wine, for in a later entry in his chronicles he praises the towns of Koblenz, Andernach, and Sinzig in similar terms (*propter vini affluentiam*).

After the Carolingian period, local rulers and aristocratic magnates owned large slices of vineyard acreage, but an even larger part came through endowments and bequests, whether through royal favor or the pious hopes of more humble owners, into the possession of the Church. The monasteries, especially, were the pioneers in the expansion of viticulture. Between the tenth and twelfth centuries monks established vineyards in Thuringia, Saxony, and Brandenburg; in the fifteenth century they spread them throughout northern Germany, even beyond the Vistula to East Prussia and the Baltic countries. That the wines grown in this inhospitable northern climate were mostly thin and sour does not seem to have mattered a great deal, as they were normally drunk mulled, spiced and sweetened with honey.

In the sixteenth century the Hanseatic League imported stronger and sweeter wines, mainly from the Mediterranean countries, which did their best to oust the inferior northern product. Further damage was inflicted on north German viticulture by the Reformation, which led to the expulsion of the monks, the closing of the monastic buildings, and the handing over of their estates to laymen, especially to Protestant princes. As a result, most of the northern vineyards must have been left to run to waste. For the first time, the price of beer fell below that of ordinary country wine. All that has survived today of north German viticulture, outside the Rhine basin, are two small wine-producing regions in East Germany, situated on the banks of the Elbe, in Saxony, and its tributary the Saale, in Thuringia. Prewar Germany had another wine-producing area, smaller still, near the town of Grünberg in Lower Silesia, now within the territories to the east of the Oder–Neisse line ceded to Poland and renamed Zielona Góra. It is situated near the 52nd parallel, now the northernmost viticultural area of the world.

All of Germany, both north and south, was seriously disrupted by the peasant wars of 1525, which are said to have destroyed more than a thousand monasteries and castles.

Nevertheless, from southern Germany, during the sixteenth century, we hear of occasional vintages so plentiful that the wine was cheaper than the casks needed to contain it, and that considerable problems of storage arose. Old chronicles record harvests when growers had to leave grapes unpicked because they did not have enough barrels in their cellars, or when the previous year's wine had to be poured into the streets to make barrels available for the new one. From the Upper Rhine we hear of the bumper harvest of 1539, when an ingenious local knight hit upon a more economical method of disposing of his old wine. He ordered his serfs to appear twice a week at his castle, each provided with his own bread and cheese, for wine-drinking corvée labor to empty his barrels. The peasants, understandably, quarreled and came to blows in the course of their labors, for which behavior their feudal master fined them appropriately. The total of the fines collected by him is said to have amounted to more than he could possibly have realized from the sale of his old wine.

All such abundance came to an end during the Thirty Years War (1618–48), the most grievous disaster that ever visited Germany, brought about by the irreconcilable antagonism between Catholic and Protestant rulers, and foreign intervention, which not only ravaged and depopulated the whole country but also, as a by-product, laid waste immense vineyard areas, destroying the wine trade as well. After the middle of the seventeenth century, what little remained of viticulture in German-speaking lands had retreated to its older homeland, the climatically favored valleys of the Rhine and its tributaries, recovering only very slowly during the following centuries. If the Germans hailed the bumper crop of 1970, nearly 10 million hectoliters (28 million bushels) and the largest in living memory, as the largest vintage since the Thirty Years War, they were, no doubt, in agreement with history.

Together with the withdrawal from unfavorable regions, a gradual but very drastic shrinkage of viticultural acreage ensued in the remaining winegrowing regions. Vines planted on more or less level ground had to give way to grain and other crops, in accordance with a general rule which said, "Where a plow can go, there no vine should grow." The wine-producing acreage about the year 1600 is estimated to have been about 300,000 hectares (740,000 acres); that recorded in the Federal Republic for the year 1971 is 75,500 hectares (187,000 acres). The most radical reduction appears to have taken place in Franconia, the region of the Middle Main, in the Middle Ages the largest winegrowing area with about 40,000 hectares (99,000 acres), now among the smallest, with only 2,750 hectares (6,800 acres). These changes signal the first beginnings of a gradual switch-over from quantitative to qualitative production. The principal obstacle to improvement had always been the miserable social position of the tenant smallholder, who was heavily burdened with rents and taxes as well as with the wine tithe enforced by the Church, and was therefore mainly interested in mass production, planting varieties producing a massive yield of inferior quality. Nevertheless, during the second half of the eighteenth century, some qualitative improvement was achieved, due in large measure to the efforts of the two Rheingau monasteries of Johannisberg and Eberbach. More promising sites were planted with better varieties, such as Riesling, Traminer, and red Burgundy, cellar methods were improved, wines bottled, and wine labels introduced. That these improvements were made in the Rheingau may not have been entirely fortuitous, for, by contrast with other areas, the Rheingau winegrower, under the crozier of the archbishop-elector of Mainz, had enjoyed the status of a free peasant since the Middle Ages.

However, some happy-go-lucky old methods still continued for a while, such as the "mixed setting," or indiscriminate planting of different varieties of vine on the same plot regardless of the different ripening times of their grapes. This has been eliminated only since the middle of the nineteenth century and been replaced by the "pure setting," the careful segregation of different varieties, not only on separate plots, but wherever possible also on different kinds of soil best suited to promote their growth and to benefit the yield and quality of their grapes.

The nineteenth century began with a severe setback to viticulture—namely, the seculariztion of 1803, by which the Church was dispossessed of all its landed property. The process had begun in the French Revolution, in which all ecclesiastical property had been declared national property. At the treaty of Lunéville, in 1801, the old German Empire had to submit to the French dictate—namely, to surrender the whole of the left bank of the Rhine to France, with the proviso that German hereditary rulers who held territories wholly or partly on the left side of the Rhine were to be indemnified on the right side at the expense of the ecclesiastical territories and free cities. As the resolution of the imperial diet in Regensburg put it, "All the estates of the foundations, abbeys, and monasteries are to be made over to the free and full disposal of the respective sovereigns for the alleviation of their finances." As far as viticulture was concerned, this meant that many centuries of devoted monastic labor, not motivated by financial interests, had come to an end. The vineyards hitherto owned by the monasteries and other ecclesiastical institutions were appropriated by various secular rulers, later to become the nucleus of the present State Domains, or partly to be auctioned to private producers, from large, titled landowners to more humble winegrowers, as well as to the wine trade.

Since the middle of the nineteenth century, European viticulture has been afflicted with a miscellany of destructive blights and pests introduced from the United States via France. Outstanding among them are oïdium, or vine mildew; peronospora, called in German *Blattfallkrankheit*, which causes leaves and grapes to shrivel on the vine and fall off; and, the most devastating scourge, phylloxera, called in German *Reblaus* ("vine louse"), a minute insect which, invisible to the eye, feeds on the roots of grape-bearing vines, damaging them so badly that they perish within a short time. It is no exaggeration to say that during the last hundred years it has been the problem of phylloxera that has had the strongest influence on viticulture. Its rate of reproduction is enormous; within one year a single insect may produce thousands of offspring. The arrival of the parasite in the 1870s caused a remarkable decline in viticulture throughout the European wine-producing countries. In France, wine production fell temporarily to a quarter of the normal yield; in one German region, Baden, planted acreage was reduced by one-half between 1870 and 1919. After years of experimentation, the remedy was at last found in the grafted vine—in German, *Pfropfrebe*. The root of the wild American vine is virtually resistant to phylloxera. For this reason, grape-bearing native vines are grafted onto supporting stems of sterile American ones. The increasing extent of phylloxera infection necessitated the restocking of large areas of affected vineyards with grafted vines, thus putting a considerable load of additional costs on wine production. The phylloxera danger still remains more or less dormant, but, on the whole, is now under control; old-established vineyards may still be partly under nongrafted native vines, but the more recent ones are, as a rule, planted only with grafted vines.

5. Christianity and Wine

Wine Essential for Missionary Labors

CHRISTIANITY was the main driving force that spread winegrowing northward. Its expansion by the monasteries throughout viticulturally unfavorable northern Germany and beyond, mentioned in Chapter 4, is most probably to be explained by ecclesiastical requirements. The essential root of the ecclesiastical concern with viticulture is the fact that wine is an irreplaceable element in the celebration of the Eucharist (literally, "thank offering"), or Holy Communion, the central sacrament of the Christian religion, which is founded on the belief in the real (not symbolic) presence of the whole Christ (*totus Christus*) in the transformed elements of bread and wine, a belief that later received its official seal with the dogma of transubstantiation, the miraculous conversion of the consecrated bread and wine into the body and blood of Christ. In the celebration of the sacrament, the shedding of Christ's blood for the remission of sins is recalled in the words of the consecration of the wine. The sacrament is, of course, derived from the account of the Last Supper in the Gospels, and the words of Christ as recorded in the Gospels have to be followed to the letter. Hence the absolute necessity of a supply of wine. Naturally, quantities of wine were also required by the monasteries for ordinary nonsacral use: Monks received modest daily rations at meals, the aged and sick had to be comforted, pilgrims and passing guests had to be hospitably received and regaled, and so forth.

Biblical References to Wine

Unlike Islam and Indian religions, which prohibit the consumption of alcohol in any form, Christianity has been intimately connected with the cultivation of the vine from its beginnings. Wine was the common drink at meals in the Holy Land throughout biblical times. It entered the intellectual world of the Christian religion from the numerous similes, metaphors, and parables used by Old and New Testament authors, who frequently illustrated their teachings by examples taken from vine cultivation. Thus, Genesis 9 tells the story of Noah's planting a vineyard and tippling too much of his own produce, with deplorable consequences. The Book of Numbers, Chapter 13, tells the story of Moses sending out the scouts to spy out the land of Canaan, and of their coming back with a cluster of grapes so heavy that it has to be carried on a staff between two of the men, a motif often represented in decorative carvings on wine barrels. In the New Testament, there is the parable of the unfaithful vine dressers, and the story of the wedding feast at Cana, where Christ performs the miracle of turning water into wine. Christ speaks of God's Kingdom as a vineyard in which we are to labor, and, again, he speaks of himself as the vine of which we are the branches and with which we are to remain closely joined. Above all, there is the account of the Last Supper, Christ breaking the bread and giving it to his disciples with the words "Eat, this is my body," and giving them the cup of wine, saying, "Drink, this is my blood of the new testament."

The equation of wine and blood is already foreshadowed in the Old Testament. Genesis 49, the blessing of Jacob's sons, mentions for the first time the expression "blood of the grapes," which is still with us. Isaiah 63:1–6 shows Yahveh treading the winepress as a symbol of his victorious battle against the enemies of Israel. "Wherefore art thou red in thine apparel, and thy garments like him that treadeth in the wine vat? I have trodden the winepress alone; and of the peoples there was no man with me: yea, I trod them in mine anger, and trampled them in my fury, and their lifeblood is sprinkled upon my garments, and I have stained all my raiment. . . . And I trod down the peoples in mine anger, and made them drunk in my fury, and I poured out their lifeblood on the earth." (The passage was destined to receive a very different exegesis by the patristic writers and medieval theologians, see p. 120.) A similar piece of imagery occurs twice in The Revelation, the end of the New Testament. In Chapter 19:13,15, Christ is shown as the victorious warrior in the final battle, "arrayed in a garment sprinkled with blood" and treading "the winepress of the fierceness of the wrath of Almighty God." But the prize of bloodthirstiness must go to the vision of Chapter 14:15ff, of the angel who is told to gather the clusters of the vine, and who "cast his sickle into the earth, and gathered the vintage of the earth, and cast it into the winepress, the great *winepress*, of the wrath of God. And the winepress was trodden without the city, and there came out blood from the winepress, even unto the bridles of the horses, as far as a thousand and six hundred furlongs."

These passages prompt the question of the derivation of the phrase "the grapes of wrath," the title of one of the most famous novels by John Steinbeck. Whether he was enough of a biblical scholar to have snatched it straight from the Scriptures may be doubted. But the *Oxford Dictionary of Quotations* may provide the intermediate link. It quotes a verse from the "Battle Hymn of the Republic," by Julia Ward Howe, whose patriotic ardor was obviously matched by her scriptural knowledge:

Mine eyes have seen the glory of the coming of the Lord:
He is trampling out the vintage where the grapes of wrath are stored.

Donations of Vineyards to Monasteries

The progress of Christianity in the Merovingian period was of great importance for the expansion of viticulture. King Dagobert (622–38) and his successor Sigibert (638–56) are known by documentary evidence to have presented vineyards in what is now northern Baden, the Palatinate, and Alsace to churches in Worms and Speyer. During the seventh and eighth centuries, the Celtic monks from Iona came to Germany and founded a number of monasteries. Outstanding among these monks were St. Gallus, who labored among the southern Alemannians in the first half of the seventh century and whose hermitage became the nucleus of the Benedictine Abbey of St. Gall, built about the middle of the eighth century, and St. Killian, the missionary to the eastern Franks, who was slain in Würzburg in 689 and became the patron saint of Franconia after his death. In the eighth century, the Anglo-Saxon Benedictine St. Boniface was not only the founder of bishoprics, such as Würzburg, and monasteries, such as the Abbey of Fulda, but is also credited with establishing a number of vineyards in the neighborhood of Mainz, where he was bishop and later archbishop before he met his death, on his last evangelizing mission, at the hands of the uncouth Frisians, in 754.

Charlemagne and his son Louis the Pious were the great protectors of the Benedictines, the oldest of the monastic orders still in existence. Beginning in the first half of the eighth century, a great number of their monasteries sprang up in German-speaking areas; for example (apart from St. Gall and Fulda), Murbach in the southern Vosges, Reichenau on an island in Lake Constance, St. Blasien in the southern, and Hirsau in the northern, Black Forest, Prüm in the Eifel hills, and others. All these monasteries, as their surviving records show, were amply endowed, by donations and bequests, with vineyards and other productive land situated, more often than not, far away from them.

One monastery remains to be mentioned in particular as

probably the greatest beneficiary of pious gifts of vineyards and other property, and because it has handed down to posterity a complete register of its acquisitions and business transactions, the *Codex Laureshamensis*. It was the Benedictine Abbey of Lorsch, originally known as Lauresham or Laurissa, situated on the Rhine plain near Bensheim, the main center of the viticultural region of the Bergstrasse. Part of it still survives, the Carolingian "Royal Hall," one of Germany's oldest buildings. Founded in 764 under the reign of Pepin the Short, Charlemagne's father, the monastery was an "abbey of the realm" under a prince-abbot. It enjoyed the special esteem and munificence of Charlemagne and his son Louis the Pious, became an economic and cultural center of the Frankish kingdom, achieving considerable political influence as well. Its religious attraction was based mainly on the relics of St. Nazarius, who had been martyred in Milan during the persecution under Diocletian (303–305). After having been preserved for centuries in the Church of San Nazario in Milan, the martyr's remains were transferred to Lorsch in 765, where they became objects of the greatest veneration, attracting pious gifts and bequests from all over the country. Entries in the *Codex Laureshamensis* usually record that donations and bequests were made in honor of St. Nazarius.

We may select three winegrowing areas often mentioned in the *Codex*. The oldest documentary evidence of viticulture on the hills of the Bergstrasse, very near the abbey, is from 765. In a somewhat long-winded and repetitious deed gift by a certain Udo, son of Lando, we read: "I hand over all my share of property at Bensheim and all that I own this day within its boundaries and is due to me by law, farms, landed property, dwelling houses, agricultural buildings, fields, meadows, vineyards, cultivated land and fallow land, woodland, mills, still and running water. . . . In the name of God, I hand over and transfer all this in its unimpaired entirety from my ownership into the possession and seigniory of the monastery . . . in perpetuity." A document dated the following year, 766, records the gift of a vineyard at Bensheim by a local nobleman named Stalan. Eight years later, in 774, the same Stalan is recorded as having given another vineyard as well as newly cleared land suitable for planting vines. The year before, 773, King Charles, the later Emperor Charlemagne, is recorded to have made over to Lorsch the whole of Heppenheim, a few miles south of Bensheim, with landed property, dwelling houses, farms and outhouses, serfs, vineyards, woodland, fields, pastures, waters, and all appurtenances. There are further entries, for 786 and 796, concerning the same two localities.

In Rheinhessen, documentary evidence of viticulture also begins in the second half of the eighth century. Some of it comes from the records of the Abbey of Fulda, founded in 744, but gifts to Lorsch considerably outnumbered those made to Fulda. In two entries in the *Codex Laureshamensis*, dated 764, the first donations of vineyards, by one Folcrad and a certain Berticus, both residents of Oppenheim, are recorded. When, in 774, King Charles appeared with his court at Lorsch for the consecration of the church dedicated to St. Nazarius, he made over to the holy man's remains the whole of his royal estate at Oppenheim. Dienheim, near Oppenheim, is down for no fewer than ninety-nine donations in as many years, from 765 to 864; Dalsheim, near Worms, with nine between 765 and 818; more than a score of donations of vineyards are recorded from other places in Rheinhessen.

The attraction of St. Nazarius extended much farther than Rheinhessen; indeed, distance seems to have made little difference in the matter. In the foothills of the southern Black Forest between Freiburg and Basel, the winegrowing area now known as the Markgräflerland, St. Gall and Lorsch were the largest vineyard owners. The scattered property of St. Gall extended north as far as Freiburg. Lorsch owned vineyards in fourteen localities, in most of them, several vineyards. As an example, the *Codex Laureshamensis* notes seven donations from Heitersheim, a place about fifteen miles southwest of Freiburg. The oldest document has the following text: "In the name of God: I, Starafried, and my son Egilbert give to St.

Nazarius, the martyr of Christ, who rests bodily in the monastery of Lorsch, within the boundaries of Heitersheim, four hides of land with fields, meadows, vineyards, and six serfs, and what we believe to possess within the same boundaries. This we have confirmed by shaking hands." The record keeper adds: "So done in the monastery of Lorsch, on the fifth of May in the ninth year of the reign of King Charles" (thus, in 777). In addition to this donation, another four are recorded from the same place during the reign of Charlemagne and a further two during that of Louis the Pious. These seven documents enumerate eight farms, nine houses, together with arable fields, meadows, and vineyards.

Wherever a larger vineyard property was accumulated by local donations and bequests, a monastery farm was built, managed, presumably, by lay brothers. In almost all the more important winegrowing communities of the Markgräflerland there were such monastic farms. It is likely that from rural centers of this kind Christian influence spread out into an as yet only partly or superficially Christianized countryside.

However, it was not necessarily from religious motives that vineyards were made over to the possession of monasteries. In the Carolingian period the freeman was a yeoman farmer who owned his own homestead and land. But at the same time he was liable to military service, following Charlemagne on his long campaigns in Italy, Spain, and against the Saxons. When he came home he found his vineyard overgrown with thistles and thorns, while that of any bondsman, who did not have to render service, was flourishing. This would suggest to the freeman to transfer his immovable property to a higher landowner, either a monastery or a nobleman, by way of a "precary contract" (i.e., a contract obtained by entreaty), by which he would get it back as a hereditary fief. For this he would have to pay the tithe in kind, but in exchange the higher landowner, whether monastery or nobleman, had to provide a substitute for him as a member of the army.

Patron Saints of Winegrowing

Considering the great significance of wine in both Chrisitan religion and Christian folklore, as well as the fact that saints were always regarded as models to strive after and friends and helpers of the living, it is not surprising that there exists a considerable hagiolatry of patrons and protectors of winegrowing. In an age of growing unbelief, winegrowers are, by and large, still religious people. A good deal of this may well be due to the very great dependence of their livelihood on the whims of nature. More than other branches of crop cultivation, viticulture depends to a great extent on climatic conditions. Whether it be frost in mid-May, storms at blossoming time in June, rain and hail when the grapes ripen, let alone blights and pests, the winegrower is always conscious of his feeling of dependence, causing strains and tensions throughout most of the year.

The senior and most widely worshiped patron saint of wine in Germany is Pope St. Urban I (222–30), whose feast day (i.e., the anniversary of his death) is May 25. The date is significant because it falls at the beginning of the vine blossom; it is also the date on which, in the Middle Ages, laborers received their share from the earnings of the previous year's produce. Statues of St. Urban are often found in vineyards. On May 25, when the dangerous "ice saints," Mamertus, Pancrace, Servatius, and, last but not least, cold Sophia (May 12 to 15), are safely over, pious vineyard owners pray to St. Urban, asking him to take care of good weather for the flowering time; and there are pilgrimages to St. Urban's chapels or processions through the vineyards.

Other patron saints, of whom only a few can be named, are of more local significance. St. Vitus, a youth of noble family in Sicily, who was martyred about 303, appears to be worshiped as a patron only occasionally. He may have achieved his dignity because his feast, on June 15, falls into the vine-blossoming season; also because of the similarity of his name with the word *vitis* ("vine"). His widespread medieval cult in the north centered about the Abbey of Corvey on the Weser River, founded in 836, and St. Vitus's Cathedral in Prague, founded in 1344. The poet Matthias Claudius (1740–1815) does not seem to have thought very highly of the young saint's taste in wine. In his "Rheinweinlied" he says:

> It does not come from Hungary, nor from Poland,
> Nor from where one speaks Frenchified.
> That's where St. Vitus, the knight, may fetch his wine,
> We don't!

But to clear him from the charge of wine jingoism, he also has reservations about other German wines:

> Thuringia's hills, for
> example, produce a growth
> that looks like wine;
> but isn't. One cannot sing with it,
> nor be happy with it.

And he goes on:

> On the Rhine, on the Rhine,
> That's where our vines grow;
> Blessed be the Rhine.
> There they grow along its banks,
> And give us this balmy wine.

Next in the Christian calendar, on July 8, follows the feast of the Irish missionary St. Killian, who, together with his companions Totnan and Kolonat, was murdered in Würzburg in 689 and later was worshiped as the apostle and patron saint of Franconia. His cult as a wine patron is confined to that region.

Mid-August has several regional or local feast days. August 8 is that of St. Cyriacus, martyred in Rome in 308. He is worshiped in the Palatinate particularly, at his pilgrimage chapel of Lindenberg, where his statue is adorned with the first early ripening grapes of the year. He is also represented on a rustic stone monument standing in the vineyards of the village of Forst and commemorating the purchase of the site of Kirchenstück ("churc piece") by a local citizen in 1656. Above the inscription there is a relief showing a touching little scene from the legendary life of St. Cyriacus. When the old hermit of Lindenberg, tired after a day of itinerant preaching, looked for a night's lodging, the town gate of nearby Deidesheim used to spring open for him of its own volition. But one evening it remained locked, and the saint realized what was wrong: On his way he had absentmindedly pulled up a vinestake and used it as a walking stick. He returned it instantly to the place of his trespass, and when he went back to Deidesheim the gate sprang wide open again for him.

August 10 is the feast day of St. Lawrence, martyred in 258, who enjoys his reputation mainly in the Moselle region, but at places on the Middle Rhine as well, where his statues are draped with early grapes. A comparative newcomer to the job is St. Rochus, who died about 1370, and who, on his feast day, August 16, is similarly honored by having his statues bedecked with early grapes. A special center of his worship is the Rochusberg near Bingen, the goal of annual pilgrimages on the saint's day. Last but not least, the Virgin Mary herself is, in addition to her other responsibilities, expected to be a patron of grape growing, her statues being adorned with early grapes on the Feast of the Assumption, August 15. On the whole, she appears in this function only sporadically; but there is at least one area, the Markgräflerland of southern Baden, where she appears to be without a rival as a guardian of winegrowing.

Finally, there is St. Martin (316–400), who enjoys great popularity in the Moselle, competing with St. Lawrence and a few others in the same region. The Moselle people share him as a wine patron with those of the Loire, where he was bishop of Tours. But on the Moselle he is also held in high regard, almost considered a local, because he is believed to have several times sojourned and worked miracles in the early Christian community of Trier. His feast day, November 11, when all the cares and toils of the winegrowers' year are happily over, is their thanksgiving day, when the first young wine of the year, still cloudy with yeast, is tasted, and the saint appealed to, to send plenty of rain as a good foreboding for next year's vintage. In earlier times, St. Martin's day was also the date for paying the wine tithe to the Church; even today, the time-honored custom of the tenant grower's paying the ground rent on St. Martin's day has not entirely disappeared.

Religious Site Names

There is a profusion of site names, to be found on older wine labels after the local name, pointing to religious symbols or wayside images, commemorating particular saints, or referring to erstwhile possession by parish churches, monasteries, nunneries, cathedrals, etc. To choose some random examples: Kreuz, Kreuzberg, Heiligenstock, Heiligenberg, Laurentiuslay, Euchariusberg, Vitusberg, Rochusberg, Kirchenstück, Kirchspiel, Kirchenpfad, Kapellengarten, Messwingert, Klosterberg, Mönchsberg, Mönchsgewann, Pfaffenberg, Bruderschaft, Jesuitengarten, Abtsberg, Abteiberg, Nonnenberg, Nonnenlay, Nonnenwingert, Frauenberg, Juffer (which is the equivalent of *Jungfer, Jungfrau,* meaning "virgin," an epithet restricted to nuns in this context), Domherrenberg, Bischofsberg, and other specimens of the kind. Most of them have disappeared from view since 1971, as a result of the radical clearance of site names by the new wine law.

Christological Exegesis of Biblical Texts

It has already been hinted (see page 110) that certain biblical passages speaking of wine, vines, the vineyard, the grape, and the winepress were interpreted by the early ecclesiastical writers, and, following them, by the medieval theologians, in a Christological fashion. It became a general custom, and indeed apparently a positive religious requirement, to

explain scriptural texts, and especially Old Testament proph-
ecies, as foreshadowing or predicting Christ's passion and his
final victory through it.

The most importnat passage in this connection is Isaiah
63:1-6 (partly quoted on page 110). With this the patristic
writers often combined the description in Revelation 19:13, 15
(quoted in the same context). At the same time, they thought
of the blessing of Jacob's sons, Genesis 49:11, where they
believed Christ's passion, purifying the faithful with his blood,
to be prefigured because "he hath washed his garments in wine,
and his vesture in the blood of grapes." Closely connected with
this was the conception of the grape as the symbol of the
suffering Christ, which emanated from Numbers 13:18ff, the
story of the scouts returning from the land of Canaan. The staff
carried by two of them was interpreted as the cross, and the
huge grape as Christ hung upon it. Thus the last and most
influential of the Greek Fathers, St. John of Damascus (eighth
century) said in a homily at the Feast of the Assumption,
"From the Holy Virgin we have received the grape of life. Her
son gave us the true paschal meal, sacrificed himself as the
Lamb of God, and was, as the grape of the true vine, crushed in
the winepress."

Ecclesiastical commentators often compared the winepress
to the Church, whose members had to suffer in it like grapes; at
the same time, they thought of Christ, who, as the head of the
Church, was crushed out first. An example is a passage from St.
Augustine (354-430) in one of his biblical commentaries: "The
first grape to be pressed in the winepress is Christ. . . . What
happens in the visible winepress happens also in the Church. . . .
When a man prepares himself for the service of God he realizes
that he has come to the winepress; he is trodden out, pressed,
utterly crushed, so that he may flow into the Kingdom of God.
He is cleansed of the skin of sensual desire. . . . All this occurs
only in the press; therefore God's churches are also spoken of as
winepresses."

Mixed up with these ideas were also reflections on passages

referring to the vineyard of God, especially Isaiah 5:1ff and 27:2ff.

From the Church Fathers the medieval theologians took over the ideas of the mystical treader in the winepress. In these ideas they recognized Christ both actively, as the victor crushing his enemies in the winepress, and passively, as freely taking upon himself his suffering like a grape in the winepress. In a slightly different way, these two mutually contradictory strands of farfetched allegory are pulled together by a twelfth-century theologian, Rupert of Deutz, in a commentary on Isaiah: "He trod the winepress in voluntarily sacrificing himself for us; he was trodden in the winepress as a grape, secreting the wine from the husk of the body under the pressure of the cross, and breathing his last."

These allegorical notions of the medieval theologians did not remain confined to scholarly disquisitions, but were widely disseminated among the laity, which absorbed their imagery in contemplation and prayer, from sermons and liturgy, Latin chants and German hymns. An example is a popular Roman Catholic church hymn known as "The Spiritual Vineyard" or "The Spiritual Grapevine," which describes how Jesus, the grape stone, fell upon the Virgin Mary, and how the precious grape came into the world on Christmas Day. However, on Good Friday the Jews crushed the precious grape. Christ himself had to carry the press beam to Calvary where he was pressed out. But his blood became the sacred draft in the Eucharist.

Christ in the Winepress

The representation of the motif of Christ in the winepress in painting, sculpture, etc., has its roots in the biblical passages referred to and their Christological exegesis. Most of the representations bear biblical inscriptions in the Latin of the Vulgate, and among them, invariably, the beginning of Isaiah 63:3: *Torcular calcavi solus, et de gentibus non est vir mecum*

("I have trodden the winepress alone, and of the peoples there was no man with me"), or a longer inscription quoting part of verses 2 and 3, or a Christological adaptation: "He hath trodden the winepress alone for all, so that all may be redeemed."

The symbol has a varied imagery. Representations may be found in almost all kinds of media and places, often replacing representations of the crucifixion: in very small primitive iron sculptures in vineyard shrines, in more elaborate wood and stone sculptures, often painted, in votive pictures, wall paintings, and stained-glass church windows, in paintings on wood and canvas, in manuscripts and missals, in woodcuts and engravings, in silk embroideries, on epitaphs, tombstones, chalices, bells, fonts, pulpits, altars, chasubles, coins, and so on.

The iconography of the subject passes through three stages. The first, from the twelfth century, is confined to German-speaking countries. In its representations, which are comparatively rare, Christ is seen standing in the tub of the press clothed in long flowing robes; in somewhat more frequent examples he is shown in the same position but in typological juxtaposition with the representation of the crucifixion. The oldest known representation is on one of the many miniatures illustrating the *Hortus Deliciarum* ("Garden of Pleasures"), a kind of theological encyclopedia or devotional book in Latin, written in the second half of the twelfth century by the abbess of the convent of Hohenburg, at Odilienberg in Alsace. In this early stage, Christ in the winepress is clearly meant to be seen as the victor. In the second stage, from the fourteenth century, the motif changes into a mystical vision of Christ's passion. He is shown with a tortured expression, wearing the crown of thorns, covered only with a loincloth, breaking down under the weight of the cross, which is pressed down on his back by the screw of the press, his blood flowing from the wounds in his side and hands and mingling with the grape mash. He appears less as the treader of the grapes than as the grape being trodden out.

In the third stage, from the fifteenth century, the representation of the passion remains essentially the same, but its eucharistic meaning is emphasized. This is indicated by one or two chalices standing in front of the tub of the press being filled with blood, and more explicitly shown by a group of saints surrounding the tub, holding chalices in their hands and drinking the blood, or the blood flowing out of the tub being gathered by angels in a chalice. Some examples of this later type are elaborate compositions showing, for instance, a vineyard in the background from which the twelve apostles carry grapes to the winepress. God the Father and the Holy Ghost press the cross down upon Christ with the screw of the winepress. The four Latin Church Fathers, Augustine, Gregory, Ambrose, and Jerome, fill the sacred blood into casks, and the four evangelists take the casks out into the world on a wagon (in this case the symbol of the Church).

In northern Germany, where wine cultivation was practiced before the Thirty Years War, the motif of Christ in the winepress is also found, though somewhat more sporadically. Some representations also belong to the post-Reformation period, which is not surprising, since Protestant churchmen adhered to Christological interpretations for a long time. However, in the long run, Humanism and the Reformation, gradually but inevitably, were bound to put aside the motif of the winepress, together with other medieval symbolical representations. On the other hand, in French ecclesiastical art, where the older forms of the motif are not represented, it was revived and even flourished between the sixteenth and eighteenth centuries.

The Virgin and Child with the Grape

Connected with the conception of Christ as the precious grape crushed in the winepress is that of the Virgin Mary as the vine, as expressed, for example, by St. John of Damascus (see page 120). An earlier reference is by St. Isidore of Seville (560–636), who, in a commentary on Numbers 13:18–25, the story of the scouts returning from the Promised Land with the giant grape (see page 110), interprets the grape suspended on the staff as Christ hung upon the cross, and the vine on which it grew as the Holy Virgin. This symbolical idea is passed on through medieval Christianity in the same way as that of Christ in the winepress. To give one example, an Alsatian predicant of the fourteenth century closes his sermon with the words: "Now we beseech the precious vine Mary that the red wine that streamed forth from her son's side and was pressed out on the holy cross may wash off all our misdeeds, and that through her intercession we may deserve to be given the wine of eternal joy in the Kingdom of heaven."

This symbolism has produced, in sculpture and painting, from the Gothic period down to the present day, a great number of representations of the Virgin and Child holding a grape in his hands. A rare medieval variation on this motif, sometimes referred to as "The Grapevine Madonna," is the representation of the Virgin Mary, crowned with stylized vine leaves and carrying the Child Jesus on her left arm, while holding with her right hand a vine with a crucified Christ suspended on its stem. This type is represented in Germany in a small number of stone sculptures, while one or two specimens in Poland are represented in alabaster carvings. In France this latter type is unkown.

Sacramental Wine

Until the later Middle Ages, not only the priest but also all the lay communicants received the chalice of consecrated wine. The withdrawal of the chalice from the laity is a medieval innovation. It began sporadically in the twelfth century but was made obligatory only at the Council of Constance in 1415. The chalice was, of course, restored to the laity by the Reformation. The Roman Catholic Church eventually returned to the original practice at the Second Vatican Council in 1963, but only under certain conditions. However, in most Roman Catholic countries, as well as in Great Britain, only occasional advantage—on special occasions—seems to be taken of the possibility of returning to the original form in place of the familiar medieval one.

Canon law requires that "altar wine must be natural wine of the grape and not corrupted." One wonders what "not corrupted" means. The *New Catholic Encyclopaedia*, edited by Catholic University of America, says under the heading "Wine": "Where fresh grapes are unobtainable, altar wine may be made from dried grapes or raisins, but not from any other fruit." And again: "Altar wine is not valid material for Mass if a notable part (more than a third) has become vinegar, or if added substances make up a notable part of it." And again: "However, in the production of altar wine, especially sweet altar wine, the Holy Office . . . has permitted the addition of alcohol distilled from grape wine if this is done before the completion of fermentation. The maximum alcoholic content for licit sweet altar wine is 18 per cent; for licit dry altar wine to which alcohol has been added, 12 per cent; for valid altar wine, 21 per cent." According to these definitions, canon law rules on altar wine appear to be a great deal less stringent than those laid down by the German wine law, old or new, for ordinary wine.

This prompts the question of the color of the wine in the Eucharist. Redness being a distinctive feature of blood, one might suppose it also to be an essential quality of sacramental wine. The sermon of the medieval preacher quoted above speaks of the *red wine* streaming from Christ's side; and all the painted representations of the motif of Christ in the winepress show the red blood in the tub and the chalices. However, according to the *New Catholic Encyclopaedia*, "Altar wine may be either red or white. Since the sixteenth century, when the use of the purificator became common, white wine has been more often used because it leaves fewer traces on the linen." (The purificator is a cloth used at Communion for wiping the chalice and paten and the fingers and lips of the celebrant.) It seems to be a peculiarly lame argument, and one is tempted to ask for an ecclesiastical decree specifically permitting the use of white wine. But it seems that no such decree has ever been issued.

6. Rheinpfalz (Rhenish Palatinate)

THE RHENISH PALATINATE includes the largest continuous wine-growing region of Germany, with a viticultural surface of about 19,500 hectares (48,165 acres). A medieval chronicler honored it by calling it "the wine cellar of the Holy Roman Empire." Indeed, it is not only Germany's largest wine region but also its largest single forest region, with the thickly wooded Pfälzerwald range, which is a continuation of the Vosges Mountains, and a magnificent nature reserve of 1,300 square kilometers (about 500 square miles) with extensive plantations of sweet chestnut trees. The Pfälzerwald divides the Palatinate into two halves, eastern and western. Its eastern slope is named the Haardt, which constitutes the main part of the Palatinate's viticultural region and is divided, from south to north, into the three cultivation zones of the Upper, Middle, and Lower Haardt. The Pfälzer Weinstrasse (literally, "Wine Street"), a continuation of the Alsatian Route du Vin, skirts the foothills of the Haardt along a length of fifty miles. It comes nowhere near the Rhine, which runs about fifteen miles to the east, between entirely flat banks.

The winegrowing belt of the Haardt fans out to a width of between two and a half and four miles into the Rhine plain, being sheltered from western and northern winds by the heights of the Pfälzerwald. It is the warmest part of Germany, having a mean annual temperature of 50.9°F (10.5°C) to 51.8°F (11°C) and an average of 1,870 hours of sunshine yearly. Sweet chestnuts, almonds, and figs flourish and ripen almost everywhere, and in some places even lemons are grown. In this favorable climate, grapes ripen in general to full maturity, so that growers only rarely have to resort to any beautifying cellar treatment.

The Upper Haardt extends from Schweigen to Hambach, now a southern suburb of Neustadt an der Weinstrasse. Everybody agrees that the Middle Haardt begins at Neustadt, but there are different views as to where it ends: Minimalists allow it to reach only as far as Bad Dürkheim, others claim Kallstadt as its northern end, and maximalists go as far north as Grünstadt. Near Bockenheim, the northern end of the Lower Haardt and of the Weinstrasse, the shelter of the Pfälzerwald recedes to some extent. The Lower Haardt is by no means a lowland; there are still protective chains of hills to the west, but throughout the centuries the plow has pushed the woodlands about eight to ten miles away from the Weinstrasse.

At the northern boundary of the Palatinate there is a much smaller viticultural subregion, the Zellertal, a valley running due west to east, at right angles to the Haardt. The Zellertal lacks the shelter of the Pfälzerwald and therefore has a noticeably cooler climate, but makes up for it by having all its vineyards situated on slopes facing due south.

There are some scattered vineyard complexes in the extreme northwest of the Palatinate, that is, on the other side of the Pfälzerwald watershed, along the little Alsenz and Glan rivers, tributaries of the Nahe. However, although the localities where they are grown are situated inside the Palatinate, the wines share the character of those grown within the Nahe region, and are therefore officially considered and labeled Nahe wines (see page 201).

The soils of the Upper Haardt are mostly heavy loam and loess with a slightly chalky admixture; and those of the Lower Haardt and the adjacent Zellertal are similar but more clayey. The Middle Haardt has a far more variegated, multilayered system of soils, including light, gravelly, and loamy ones: dry, chalky sandstone, marl and red marl, shell lime, granite and basalt, gneiss, and micaceous schist.

The range of wines, both in variety and quality, is correspondingly wide. Silvaner is still the predominant variety, especially in the Upper Haardt, where it is juicy and full-bodied, sometimes a bit heavy; and in the Lower Haardt, where it tends to be milder. It is closely followed in both zones by fresh Müller-Thurgau, red Portugieser of medium quality, and the rarer, higher-quality Ruländer, Traminer, Muscatel, and Morio-Muskat. Riesling is virtually confined to the better soils of the Middle Haardt. However, all Palatinate wines, whether simple consumer wines or the most select and sophisticated ones, have great attraction for most drinkers because of their slight acidity.

The Weinstrasse begins at the Deutsches Weintor ("German Wine Gate") at Schweigen, a tiny village facing Wissembourg (Weissenburg) in Alsace. The Deutsches Weintor is not tiny, but in fact a massive monstrosity of the Nazi era that was regrettably rebuilt, though minus swastika, after World War II. From here, the Weinstrasse gently undulates and meanders northward across the attractive hill country of the Upper Haardt. The next locality of consequence is Bad Bergzabern, an old spa town of about six thousand inhabitants. Farther on, the large village of Klingenmünster produces wines that are among the best of the Upper Haardt. Its origin is dated by the foundation of a monastery prior to Charlemagne's reign, thus at about the same time as the Benedictine abbeys of Lorsch and Wissembourg. Leinsweiler is one of the prettiest winegrowing villages of the Palatinate, situated at the foot of a vineyard site rising up to the Slevogt Hof, formerly the home of Max Slevogt, an outstanding German Impressionist painter, who died in 1932. The town of Landau, with about thirty thousand inhabitants, situated to the east, just outside the vineyard belt, would seem to be the most convenient base from which to explore the Upper Haardt.

Returning to the Weinstrasse, the Geilweilerhof estate, near the village of Siebeldingen, is the home of a Federal Research Institute. Westward, a road leads up to the town of Annweiler and, high above it, Trifels Castle, which in the twelfth and thirteenth centuries was an important political center and the repository of the imperial insignia of the emperors of the Hohenstaufen dynasty. On the Weinstrasse again, we reach the pretty village of Rhodt, situated at the foot of the ruined Rietburg, which, among other wines, specializes in growing Traminer, and besides has the distinction of possessing the oldest vineyard in Germany, more than three hundred years of age. Edenkoben, a town of about seven thousand inhabitants, is recorded as a winegrowing center in the *Codex Laureshamensis* for the year 769. The vine-planted surface of the town covers 500 hectares (about 1,200 acres).

Situated a short distance to the west of the Weinstrasse, and at the foot of the thirteenth-century Kropsburg, St. Martin, tucked away in a narrow valley, is undoubtedly the most beautiful village in the Palatinate. Its parish church houses a Renaissance stone sculpture of impressive beauty. Maikammer is a large village of about four thousand inhabitants, which, however, with the well-kept town houses, offices, and cellarages of a number of large-scale producers, presents a partly urban character. Its wine production is the highest of the Upper Haardt, more than that of the much larger town of Edenkoben; indeed, 95 percent of its cultivated ground is under vines. Maikammer's war memorial in front of the parish church offers a novel and imaginative approach to the imagery of re-membrance, with a bronze group representing the Four Horse-men of the Apocalypse.

North of Maikammer, we enter the outskirts of Neustadt an der Weinstrasse, the center of Palatinate viticulture. In 1969, eight winegrowing communes allowed themselves to be incor-porated as suburbs of Neustadt. Of these, four are within the Upper Haardt zone, south and southeast of Neustadt; and four, to the north of Neustadt, together with Neustadt itself, are in the Middle Haardt zone. By incorporating these villages, Neustadt has increased its population to about fifty-five thou-sand, nearly double its original number, while at the same time increasing its vine-planted surface from a mere 180 hectares (about 450 acres) to a total of 2,013 hectares (about 5,000 acres), making it the largest winegrowing community of Germany. However, the eight incorporated communes retain their independence as viticultural producers and continue to use their separate wine labels.

The southernmost of these rural suburbs is Diedesfeld, a winegrowing community in Roman times, as has been borne out by a series of archaeological finds. Hambach, more than twice the size of Diedesfeld, is situated at the bottom of a hill bearing Hambach Castle, first built by the Salian emperors in the eleventh century. The present new-Gothic style in which the castle was renovated after World War II does not seem to do justice to the monumental old building of the Middle Ages, but the view from its terrace across an apparently boundless expanse of vineyards is one of the most beautiful of the Palatinate. Some miles to the southeast of Neustadt, in the Rhine plain, are the villages of Lachen-Speyerdorf and Geinsheim, both old winegrowing communities dating from the eighth century, but nowadays also engaged in tobacco growing, a major agricultural activity of the plains.

The urban center of Neustadt is situated precisely at the middle of the Weinstrasse, twenty-five miles from its southern and twenty-five miles from its northern end. It is here that the Middle Haardt begins. The view of the town is dominated by the twin towers of the fourteenth-century Stiftskirche, which serves both religious confessions. Tucked away in a labyrinth of old houses and courtyards, the thirteenth-century synagogue, Germany's only medieval Jewish place of worship to have escaped the attention of the Nazis and to have survived, was rediscovered in the early 1960s. As the center of Palatinate viticulture, Neustadt is the seat of an Enological Research and Teaching Institute. The main vineyard sites of the town are Mönchgarten, Grain, and Erkenbrecht. Not far to the west of Neustadt, near the little town of Lambrecht, is the Lindenberg shrine—according to legend the hermitage of St. Cyriacus, the local wine patron—the goal of the annual pilgrimages of Palatinate winegrowers.

Haardt, the first of the four incorporated villages in the Middle Haardt, is a very attractive place, virtually a single-street village and almost a mile and a half long, situated exactly on the edge of the woods and vineyards and overlooking the Weinstrasse to the east of it. Because of its elevated situation with a view of the broad plain, Haardt is called the "Balcony of the Palatinate." Its main vineyard sites are Herrenletten and Mandelring. It is here, on the stretch between Neustadt an der Weinstrasse and Bad Dürkheim, that Germany's mildest and warmest climate is found.

Gimmeldingen can prove its descent from a Roman settlement by a stone relief of the Persian sun god Mithras, erected and dedicated with an inscription by a certain Marterninus Faustinus in the year 325. The original is in the Historical Museum in Speyer, but a replica can be seen in the village. Gimmeldingen's most widely known vineyard site is the Meerspinne ("Sea Spider"), a puzzle of a name, for which a number of different explanations have been suggested.

Königsbach, like Haardt, is situated on the edge of the woods, with a charming view of the Rhine plain and well away from the traffic of the Weinstrasse. Its parish church contains a very beautiful and valuable altar painting by an unknown master, a representation of the crucifixion, dating from about 1475. Königsbach's best-known vineyard sites are Idig, Jesuitengarten, and Reiterpfad. Its production also includes a considerable percentage of red wines, mostly the humble Portugieser.

The large village of Mussbach is situated on the other side of the Weinstrasse, on the Rhine plain. Its first documentary mention as a winegrowing community, in the records of the Benedictine Abbey of Wissembourg and in those of faraway Fulda, is dated 753, that is, during the reign of Pepin, Charlemagne's father. Mussbach's best-known vineyard site is the Eselshaut ("Donkey's Skin"), another curious name.

We have now left the rural outskirts of Neustadt to enter upon a stretch of the Weinstrasse, from Ruppertsberg to Wachenheim, that may well be called the heart of the Middle

Haardt. That we are now in the most favored stretch of the Middle Haardt is made clear by the presence of the large estates of the houses of Bürklin-Wolf, von Buhl, and von Bassermann-Jordan. The "Three B's," as they are locally named, apparently scorn the rest of the Middle Haardt, let alone the Upper and Lower Haardt. There may not be any noticeable difference in climate as compared with the rest of the Middle Haardt to the south and north of this area; what counts mainly is the difference in soil composition. Ruppertsberg is situated slightly to the east of the Weinstrasse, on the Rhine plain. As local archaeological finds prove, its winegrowing goes back to Roman times. Its principal vineyard sites are Gaisböhl, Nussbien, and Reiterpfad, and some of its wines are of a quality equal to the celebrated products of nearby Deidesheim.

Documentary evidence of winegrowing at Deidesheim goes back to the year 770. Deidesheim is a most attractive little town, with a marketplace dominated by the parish church of St. Ulrich, a late Gothic building of the fifteenth century, and bordered by a handsome town hall, opposite which is the Kanne ("tankard"), a twelfth-century inn, the oldest in the Palatinate. There are, besides, several excellent hotels.

There could hardly be a greater contrast than that between graceful Deidesheim, with its comfortable hotels, and, only about two and a half miles to the north of it, the tiny and rather dreary-looking one-street village of Forst, without even a simple inn in which to spend the night, but with two restaurants. Yet the two unlike neighbors rival for recognition as the highest-quality producers of the middle Middle Haardt, and not a few connoisseurs would give their vote to Forst. From its famous vineyard sites of Jesuitengarten, Kirchenstück, Ungeheuer (not literally "monster", but derived from a family name), Freundstück, Pechstein, and others, it produces some of the most noble Rieslings of Germany. The best Rieslings of Forst are virtually in a class of their own, more full-bodied, more fiery, and richer in bouquet than those of any other place in the Palatinate. The superior quality of Forst's wines is ascribed to the ancient fires of the extinct volcanic Pechsteinkopf above the village, which threw up a large outcrop of basalt from which for centuries the local growers have helped themselves to provide heat storage for their vines, so that the whole of their vineyard soil has gradually become saturated with the stuff.

About two miles farther on, Wachenheim is a pretty little town about the same size as Deidesheim but with a much less urban character. Its first documentary mention is dated 765, when it belonged to the hereditary estate of the Salian dukes. Its best-known vineyard sites are Gerümpel, Goldbächel, Luginsland, and Bischofsgarten.

After about three miles or so, we reach Bad Dürkheim, after Neustadt the second-largest town on the Weinstrasse, and before Neustadt outstripped it by incorporating its eight outlying villages, the largest winegrowing community of Germany; besides, it is a spa of some importance. Among Dürkheim's vineyard sites, Spielberg, Hochbenn, Herrenmorgen, Nonnengarten, and Steinberg should be mentioned, but probably the best known is Feuerberg. About a third of Dürkheim's production consists of red wines, mostly Portugieser from the Feuerberg site. However, many ordinary Portugiesers from elsewhere prefer to identify themselves with this well-known site, and a so-called Dürkheimer Feuerberg may well be a *mixtum compositum* of produce coming from a number of other localities.

The village of Ungstein has, among its total production, an even higher percentage of red Portugieser than Bad Dürkheim. Among its vineyard sites are Herrenberg, Nussriegel, and, the best known, Honigsäckel. Kallstadt is a village about the same size as Ungstein. Its best-known vineyard sites are Saumagen and Annaberg, producing high-quality wines that make it obvious that Kallstadt is still within the Middle Haardt zone.

At the small village of Herxheim am Berg we enter upon the subregion of the Lower Haardt. From its large churchyard we have a splendid view of Freinsheim, situated to the east of the Weinstrasse, and a panorama of the Rhine plain beyond it.

Freinsheim, a much larger village, is mentioned in the records of the abbeys of Lorsch and Wissembourg. Parts of its medieval defense walls still remains, and an impressive stone votive crucifix is to be found standing at a crossroads in its neighborhood. After passing through the village of Kirchheim, we cross the Mannheim-Saarbrücken road and reach Grünstadt, a town of about nine thousand inhabitants and the center of the Lower Haardt, though itself insignificant as a winegrowing community.

At the village of Bockenheim we have arrived at the northern end of the Weinstrasse. Its Roman Catholic church of St. Lambert contains a graceful representation of the Virgin and Child, who holds a grape in his hands. A short distance to the west of Bockenheim and the Weinstrasse, the small village of Kindenheim is also at the northern end of the Lower Haardt.

The northernmost part of the Palatinate region, the Zellertal valley, running at right angles to the Haardt, has soils of mixed loam and clay producing pleasant and spicy wines. The main winegrowing villages are, from east to west, Niefernheim, Zell, Harxheim, Einselthum, and Albisheim. The best-known vineyard site is the Schwarzer Herrgott of Zell, named after the black crucifix that dominated it in earlier times.

Speyer, the capital of the Palatinate, is situated on the Rhine. The heart of Speyer is its red-sandstone Kaiserdom ("Emperor's Cathedral"), begun in 1030, the most magnificent Romanesque edifice in Germany. For nearly three centuries, the cathedral served as a tomb for eight German emperors, three empresses, and an imperial princess. Not far from the cathedral, the Historical Museum of the Palatinate includes, as a separate department, a Wine Museum, the richest of its kind in Germany. In seven large rooms, together with a courtyard linking it with the main part of the museum, it contains a unique collection providing an interesting survey of the whole range of objects connected historically with wine cultivation, including a complete cooper's workshop, cellar master's equipment, heraldic objects connected with wine, a large collection of drinking glasses and vessels for containing and serving wine, a collection of early wine bottles from the late eighteenth and early nineteenth centuries, a collection of early wine labels, as well as other memorabilia.

7. Rheinhessen

In TOTAL land surface, Rheinhessen is only about a quarter of the size of the Palatinate; nevertheless, the size of its winegrowing surface, about 18,300 hectares (45,300 acres), comes close to that of its larger southern neighbor. The reason is that the wine-producing areas of the province are scattered virtually all over its surface, while those of the Palatinate are more or less strung out along, and confined to, the Haardt belt and a short, narrow strip to the north of it. In the east and north, between Worms, Mainz, and Bingen, Rheinhessen is surrounded in a wide semicircle by the Rhine; in the west it reaches the Nahe River, a tributary of the Rhine; and in the south it passes over into the Palatinate without any natural geographical boundary.

Viticulturally, Rheinhessen may be divided very roughly into five subregions: the Bingen area, extending a short distance along the lower Nahe; the Ingelheim area, between Bingen and Mainz; the Rhine Front, extending from Mainz to Worms; the inland area of Worms (or Wonnegau; a name that has displaced the older one of Wormsgau); and the interior area, on both sides of the Selz, the only river that traverses the province, running northward through the town of Alzey to join the Rhine near Ingelheim.

Climatically, Rheinhessen is as favored as the Palatinate. It may not be quite so warm as the part to the east of the Haardt; instead, it is probably the driest region of West Germany. The hill ranges of the Taunus, Hunsrück, and Pfälzerwald shelter it from rainy winds, so that the average annual precipitation is only 52 centimeters (20.8 inches). Climate and fertility, however, are the only natural features that the adjoining regions have in common. Rheinhessen is a flat, low plateau with only slightly undulating hills, with very few and small wooded areas in the southwest, on the spurs of the Donnersberg, and in the northeast near Mainz. Excepting the short stretch of the Rhine Front, the scenery is a little dull, and consequently the interior is a terra incognita to the outsider and of no interest to tourist traffic.

Of all German viticultural regions, Rheinhessen has the most diverse composition of soils, a heritage of its geological past. To geologists, it is the Mainz basin (Mainzer Becken), a depression created in the Tertiary period in connection with the formation of the rift valley of the Rhine. It is surrounded by the Taunus range in the north, the Hunsrück in the west, the Palatinate hill country in the south, and the Odenwald in the east. In the first half of the Tertiary period, the sea penetrated this depression, filling the whole basin, while at the same time rivers and streams from the surrounding heights discharged their water into it. After new movements and displacements in the earth's crust had shut off the basin from the sea, a lake of first brackish and then fresh water came into being about the middle of the Tertiary period, which became dry land in the later Tertiary period.

Considering their diversity, any general description of Rheinhessen's wine is bound to be inadequate, but it may perhaps be said that, by and large, they are softer, milder, more delicate, and less pithy than those of the Palatinate. Silvaner, traditionally the predominant variety, and still higher in quantity of production than in the Palatinate, has been drastically reduced and overtaken by Müller-Thurgau. Riesling constitutes only 6 percent of the total, substantially less than in the Palatinate; it is largely confined to the favorable sites of Bingen, Nackenheim, Nierstein, Oppenheim, and Worms. Ruländer, Traminer, Morio-Muscat, and Scheurebe have their places among the minorities; other new crossbreeds, such as

Faber, Kanzler, and Huxelrebe, are as yet pretty rare in the assortment of local wines. Of red wines, Portugieser represents 6 percent of the total production. The main producer and specialist in red wines is Ingelheim, which besides Portugieser also grows quantities of Frühburgunder and Spätburgunder.

Apart from the State Domain in Mainz, which has extensive vineyard estates near Bingen, Bodenheim, Nackenheim, Nierstein, and Oppenheim, there are few large producers in Rheinhessen. The bulk of the viticultural surface is parceled out among small holders who combine viticulture with agriculture. Exclusively viticultural properties are found particularly in places like Bingen, Nackenheim, Nierstein, Oppenheim, and Worms.

The city of Worms is surrounded by vineyards; it is, in fact, following the recent incorporation of a number of villages, the third-largest German winegrowing community. The Middle High German Nibelungen saga tells us that at the Burgundian royal court in Worms "a good wine was served, the best that could be found along the banks of the Rhine." But the wine with the oldest, most-famous name, Liebfraumilch, a name that has an almost magic ring to it, is associated with the Liebfrauenkirche, the late Gothic, fifteenth-century church situated at the northern end of the city. The church is surrounded by a small number of entirely flat vineyards on a soil of gravelly clay, each protected by stone walls. The entire vineyard area is no larger than about 3.7 acres. The wines grown there, formerly known as Liebfraumilch, are now exclusively named Liebfrauenstift wines, so called because the Liebfrauenkirche was a *Stiftskirche*, that is, a collegiate church with a chapter. The genuine Liebfraumilch, nowadays under the protected name Liebfrauenstift, is undoubtedly a very pleasing wine, mild, delicate, and fragrant, but rather deficient in fire and pithiness; moreover, it has a slight earthy taste that not all wine lovers appreciate. It certainly does not rank among the peak wines of Germany, or even of Rheinhessen.

The name Liebfraumilch has covered an increasing range of

viticultural produce. Originally confined to the Riesling grapes grown within the precincts of the Liebfrauenkirche, it became a fancy name by being extended regionally to cover wines derived from a perimeter of ten to eleven miles around Worms, by no means all Rieslings. Up to about 1950 the practice of the wine trade confined it to white-wine blends "of good quality and pleasing kind" from the whole of Rheinhessen, with Silvaner as its main ingredient. Since about 1955 it may also include mild and not-too-sweet wines from the Palatinate, Rheingau, Middle Rhine, and Nahe regions, more or less fairly priced. On the whole, these wines tend to be a bit low on acidity, since generally they do not cater so much to the experienced wine drinker's palate as to the aspirant's.

To the general fancy name Liebfraumilch, another fancy name, that of the proprietary brand, is often added. Thus, in the United Kingdom the customer is offered the choice between Goldener Oktober Liebfraumilch, Hanns Christof Liebfraumilch, Three Kings Liebfraumilch, Blue Nun Liebfraumilch, Crown of Crowns Liebfraumilch, even Wedding Veil Liebfraumilch, *e tutti quanti*. The first-named of the lot is produced at the St. Ursula Weinkellerei in Bingen, not by a specialist vintner, but as a sideline of a dairy firm. All these mass-produced proprietary brands are standardized by blending, sugaring, and other cellar treatment, thus ensuring invariable quality over the years, rain or shine. In the United Kingdom and other European countries, Liebfraumilch wines are at least fairly certain to have been produced from German grapes. This, however, cannot always be taken for granted in the case of wines offered under this name overseas, say, in the United States or Canada, South Africa or Australia.

On the whole, English-speaking countries, or for that matter the Netherlands and the Scandinavian countries, are, alas, not very familiar with other German wines. On wine lists usually resplendent with good Burgundies and Bordeaux wines, German produce is often enough represented only by the inevitable Liebfraumilch, perhaps with Niersteiner Domtal and Bern-

kasteler Riesling as close seconds. There is even a rumor that
the late Dr. Konrad Adenauer, chancellor of the Federal
Republic, and a wine expert besides, was feted with Liebfraumilch at a Guildhall banquet given in his honor in London.

The new German wine law requires that fancy designations
of proprietary brands must always be unequivocally recognizable as such in order to protect the consumer from being misled
into believing that a wine of this kind comes from a particular
vineyard site, particular locality, or even from a particular
geographical area. Additional designations suggesting a particular derivation are held to be inconsistent with the nature of a
fancy designation, and are therefore banned. The same holds
for illustrations representing a particular landscape, church, or
other recognizable feature on the label. This will be hard on
such Rheinhessen names, previously accepted as *Gattungsna-
men* ("generic names"), as Oppenheimer Krötenbrunnen, Niersteiner Domtal, and Binger Rosengarten, each applied to wines
grown, or supposed to be grown, within a perimeter of five miles
of the respective town. The first two, incidentally, overlap, the
two towns being separated by little less than half a mile.
Oppenheim has a vineyard site named Krötenbrunnen ("Toads'
Well")—and, indeed, a very good one—but if the floods of
proprietary brands have anything to do with it, it can only be
very little. So it runs counter to the new law on both counts, site
and locality. Niersteiner Domtal ("Cathedral Valley") could be
disqualified on only one count, the local name, for there is no
valley of that name, nor, indeed, a cathedral at Nierstein. The
same applies to Binger Rosengarten.

The stretch between Worms and Mainz is named the Rhine
Front. Here, beginning at Osthofen, the undulating plateau of
the interior breaks off into the Rhine plain, for the greater part
of its length as a low ridge with gentle slopes bearing the
vineyards, mostly with a southeasterly exposure. Osthofen and
the string of villages to the north of it—Mettenheim, Alsheim,
Guntersblum, Ludwigshöhe, and Dienheim—are all situated on
the plain, standing in front of their vineyard slopes on soils

mostly composed of loess, Guntersblum has a special object of interest in its Kellerweg, a lane behind the village leading past a number of vaults excavated at the base of the vineyard slope that serve as storage cellars for the wine barrels. The reason for this exceptional arrangement is that the village is very low-lying and not safe from the danger of occasional Rhine floods.

The wines grown in these places are in great part fair table wines, but also, in part, good, full-bodied wines with fine bouquet. Those of the best sites may be said to be comparable in quality to Oppenheim or Nierstein wines of middling sites. This is true especially of the wines of Dienheim, situated nearest to Oppenheim, whose best sites produce wines that are nearly equal to those of the latter town. On the whole, Silvaner and Müller-Thurgau predominate, but the proportion of Riesling is a good deal higher than in most of the interior tableland. Besides, smaller quantites of Ruländer, Morio-Muscat, Scheurebe, and occasionally Traminer are grown. The proportion of red wine, almost all of it Portugieser, is probably not much more than 5 percent.

Most of the Rieslings are grown on the short Rhine Front stretch between Oppenheim, Nierstein, and Nackenheim, and some of them rank among the finest of Germany. The old town of Oppenheim is built on a ledge of the plateau above the Rhine valley. Its many-angled streets lead up to the red-sandstone church of St. Catherine's, built in the early fourteenth century, one of the most beautiful Gothic churches of Germany.

Oppenheim's soil consists predominantly of Tertiary Cyrene marl, covered by a layer of chalk and topped with loess. Cyrene marl, which also forms the main geological substratum elsewhere in Rheinhessen, is very permeable, with a high capacity for absorbing water and nutrients, so that even in dry years it still provides good growing conditions for the vine. But Oppenheim's particular Cyrene marl differs somewhat from that of other places in its granular structure and calcareous and other mineral content. Even where similar geologic conditions exist elsewhere, the microclimate conditions cannot compete with those of Oppenheim, whose vineyard sites have the most favorable southerly exposure and are protected against rough winds by chains of hills that catch the sun's rays and store its warmth. Moreover, the local microclimate is characterized by a relatively high atmospheric humidity in late autumn, providing the prerequisite for the advent of "noble mold," which very considerably improves the quality of the harvest yield. Among the wines grown in Oppenheim's vineyards, Rieslings such as Reisekahr, Sackträger, Daubhaus, Kreuz, Zuckerberg, Herrengarten, Schlossberg, and others are in the highest-quality class of German wines.

Less than a mile farther north, at Nierstein, we reach the stupendous "Red Mountain," which in one direction stretches as far as Nackenheim, three miles beyond Nierstein, and in the other turns for a short distance inland to Schwabsburg, bypassing Oppenheim. Between the two first-named towns, the ridge that forms the western border of the Rhine plain becomes much higher and steeper and, almost forming a steep bank, closely approaches the river, thus benefiting from its reflection of light and warmth.

Red Mountain belongs to the Permian formation, and thus is far older than Oppenheim's Cyrene marl of the Tertiary period. Its soil is often mistaken for red sandstone, but is in fact red argillaceous slate. It crumbles into flat pebbles, which produce a rather dangerous scree on the steep slopes in spite of the terracing. Nor is it really red, but more of a dark purplish color; but when, in heavy thunderstorms, some of it is washed down into the Rhine, it stains the water crimson for miles. This soil stores the heat of the sun in the daytime and gives it back again to the vines at night. It is rich in nutritive substances, especially iron. On the other hand, it is deficient in calcareous content. This deficiency, however, is repaired by nature, on the upper reaches, in the form of an admixture of loess, which comes down from the plateau above with wind and rain; on the lower slopes the calcareous matter has to be added by human labor.

Nierstein's vineyard surface includes about 550 hectares (1,350 acres). It was the largest winegrowing community of Rheinhessen before Worms overtook it by incorporating all of the villages in its immediate neighborhood. Its surface is now also smaller than that of Ingelheim, which, since the administrative merger of Ober-Ingelheim and Nieder-Ingelheim, measures about 665 hectares (1,540 acres). Among its Rieslings, Glöck, Auflangen, Rehbach, Pettenthal, Kranzberg, Orbel, Hipping, Zehnmorgen, and Rosenberg may be mentioned. Glöck is especially noteworthy. It comes from a tiny piece of vineyard, less than 1 hectare (about 2 acres) in size, lying below the church—the name Glöck was probably taken from the ringing of the church bells. In spite of its small size, it has managed to survive the drastic massacre of site names by the new German wine law, benefiting from a clause that states that if the wine from a smaller site has contributed outstandingly in spreading the reputation of German wines, that site will be allowed to keep its old name.

Nackenheim is a much smaller town than Nierstein. Its best-known Riesling sites are Rothenberg and Fenchelberg. At the other end of Red Mountain, the viticultural acreage of Schwabsburg is a continuation of that of Nierstein, sharing the same kind of soil; therefore, some of Schwabsburg's wines come up to the standards of Nierstein's.

It is an interesting experiment to compare two good Rieslings, one from Oppenheim—say, Herrengarten—the other from Nierstein—say, Rosenberg—both of the same vintage, from the same producer, and developed in the same cellar, neither, perhaps, in its respective locale of a peak-quality grade. They are of the same general quality mainly because they share a more or less identical microclimate. Yet they are different in their respective individual flavors and tastes, having been grown on entirely different kinds of soil.

In the northern section of the Rhine Front, the plateau again slopes down gently onto the Rhine plain, which here becomes much wider again. The small old town of Bodenheim, about two miles from the river, has a substantial viticultural acreage within its boundaries; while that of Laubenheim, somewhat closer to the Rhine, is a good deal smaller. Both places produce predominantly wines of a fair, middling quality, though their better sites may yield quite good mild wines with a delicate bouquet. In both places, wine cultivation goes back at least to the early Middle Ages.

Since the late Middle Ages, the epithet of "Golden Mainz," as a counterpart to that of "Holy Cologne," has been in popular use, although industrialization and other modern developments have somewhat tarnished both the "golden" and the "holy" reputations. However, having been rebuilt after the destruction of World War II, Mainz still remains a beautiful city. Its cathedral of Sts. Martin and Stephen, begun about 1000 and completed in 1137, forms, with those of Worms and Speyer, the triad of great Romanesque "emperors' cathedrals," although, in fact, no medieval German emperors are known to have been buried in it.

In recent years, Mainz has become a winegrowing community again, though only on a moderate scale, by the incorporation of some villages in its neighborhood. But it has always been an important center of the wine trade, as well as the seat of several institutions of the official wine organization. In the Haus des deutschen Weines ("House of German Wines"), on Gutenbergplatz, nearly three hundred wines from all German viticultural regions are on sale. The same building also houses the German Winegrowing Institute and the Stabilization Funds for Wine, both concerned with the promotion of wine marketing. Just around the corner, in the Fust-Strasse, a narrow lane named for a fifteenth-century printer closely associated with Gutenberg, are the offices of the German Wine Information bureau, which, besides other publicizing activities, issues a popular periodical entitled Der Weinfreund ("The Wine Friend"). Johannes Gutenberg University, reopened after World War II after having been closed for about a century, is the only German university that has an institute for wine research devoting itself specifically to the investigation of the physiological processes of fermentation. The Museum of Roman-Germanic Antiquities and the Middle Rhine Museum are concerned with ancient and medieval viticultural history.

At Ingelheim, halfway between Mainz and Bingen, the Selz River leaves the hills to join the Rhine. Near their junction Charlemagne built his palace in 770; today only scanty remains indicate the site of his residence. Now constituted as a single town, Ingelheim consisted in the past of the separate communities of Ober- and Nieder-Ingelheim. Their union has given Ingelheim the second-largest wine-planted acreage of Rheinhessen. It is the province's main center of red-wine production. Its Frühburgunder and Spätburgunder are great quality wines with fine bouquet, but a great deal of Portugieser is also grown. Its white wines are, on the whole, light table wines with mild acidity, which, however, in better vintages may be of quite good quality. The main red-wine vineyard sites are Pares, Horn, Höllenweg, and Steinacker.

Neighboring Gau-Algesheim, situated like the upper part of Ingelheim on a soil mostly consisting of loess and Cyrene marl, and with a considerable acreage of vineyard land, grows more white than red wines. On the whole, its white wines are superior to those of Ingelheim, while its red ones are about equal in quality. Among its vineyard sites, Goldberg and Pares (the latter a part of Ingelheim's site) may be mentioned. In the past, Gau-Algesheim's inhabitants were almost wholly dependent on the outcome of their vintages; in contrast to the interior plateau, there was virtually no ordinary agriculture to fall back on.

The town of Bingen is most beautifully situated at the junction of the Nahe and the Rhine and at the foot of the Rochusberg, a ridge extending eastward as far as Kempten. It also sits at the intersection of four viticultural regions, that of its own Rheinhessen, that of the Nahe, that of the Middle Rhine, on the left bank of the Rhine below the junction of the Nahe, and that of the Rheingau, on the right bank of the Rhine. Since the incorporation of Büdesheim, on its southern side, and of Kempten, on the east, it has been a winegrowing community of considerable size; besides, it is a major center of the wine trade and of industries connected with wine production.

The composition of its vineyard soils is variable, but quartzite slate predominates. The quality of the local wines varies in accordance with the diversity of soils and sites. The vineyard sites situated on the partly very steep slopes of the Rochusberg—for example, Schlossberg and Schwätzerchen ("Little Babbler")—produce wines with a fruity acidity and fragrant bouquet. Kempten's main site, on the eastern slope of the Rochusberg, is the Kapellenberg, named for the Rochus chapel above it. The Eiselberg site along the Nahe produces an especially spicy wine, considered one of the finest of Rheinhessen. Büdesheim is one of the most outstanding winegrowing areas of the province. Lying below the large Scharlachberg ("Scarlet Hill"), the southern slope of the Rochusberg, it produces Rieslings and red Burgundies that are in the top bracket of Rhine wines.

In Bingen and its neighborhood, a corkscrew is known as a "Bingen pencil." This expression goes back to a local anecdote about a meeting of the town council at which none of the members had a pencil. So the proceedings had to be discontinued, and it was decided to withdraw to the town hall's cellar instead, to have an already overdue tasting of some of the wines. When the mayor wanted to open the first bottle, he found that he had no corkscrew ready and asked for one, whereupon every one of the councilors pulled one from his pocket. Various versions of this story are found in most popular German wine books as well as in some English ones. Even more overdone through repetitious quotings is Goethe's description of the St. Rochus festival at Bingen on August 16, 1814, and of the story, told him by somebody on that occasion, of the local bishop's Lent sermon, in which that dignitary explicitly approved of wine drinking, even of an astonishing degree of indulgence, as long as the drinker managed to stop short of beating up his wife and children afterward.

It is impossible to mention, let alone describe, all the many winegrowing localities of the interior tableland; only a few of them can be chosen for consideration. While it is true that part of the interior consists of more or less impermeable soils of stiff, clayey marl, which are not friendly to the vines, especially in wet years, the old prejudice that marl produces only modest wines for local consumption is certainly not justified. There are many tracts of Cyrene marl and chalk and other favorable soils here, producing good wines, which in some cases even come up to the standards of the Rhine Front. Even where soil conditions are not especially favorable, advances in modern field and cellar techniques have achieved a general improvement in quality.

Gau-Bickelheim, a large village in the west-central part of the province, deserves special attention. Lying on Cyrene marl and chalk, at the foot of the broad, sun-drenched southerly slope of the Wissberg, this village produces some of the best wines of Rheinhessen, vigorous, full-bodied, juicy, and fragrant. The long stretch of the hillcrest provides distant views of the fertile land. In the middle of the Wissberg the foundations of a Roman country house, or *villa rustica*, have been discovered; in addition, quantities of fragments of amphorae and other vessels and coins dating from Augustan times to those of Constantine the Great have been found. Following the Romans, the Franks, to judge from recorded donations of local vineyards to Lorsch Abbey, appear to have greatly expanded winegrowing. In the twelfth century, Rupertsberg, the convent of St. Hildegarde of Bingen, owned a large acreage of vineyard land on the slopes of the Wissberg. Coming back to modern times, Gau-Bickelheim possesses the oldest winegrowers' cooperative in Rheinhessen, founded in 1897. It has developed into a remarkably large central cellarage with completely up-to-date equipment, and is supplied by sixty-odd other cooperatives, constituting an additional attraction of the town.

Westhofen, in rolling hill country a few miles inland from Osthofen on the Rhine Front, may be said to be a typical winegrowing village of the Wonnegau area. On good soils of

Cyrene marl covered with chalk and loess, it produces predominantly white wines, including a high proportion of Riesling and Ruländer, as well as smaller quantities of red ones, mostly Portugieser but also Burgunder. In the Middle Ages, the Benedictine Abbey of Wissenbourg in Alsace owned a large share of the local vineyard land. A short distance to the west of the village, Gundersheim is the main red-wine producer of the Wonnegau.

Alzey, on the Selz River in the south-central part of the province, is a medium-sized town lying at the foot of its castle, which was built on the ruins of an earlier stronghold of the Palatine counts. Alzey is one of Germany's oldest towns, of Celto-Roman origin, and in the early Middle Ages enclosed a Merovingian and Carolingian royal estate. Under the Hohenstaufen dynasty, in the twelfth and thirteenth centuries, Alzey was far-famed for the splendors of its knightly pageantry, its tournaments, and its minstrelsy. Today it is an important center of the Rheinhessen wine trade, as well as the seat of a State Research Institute specializing in the breeding of new vine varieties.

8. Mosel-Saar-Ruwer (Moselle-Saar-Ruwer)

THIS is the third-largest viticultural region, following Rheinhessen at a considerable distance, however, covering only about
11,000 hectares (27,100 acres) as compared with Rheinhessen's
18,300 hectares (45,300 acres). The French and English form
(Moselle) of the name of the principal river is derived from its
Latin name, Mosella, which is a diminutive of Mosa, the Latin
name of the Meuse. The shorter German form of the name
(Mosel) is pronounced with the accent on the first syllable. The
Moselle rises on the Col de Bussang in the southern Vosges;
after a northwestern sweep through Lorraine it turns in a
general northeasterly direction at Thionville (Diedenhofen),
first forming the frontier between Germany and southeastern
Luxembourg and then entering Germany; it takes up its bigger
tributary, the Saar, a few miles above Trier, and its smaller one,
the Ruwer, a short distance below that city, finally joining the
Rhine at Koblenz.

The soils of the Upper Moselle (from the viticultural point
of view, the stretch from the village of Perl at the beginning of
the Luxembourg frontier to Trier) consist predominantly of
heavy shell lime. This section of the river is also called the
White Moselle. Because of the light color of the soil its storage
of warmth is relatively scanty; also, its high alkaline content
makes it unsuitable for Riesling vines. In the Trier basin, from a
short distance above the mouth of the Saar to the small market
town of Schweich, the shell lime changes into grayish-red

sandstone. From Schweich to its junction with the Rhine, the river runs through a narrow, more or less steep-sided valley between the Eifel hills and the Hunsrück range, both part of the Rhenish Slate Hills complex (Rheinisches Schiefergebirge), which is a Devonian formation, meandering capriciously most of its way in a series of narrow U-bends. The upper half of this stretch is, viticulturally, the Middle Moselle; the lower half, the Lower Moselle. The former section is made up geologically of permeable bluish-gray argillaceous slate; the latter section of harder and more or less impermeable reddish graywacke slate. The argillaceous slate of the Middle Moselle crumbles easily into a nutritive, moisture-retaining soil. The graywacke slate of the Lower Moselle is interspersed with iron and weathers insufficiently; thus, it is poor in nutritive substances and has a low moisture-retaining capacity. Another disadvantage of the Lower Moselle is that that part of the river, below Cochem, assumes a much straighter northeasterly course and slopes with a southerly exposure become rare.

While in the low hill country of the Luxembourg frontier and throughout the level stretch of the Trier basin agriculture can be carried out alongside viticulture, the Middle and Lower Moselle, as well as the Lower Saar valley and that of the Ruwer, are virtually one-crop tracts, the narrowness of the deep valleys making any other form of cultivation besides viticulture all but impossible. By contrast with the Palatinate, Rheinhessen, and most other regions where the usual method of training vines is by means of frames connected by wires, the vines on the slopes of the Moselle, Saar, and Ruwer are trained on individual vine stakes. One of the reasons for this traditional method is the steepness of the slopes; another, the need to renew the slate cover beneath the vines every few years with slate rubble brought up from pits in the valleys.

The whole region produces white wines exclusively—Riesling, Müller-Thurgau, and Elbling. In the eighteenth century all sorts of wines—white and red, good, bad, and indifferent—were grown; but an edict issued in 1786 by the last archbishop-elector of Trier, Clement Wenceslas, a man of high birth (son of Frederick Augustus II, elector of Saxony, and, as Augustus III, king of Poland) and probably of refined tastes, ordered the rooting out of the prolific but inferior "Rhenish grape" (no doubt the plebeian Elbling) and other varieties, and their replacement by Riesling wines.

Obviously such an order could not be complied with in a hurry, especially since the archbishop's rule was itself replaced by that of French authorities only two years later; nevertheless, Riesling cultivation increased remarkably during the nineteenth and the first half of the present century, until in the last two decades it went down again in favor of its competitor Müller-Thurgau. (The official figures for 1963, 1964, 1968, and 1971 are, respectively: Riesling 87 percent, Müller-Thurgau 4 percent; Riesling 77 percent, Müller-Thurgau 9 percent; Riesling 77 percent, Müller-Thurgau 12 percent; Riesling 71 percent, Müller-Thurgau 16 percent.)

Müller-Thurgau, which is usually planted at and near the bottom of the slopes, has especially profited from the canalization of the Moselle, carried out mainly for the purpose of connecting the iron ore of Lorraine with the coal of the Ruhr, and completed in 1964; there are now fourteen locks between Thionville and Koblenz, overcoming a difference of nearly three hundred feet in water level. By damming up the river, the locks greatly enlarge the water surface, which is also to the advantage of the vineyards because the climatic conditions are improved— the larger water surface reflects more sunlight onto the vines.

The proportion of the planted surface occupied by the humble Elbling remained stationary at 11 percent between 1964 and 1971; it is grown mostly on the Upper Moselle and in the Cochem Krampen, but because Müller-Thurgau is increasingly planted on the heavy shell-lime soils, its days are probably numbered.

The Moselle countryside is one of the most beautiful river landscapes on the Continent. Its peculiar charm rests mainly on the countless turns in the river's course, providing constantly

changing views, with vineyards and woods or meadows succeed-
ing each other at every new bend. Wherever there is a southerly
exposure—sometimes on the left and sometimes on the right
bank, according to the river's change of direction—the steep
slopes are planted with vines. The tranquil beauty of the
landscape is enhanced by the mild climate, the soft, clear air of
the valley, and the relatively clean water, in which it is still
possible to swim.

A quality that often seems especially enchanting is that the
atmosphere of the valley almost appears to be "breathing slate."
As a German poet, Rudolf Binding, has described it, "One
tastes the slate in the wine, breathes it in the air, smells it after a
fleeting rainfall, when the sun dries the porous layers." Local
and vineyard names endlessly recall slate by including the word
Lay, still understood here as denoting "slate," though it is
obsolete elsewhere in Germany. The word occurs by itself only
occasionally as the name of a village or vineyard, but there are
hundreds of site names in which it forms part of a compound,
such as Schwarzlay, Urlay, Kranklay, Günterslay, Hubertuslay,
Eulenlay, Busslay, Herzlay, Klosterlay, Münzlay, Geyerslay, and
Burglay. The old villages and towns with their half-timbered
houses and medieval churches surmounted by castle ruins, and,
of course, the Roman and medieval remains of ancient Trier are
beautiful to see.

Moselle Rieslings are on the whole lighter, somewhat less
alcoholic, and less full-bodied, but rather more airy and fragrant
than those of most other regions. They generally have a very
pleasant fruity acidity. Those of the Saar, especially, are
remarkable for their naturally sparkling, prickly taste. All
Rieslings of the Moselle region have a basic individuality of
their own, which makes it relatively easy to distinguish them
from those of other regions. However, partly owing to the many
snaky undulations in the course of the river, and partly to
differences in the subsoil below the slate, the natural conditions
of different sites vary a good deal, and this accounts for a
considerable variability in the flavor of individual local wines.

There is a popular German saying, *Wer die Wahl hat, hat die Qual,* which may be translated as "The larger the choice, the greater the agony." The insufficiently initiated wine lover, faced with a list of hundreds of site names, may well despair. But there are plenty of firms here, too, which are only too happy to relieve him of his agony by offering him their artificially homogenized proprietary brands with fancy names. For instance, our old friend Goldener Oktober appears not only as a Rhine wine in brown bottles, but also as a Moselle in green ones. There is one product with the modest name Mosel-blümchen ("Moselle Floweret") and another with the more pretentious one of Himmlisches Moseltröpfchen ("Heavenly Moselle Droplet"). Bernkasteler Riesling may have been grown anywhere within a five-mile radius of that town, perhaps somewhere up in the Eifel hills, but is rather unlikely to have come from any site at its alleged origin. Kröv's somewhat coarsely named Nacktarsch ("Bare Bottom"), a nonexistent site, gives that name to the less satisfactory produce from any of the town's vineyards. Zell's widely known Schwarze Katz ("Black Cat") might mistakenly be thought to have been grown in a local vineyard of that name; in fact, it is a *mixtum compositum* from any number of the town's sites.

The Upper Moselle enters Germany at the village of Perl, the "Dreiländereck" ("Three Counties' Corner"), and forms the frontier between Germany and Luxembourg as far as its junction with the small Sauer River. It is a countryside of meadows, fields, and orchards, with low hills bearing the vineyards, which are planted mostly with the age-old Elbling and the new Müller-Thurgau vines. The village of Nittel has the largest vineyard acreage. The countryside is not unattractive, in places even picturesque, but the wines grown there may safely be left to the natives to drink; they are used to them. The Upper Moselle is really more interesting to the archaeologist than to the wine lover.

There is an old local saw that in a good year the best Moselles grow on the Saar. There is something to be said for this, but it has to be a very good year indeed. The Saar joins the Moselle at the little town of Konz, opposite the village of Igel. Its wines do not belong to the federal state of Saarland, as they grow on the lower course of the river, a stretch of about eighteen miles' length situated in the state of Rhineland-Palatinate. The topsoil of the Lower Saar slopes consists of argillaceous slate like that of the Middle Moselle, but is harder, being interspersed with quartz and therefore not weathering so well. This is a disadvantage affecting more the quantity of the yield than its quality. On the other hand, there is also a climatic disadvantage. The river has a general northward direction, and parts of the valley are therefore exposed to the cold winter blasts coming down from the Eifel hills; other parts, however, are in well-protected, warm, basin-shaped valleys formed by loops of the river. On the whole, Saar wines are characterized by a comparatively low alcohol content, a slightly higher degree of acidity, freshness, prickliness, a naturally sparkling quality, and, in good vintages, by a pleasant pithiness, fruitiness, and fragrant bouquet.

Traveling from north to south, the first village worth mentioning is Kanzem. It is situated on the left bank, surrounded by a narrow loop of the river, but having its best sites, with well-protected southerly slopes, on the opposite bank. Wiltingen, higher up and on the right bank, has the largest acreage of wine-planted surface and is, with its famous Kupp and Scharzhofberg sites, in the highest-quality bracket of Saar wines. Ockfen, lying at the foot of the steep southerly slopes of its Bockstein and Herrenberg sites, justifiably rivals Wiltingen for recognition as the producer of the best wine on the river. Opposite Ockfen and Wiltingen, but at some distance from the Saar, the villages of Ayl and Wawern have some good sites on the slopes above an old river bed, now a valley of fertile fields and lush meadows. A short distance above Ayl, also on the left bank, the old and attractive town of Saarburg is the largest community on the lower Saar. Its dry, prickly wines are of a pleasant quality only in good vintages.

A little higher up, but again on the right bank, the vineyards of the little town of Serrig lie at the base of, and on the slopes rising to, the modern castle of Saarfels, used by a firm manufacturing Sekt (sparkling wine). Serrig has an extensive acreage of vine-planted surface, but the quantity of its produce is not matched by quality. Serrig lies within a stretch of the valley that is most exposed to the northern winter winds, and its wines require a hardened connoisseur of acidity and steeliness to do them justice. It may be presumed that a good proportion of them end up in the Sekt cellars of Saarfels castle, where thinness, steeliness, and acidity can be dealt with, and natural prickliness is a positive asset.

Trier's own wines are of only moderate quality, but the city is the principal center of the wine trade in the valleys of the Moselle and its tributaries. It houses more than a score of large cellars belonging to the great estates. Representatives of the trade attend the annual spring and autumn auctions. Among the local owners of large estates all over the region are the cathedral, the episcopal priests' seminary, the episcopal hostel (all of which were given back part of their old estates or purchased new ones at sometime or other after secularization), the State Domain, the municipal homes for the aged and infirm, and Friedrich Wilhelm Gymnasium (a grammar school whose most famous graduate was Karl Marx). As the center of the region, Trier is also the seat of an enological Research and Teaching Institute. Trier's most distinctive landmark is the Porta Nigra ("Black Gate"), the northern city gate whose remains date from the fourth century. The oldest of Trier's Roman ruins is the oval amphitheater, built about A.D. 100 as an arena for gladiatorial combat and fights between wild beasts.

The Ruwer is not much more than a large stream, and its viticultural area is only about six miles in length. In the upper part of the valley, the hard slate is interspersed with quartz like that of the Saar, while the lower reaches have the crumbling argillaceous slate rich in nutritive substances as good as any, and better than most, in the Moselle valley itself. All the villages are on the right bank. The main towns on the lower course are the tiny village of Eitelsbach and the neighboring, much bigger Mertesdorf. The best Eitelsbach vineyard site is the Karthäuserhofberg, which takes its name from a former Carthusian monastery. Mertesdorf has a number of good sites in its neighborhood, but the largest, and by far the best, the Maximin Grünhaus, named for the former Benedictine Abbey of St. Maximin, is situated on the opposite side of the valley.

A little higher up, at Kasel, the harder soil begins, and the wines of the village are, in color, flavor, and taste, remarkably similar to those of the Saar. Still higher up is Waldrach, the largest Ruwer village and its largest producer; probably a considerable proportion of its produce finds its way to the cellars of the Sekt manufacturer. This also applies to the only vineyard of Sommerau, the highest village in the area, on the edge of the densely wooded Hunsrück slopes. There is, however, one larger vineyard complex at the village of Avelsbach, far to the west of the Ruwer valley and in the immediate neighborhood of Trier, which shares the same kind of soil with the lower Ruwer and produces wines of the same fine quality.

The definition of what constitutes the Middle Moselle is a little controversial. It is at Schweich that the river first knocks against the spurs of the slate hills, so this little town is often called the gate to the Middle Moselle; however, Mehring, a little lower down, might be given the benefit of the doubt. Turning around the first big bend of the river, we arrive at Klüsserath, which stretches for a long distance between the stream and its vineyards. Its largest and best-known site is Bruderschaft.

On the right bank, at the beginning of the next great loop, lies Leiwen, with the Laurentiuslay as perhaps its best-known site. The apex of the loop is occupied by Trittenheim. Its main sites are Apotheke, Altärchen, and Laurentiusberg, the last-named vineyard dedicated to the patron saint of winegrowers, whose special place of worship, St. Lawrence's chapel, is on the top of his hill. From the bridge at Trittenheim a new road leads up to a restaurant whose terrace commands one of the finest views of the Moselle valley.

Continuing on the right bank, we soon reach Neumagen, where replicas of the famous "Neumagen finds"—Roman antiquities on display in the Landesmuseum in Trier—may be admired all over the town, even in the local school; the local wines, however, do not command the same admiration. Those of nearby Dhron are better. The village lies at the junction of a brook of the same name with the Moselle, and its vineyards extend for some distance on southerly slopes along the river's right bank. Niederemmel has no vineyards worth mentioning, but it is the site where a large Roman glass vessel decorated with filigree work, today a precious possession of Trier's Landesmuseum, was discovered. Niederemmel also provides a marvelous view of Piesport and its famous Goldtröpfchen site, a vast amphitheater of steep, sun-drenched vineyard slopes on the opposite bank. Goldtröpfchen ("Golden droplets") sounds like another fancy name, but is nothing of the sort. It is true that it is often unduly extended to cover wines from other vineyards of the village, but some of the original article was worthy of gracing the festive table at Queen Elizabeth's coronation.

On the right bank we now come to Wintrich, whose vineyard sites are Geierslay—a large rugged rock of hard quartzite slate for a change—Ohligsberg, Grosser Herrgott, and others. Farther down, Brauneberg has its vineyards on the opposite bank of the river, the best-known site being Juffer. Lieser follows on the left bank, where the river is joined by a little stream also named the Lieser. Schlossberg, its main site, faces the Moselle, and others extend for some distance up the river.

After another of the Moselle's bends we come to the twin towns of Bernkastel-Kues, the first-named the most celebrated winegrowing community of the Moselle, and the second, across a bridge, more renowned as the hometown of the great fifteenth-century theologian, Cardinal Nicolaus Cusanus. Bernkastel is dominated at its southern end by the ruined castle of Landshut, and on the north, beyond a gorgelike intervening valley, by its very high, steep-sloped vineyard hill, locally called the Doktorberg ("Doctor Hill") after its most famous site. The little town is a charming old place, having a most intimate market square with timber-framed houses and a Renaissance town hall, although it may be felt to be a bit spoiled by too many coaches bringing in too many day-trippers. The far-famed "Bernkasteler Doctor" grows on an exclusive site at the bottom of the slope, immediately above the town's roofs. This vineyard measures only about one and a third hectares (about three acres), which is an exception to the rule of the new wine law that a site, to be allowed to retain its old name, must have a minimum surface of five hectares. This exception is based on the same grounds as the clause applying to the tiny Glöck site of Nierstein (see page 143). Besides the "Doctor," there are, of course, a good many other sites, some of nearly equal quality, such as Graben, Badstube, Lay, and Bratenhöfchen.

The floor of the cellar belonging to the largest of the three estates sharing in the "Doctor" site is decorated with an old stone mosaic inscribed with the Latin tag *Vinum Mosellanum omni tempore sanum* ("Moselle wine is healthy at any time"), which refers primarily to the health-giving quality of the "Doctor's" wine. The name of the site is derived from a legendary event. In the mid-fourteenth century the archbishop-elector Boemund II of Trier used to spend much of his time at Landshut, his castle above Bernkastel. On one of these occasions he fell gravely ill, but was miraculously restored to health by a mighty draft of the "Doctor's" wine. And this was not its only success. In the first decade of the present century it is said to have had its ancient luster refurbished when King Edward VII had his physician prescribe it for the good of the royal liver.

At Bernkastel the Moselle takes a turn to the northwest, but the slopes on its right bank have on the whole a more southerly than southwesterly exposure. The next village is Graach, which specializes in theological and ecclesiastical names for its sites: Himmelreich, Petrus, Domprobst, Abtsberg, and so forth.

Wehlen, situated on the left bank of the river, but having its vineyards of course on the right, immediately adjoining those of Graach, is best known for the site of Sonnenuhr, named for a large sundial that stands in its center. Zeltingen-Rachtig follows with contiguous vineyard slopes that produce the largest harvest yield along this whole stretch. Zeltingen has another Himmelreich and another Sonnenuhr.

Now the Moselle turns eastward again, and the vineyard slopes rise on its left bank. The first village on this stretch is Ürzig, best known for its site of Würzgarten. What is not so well known, not only to all writers in English but also to most of them in German, is that the name of this site does not, as it seems to do on the face of it, mean "Spice Garden." The medieval Ursiacum belonged to the Benedictine Abbey of Echternach (then Epternacum) in Luxembourg, and the thirteenth-century records of this abbey contain an entry referring to a certain "Godefridus filius Th. vurzegard" as the first hereditary tenant of its vineyards at Ursiacum. Near its eastern boundary, where its slopes pass over into those of Erden, Ürzig has a large sundial affixed to a slope just above the road, but the vineyard is not named after it; it bears the name of Urlay and is now merged with the Würzgarten.

There is a striking difference in the shape of the slopes between Bernkastel and Zeltingen-Rachtig and those between Ürzig and Erden. The former sweep down in a series of gentle arches; the latter offer a rugged, craggy, irregularly broken surface, as if piled up by some Cyclopean hand. The best-known Erden site name, Treppchen ("Little Steps"), is an attempt to describe the appearance of its vineyard slopes, although the diminutive form seems to have a ring of irony to it. The village is situated on the opposite bank of the river, connected with its vineyards by a ferry. The whole of this stretch from Bernkastel to Erden, despite the physical differences, may be said to be the very heart of the Middle Moselle, very occasionally approached but never surpassed in the quality of its wines by other places higher up or lower down the course of the river.

Below Erden, there is a gradual falling off in the quality of local wines. This is only slightly marked at Kinheim, with its sites Hubertusberg and Rosenberg, but more noticeable at Kröv, which sells the produce of most of its sites under the somewhat coarse-sounding name of Nacktarsch ("Bare Bottom"), with a label showing an angry father walloping his young son's posterior. Another very narrow loop surrounds the twin towns of Traben-Trarbach on opposite banks. Unlike the rest of the Moselle, this community has a predominantly Protestant population. Traben, on the left bank and facing due south, is surmounted by the broad-fronted Mont Royal with the ruins of a fortress built under Louis XIV; Trarbach is dominated by the ruins of the medieval Grevensburg Castle. Trarbach's Schlossberg would probably qualify as the twin towns' best site. One of Traben's sites is the Gewürzgarten, probably named after that of Ürzig but in the belief that the name really means "Spice Garden." Enkirch, a little farther down the river, on the right bank, a very attractive village with many half-timbered houses, has a very large acreage of vineyard land, and, with its sites of Steffensberg, Herrenberg, and Klosterberg Monteneubel, some of the best wines below Erden.

Zell, situated toward the end of another narrow loop, is one of no less than twenty-three towns in the Federal Republic bearing that monastic name (not to mention those in other German-speaking localities). The valley is extremely narrow, and consequently the old town, with its handsome castle, stretches very far along the river bank. It has a number of vineyards producing fair wines—though none so good as those of Enkirch—but prefers to swamp the market with a wine going by the name of one of its vineyards, Schwarze Katz ("Black Cat"). This name vies in popularity with that of Kröv's Nacktarsch, but caters mainly to a different kind of customer. It appeals to children, who invariably pester their elders and betters to buy the stuff because of the plastic black cat attached to the top of the bottle.

Our next stopping places are Bullay on the right and Alf on

the left bank of the river. A steep hill crowned with the ruined castle of Arrasburg rises to the west of Alf, the southern slope of the hill producing a very acceptable wine. To the south of Alf, the neck of the river loop is surmounted by another ruin, that of Marienburg Castle, once one of the most picturesque sights of the Moselle valley. Here the main interest is not viticultural but archaeological. At the end of World War II, Marienburg was smashed to bits by a direct hit, however stray the bomb that hit it. This event was greeted with joy and gratitude by archaeologists, for beneath the moldering ruins they discovered the far more interesting foundations of the old fortified monastery build by the Premonstratensians in the twelfth century.

The Middle Moselle is usually reckoned to extend as far as Bullay and Alf. Actually there is no sharp border between the bluish argillaceous slate of the middle reach and the reddish graywacke of the lower one. About three miles below Bullay, the village of Neef lies at the foot of the very steep, broad southern slope of the Frauenberg. The rock is reddish to look at, but when crushed in the hand it turns out to be more bluish underneath. Neef is so tightly hemmed in between the river and the Frauenberg that it has no room for a cemetery; its dead are buried in a beautifully situated churchyard surrounding a chapel, built about the middle of the twelfth century, on the top of the Frauenberg. Since 1960 there has been a road winding up to the top; before that time, coffins had to be carried up on a steep vineyard path. The name Frauenberg ("Women's Hill") dates from the year 1136, when it was given to the aristocratic Augustinian convent of Stuben (founded in 1131) by a wealthy local nobleman named Egilolf. The site remained in the possession of the convent until its dissolution in 1788.

The Frauenberg site faces due south, and its vineyards produce some very fine Rieslings. Few sites on the Moselle are normally sprayed from a helicopter, which has to be done by flying at a dangerously low level, but the owners of the Frauenberg vineyards can afford to have the site sprayed, and hire an American stunt pilot—which must cost a tidy sum; flying aces performing breakneck jobs do not come cheap. Another sign of quality is the fact that at least some of the vineyard owners are not bound to label their bottles Neefer Frauenberg, but are allowed to name their product simply Frauenberger, without indication of locality, a rare distinction in Germany.

Immediately below Neef, the Moselle executes another of its bizarre hairpin bends, with the little town of Bremm at its apex. The hillside opposite Bremm, and included in its boundaries, is the very gentle northern slope of the Frauenberg, formerly wooded but now planted with the local growers' vines, mostly Elbling. At the bottom of the hill, just above the river, the melancholy, scorched ruins of the Stuben convent may be admired.

The Lower Moselle valley is characterized by the harder, reddish graywacke slate which weathers only insufficiently, thus offering the vine roots merely a thin layer of nourishing soil. Here the winegrower's work is extremely hard. In an extensive and intricate terracing system built up over centuries, every little crumb of the precious weathering surface has to be carefully saved from slipping down. On the other hand, what the soil lacks in porosity and nutritive substances is occasionally compensated to some extent by the greater steepness and consequently more intensive solar irradiation of the slopes. There are also some good southerly exposures—where the river bends, and in a small side valley. Thus, in spite of the meagerness of the rocky soil, a wine full of character may be grown in some parts of the Lower Moselle.

The Calmont site (the name probably derives from the Latin *Calidus mons*, "Hot Mountain") swings in the form of a semicircle, two and a half miles in length, between Bremm and Eller. It rises nearly 1,240 feet, is planted with vines to a height of more than 660 feet, and, with an overall gradient of sixty-five degrees, is the most precipitous vineyard site in Germany, and possibly in the world. To observe men and women working on its surface, carrying manure in shoulder baskets up the terraces, or loads of grapes down, almost makes one's head swim. Eller's half has the better southerly exposure. The Calmont marks the beginning of the Cochem Krampen (literally, "cramp" or "staple"), a large eastward bulge of the river.

Practically next door to Eller lies Ediger, a small place that has, however, held township rights since the fourteenth century. Its best-known site, with a good southerly exposure, is Osterlämmchen ("Paschal lamb"). High up on the hillside, above the last vineyard, lies the old Kreuzkapelle ("Chapel of the Holy Cross"), which contains a sixteenth-century stone relief of Christ treading a winepress. The Kreuzkapelle is now easily accessible by means of a new road from Eller and Ediger over the hills of Cochem. Halfway down the Krampen, and again on the Moselle's right bank, lies tiny Beilstein, with not many more than two hundred inhabitants, yet also holding township rights since the fourteenth century. It is a charming medieval fairyland place, although there is nothing fairylandish about its wine, the neighborhood being one of the main homes of the Elbling vine. Beilstein lies at the foot of the ruined castle of Metternich, where in the seventeenth century the Metternich ancestors used to earn their keep by the peculiar trade of protecting the local Jews. Valwig, near the end of the Krampen, has southerly slopes again, and more favored sites.

Cochem, beautifully situated on the river's left bank, is the largest town of the Lower Moselle and a busy tourist center. Its medieval castle, razed in 1689, was rebuilt in the nineteenth century. Below Cochem the graywacke slate becomes harder still, and southerly slopes become rare. Karden is noted for St. Castor's, consecrated in 1121 as a collegiate church, which, historically and architecturally, is the most important church between Trier and Koblenz. St. Castor was the apostle of the Moselle; he was sent here (the Roman Vicus Cardena) as a missionary by Bishop Maximinus of Trier (336–46), ending his life as a hermit. In 836 his remains were interred in St. Castor's Cathedral at Koblenz, which was consecrated on the same occasion.

About three miles from Moselkern, on a stream called the Eltz, which descends the Eifel hills, lies Eltz Castle, a show-piece among German Schlösser, still owned by the counts of Eltz. Hatzenport's landmark is a thirteenth-century Gothic church rising high above the town on the steep vineyard slopes. Alken is situated on the Moselle's right bank and has a short side valley with a broad southerly slope producing a fair wine. The hill is surmounted by Thurant Castle, built about 1200, now partly restored and privately owned. Kobern and Win-ningen, again on the left bank, are situated on the last great loop of the river. Their vineyard slopes have a good southerly exposure and produce wines of better quality than most places on this last stretch of the Moselle. Winningen enjoys a certain fame for its annual wine festival, celebrated here with particular pomp and circumstance.

9. Baden

WITH a total vine-planted surface of more than 10,100 hectares (24,900 acres), Baden's production closely approaches that of the Moselle-Saar-Ruwer region. The region, now part of the federal state of Baden Württemberg, is long and narrow in shape, forming a semicircle around Württemberg. Its east–west extension, from Immenstaad, on Lake Constance, to Wyhlen, near Basel, is 81 miles; its northern extension, from Wyhlen to Laudenbach, on the border of Hesse, is 146 miles; while its northeastern extension, from Wyhlen to Dertingen, on the Bavarian border, is 176 miles. Baden has 309 winegrowing communities of varying size and varying vine-planted acreage, 50-odd others having gone out of the viticultural business in the years following World War II because of increasing industrialization.

Unlike the Palatinate, Rheinhessen, and Moselle-Saar-Ruwer regions, Baden does not have a surplus production of wine. What with local needs and those of the numerous holiday visitors to the Black Forest and Lake Constance, added to by the neighboring Württembergers and Baselers enriching their wine lists with Baden wines, total consumption is almost double that of total production, so that Baden has to import considerable quantities from elsewhere to meet demands. Thus, since there is no need to sell Baden wines in other parts of Germany, they are not as well known elsewhere as their quality would seem to deserve.

Although Baden and Württemberg have been politically

merged into a single federal state, their respective wine regions have not been merged. Each one is extremely jealous of the separate identity of its wines. At the same time, there can be no greater local diversity than exists among the different wines included in the category of Baden wines. The country is not a single winegrowing region but an agglomeration of separate areas strung together like the links of a chain. There are certain exceptions, however. For example, although Baden is separated from Württemberg by the Black Forest, nevertheless in the north, where the Neckar crosses over from Württemberg into Baden, there is little difference among the wines grown along adjacent stretches of the river. Again, in the extreme northeast, where the Tauber valley joins that of the Main, the character of the Tauber wines of Baden blends with that of the Franconian wines of Bavaria.

In the whole Baden region, twelve main subregions may be distinguished. These are, from south to north: (1) Lake Constance (Boden See); (2) the Hohentwiel; (3) the High Rhine (Hochrhein) (this term being used for the stretch of the river above Basel, in contrast to Upper Rhine [Oberrhein], the section ending at the Palatinate border, where the Middle Rhine [Mittelrhein] begins); (4) the Markgräflerland or Markgrafschaft, in the foothills of the Black Forest between Basel and Freiburg; (5) Kaiserstuhl-Tuniberg, an isolated massif in the middle of the Upper Rhine plain northwest of Freiburg; (6) the Breisgau, in the foothills of the middle Black Forest from Freiburg to beyond Lahr; (7) the Ortenau, in the northern Black Forest as far as Baden-Baden; (8) the Pfinzgau-Enzgau, to the east and southeast of Karlsruhe-Durlach (to be distinguished from Durbach in the Ortenau) as far as beyond Pforzheim; (9) the Kraichgau, the area from Durlach northward to near Wiesloch, and northeastward to near the Neckar River, with Bruchsal as its largest town; (10) the Badische Bergstrasse, the southern half of the Bergstrasse along the foothills of the Odenwald, plus its artificial southern extension from Heidelberg to Wiesloch; (11) the area of the Neckar valley in Baden extending for only a few miles and including a short strip of the Jagst, a tributary of the Neckar; (12) Baden-Franconia (Badisches Frankenland), the northeasternmost part of Baden, with the valley of the lower Tauber River and the towns of Tauberbischofsheim and Wertheim.

The whole viticultural region has a warm climate, differing in some parts mainly in the degree of humidity and amount of precipitation. Most of the northern section, the Kraichgau, Bergstrasse, and Tauber valley, is relatively dry, and the Kaiserstuhl is extremely dry as well as being the warmest part of Baden. The areas along the Black Forest foothills get more rain—Freiburg and the Breisgau being the wettest—while the Ortenau to the north and the Markgräflerland to the south get somewhat less rain. Lake Constance gets a lot of rain, while the Hohentwiel is dry.

Baden's soils are more diverse in composition than those of any other region; consequently—in marked contrast to Moselle wines in particular—the wines of Baden have no unity of character, although almost all of them are relatively low in acidity.

Vineyards in Baden are mostly parceled out in small holdings of between half an acre and two acres, and are owned and worked mainly by part-time winegrowers. There is a corresponding density of growers' cooperatives. The first of these was founded in 1881 by a Freiburg priest, Heinrich Hansjakob, at Hagnau on Lake Constance; his idea of helping the small grower has resulted in a present-day total of 126 cooperatives all over Baden, which jointly control 80 percent of the country's total wine production. The smaller cooperatives, which cannot afford expensive modern cellar machinery, deliver their grape harvests for processing and storing to the Central Cellarage of Baden Winegrowers' Cooperatives (Zentralkellerei Badischer Winzergenossenschaften, or ZBW), founded in 1952 in the small cathedral city of Breisach, south of the Kaiserstuhl hills. This plant, utilizing the most up-to-date machinery, is equipped with giant tanks having a total capacity (in 1972) of 60 million litres.

Of the larger estates, the biggest are run by the state—for

example, the Meersburg State Domain on Lake Constance with 108 acres, plus another 15 acres on the cone-shaped Hohentwiel in the Hegau, and the Blankenhornsberg Domain in the Kaiserstuhl hills, with about 50 acres. About 75 acres of the State Viticultural Institute in Freiburg, scattered over various subregions, are also state-owned. (In addition to this institute, the State Viticultural Institute at Karlsruhe-Durlach specializes in the improvement of existing vine varieties and the breeding of new ones.)

Of the privately owned estates, that of the margrave of Baden, comprising about 60 acres, appears to be the most extensive. Its largest single unit includes Straufenberg Castle, above Durbach in the Ortenau; smaller ones are located on Lake Constance. Other large estates in aristocratic ownership are confined mostly to the Ortenau area.

Lake Constance (Boden See), at an altitude of 1,320 feet above sea level, is near the upper limit of vine cultivation north of the Alps. At the present time only Meersburg, with 124 acres, and nearby Hagnau, with 89, remain as winegrowing communities of any size. At Meersburg, the vines stand on a soil of moraine till; at Hagnau, on light loam, gravel, and sand soils. The handicap of poor soils is, however, offset by a very favorable climate, albeit with a relatively high rainfall, but with a summer-like warmth remaining in October; a generally southerly aspect of vineyard slopes, which often extend down to the lakeshore; and the reflection of sunlight from a very large sheet of water, as well as the effect of the lake in equalizing temperatures.

In the past, *Seeweine* ("lake wines") were sometimes considered a bit raw by outsiders, if not by locals, but a substantial improvement has been achieved in the last few decades, due in a large part to the untiring efforts of the State Domain at Meersburg, which grows wines of high quality. The Meersburg Domain is the oldest of its kind in Germany, consisting of the former vineyard estates of the prince-bishops of Konstanz, which in the course of secularization were taken over by the margrave of Baden in 1802, and have been managed by the subsequently established State Domain administration since 1812. At the present time, the planted area of the State Domain, which owns 109 of Meersburg's 124 acres, is divided as follows: 55 percent, Spätburgunder, used for red wine as well as for Weissherbst (Rosé); 30 percent, Müller-Thurgau; and 10 percent, Ruländer. The remaining 5 percent consists of Riesling and Traminer plantations. Meersburg's best-known sites are Rieschen and Bengel.

The town presents a picturesque aspect from the lakeshore, rising up to a castle—with its mighty keep, the Dagobertsturm—said to be the oldest in Germany, having been built by the Merovingian king Dagobert. The vineyards reach down on steep slopes right into the town.

Elsewhere on Lake Constance very little is left of the extensive, flourishing viticulture of the past; vegetable gardening, fruit growing, and, of course, increasing industrialization have taken its place. The island of Reichenau, near Konstanz, from whose former Benedictine abbey monks propagated winegrowing far and wide from the eighth century onward, has only about twelve acres of vineyard left; the rest of its soil is planted with vegetables and fruit trees. Konstanz itself, which in the 1950s had a few acres more than Reichenau, probably has a good deal less since its development into a modern university city and computer-building center, with all the brick-and-mortarizing that goes with it. Immenstaad, at the eastern end of the Baden section of the lakeshore, has only tiny remnants. Überlingen, which stands on a Molasse formation of fine-grained gray sandstone, has also lost most of its formerly extensive vineyards. Before the Thirty Years' War, its entire boundary was planted with vines, and the town boasted that not a single plow could be found within its walls.

The countryside at the western end of Lake Constance and extending into the Swiss canton of Schaffhausen is known by its ancient name of Hegau. Here the industrial town of Singen lies at the foot of the Hohentwiel, a steep, cone-shaped phonolite rock 2,270 feet high, which is covered with a coat of volcanic ashes, or tuff. The vineyards on its south face, climbing to a height of 1,735 feet, are the second highest in the Federal Republic. They would climb even higher if the upper reaches were not out of bounds, a nature reserve for rare plants. The total viticultural surface is about thirty acres, of which fifteen are owned and worked by a Meersburg State Domain. The sites belonging to the Domain are Olgaberg and Himmelreich; they are planted with the same vines and in the same proportion as those at Meersburg. The main site of the rest of the surface, also planted with the same varieties, is Elisabethenberg. In spite of the altitude at which they are grown, the wines are of high quality.

The Hohentwiel is the smallest separate winegrowing area not only of Baden but also of the whole of West Germany, mostly unknown and not even mentioned in most publications on German wines. If mentioned at all, it is usually included in the Lake Constance area. This, however, could only be justified on the grounds of its nearness to the lake. Its soil composition is different, its climate is much drier, with an average annual rainfall of 700 millimeters (28 inches) as compared with Meersburg's 850 millimeters (34 inches), and its wines have a distinct character of their own.

Farther down the High Rhine, the countryside to the west of the Hegau is the Klettgau, partly in Baden and partly in the canton of Schaffhausen. The only Baden winegrowing community of any size is the village of Erzingen, situated right on the southwestern border of the Swiss canton.

From the viticultural point of view, the Markgräflerland (or Markgrafschaft), in the Upper Rhine plain and the foothills of the southern Black Forest, extends from Weil am Rhein, immediately adjoining Basel, to a short distance south of Freiburg. It contains seventy-six winegrowing communities. It has a warm, humid climate with an average annual precipitation of between 850 and 900 millimeters (34 to 36 inches), but the lower, western parts are on the whole a good deal drier than the higher, eastern ones. The southern section of the plain is extremely narrow as far as Bad Bellingen, where it widens out. The narrow stretch from Efringen-Kirchen northward is bounded by the Istein ridge of Jurassic rock; and Kleinkems, north of the village of Istein, has large jasper quarries emitting clouds of white dust, which settles on the grapes of the surrounding vineyards. The low, western foothills are covered with calcareous loess; in the more eastern, higher parts, the calcareous content decreases, leaving deep, fertile loess-loam soils. The inclination of vineyard slopes is mostly toward the west and southwest, but there are also a good many slopes facing due south.

According to statistics issued a few years ago, the respective share of vines was 70 percent for Gutedel; 13 percent, Müller-Thurgau; 7 percent, Silvaner; 4 percent, Spätburgunder; and 6 percent for others, including Ruländer and Traminer. Small quantities of Traminer are occasionally planted on the most favored southerly slopes of Grenzach and Haltingen, just north of Basel, as well as at Efringen, Istein, Auggen, Hügelheim, Sulzburg, and Staufen. Since the time of the statistics mentioned above, the cultivation of Spätburgunder is certain to have increased considerably; while that of Silvaner, which in these parts gets satisfactory "must" gravities only in very good vintages, appears to be receding.

Gutedel remains the predominant variety. It is so closely connected with the area that the general name Markgräfler, which should refer to all varieties grown in the area, has become a synonym for Gutedel wines. Of course, they vary in taste and quality in accordance with particular soil and climatic conditions; nevertheless, by and large they have a sufficiently uniform character of their own. They are characterized by ample and regular yields and have the advantage of a relative evenness of quality over time; in good and bad years they deviate less from their normal value than do other varieties. They are light in alcohol content, mild, with little acidity and a very gentle bouquet. Their favorable relationship between alcohol content and acidity makes it possible to avoid artificial sugaring in almost every year. In addition to their inherent qualities, they are most carefully cultivated by local growers. They were the first Baden wines to meet with appreciation outside Baden's frontiers and began to be exported about the middle of the nineteenth century.

The Markgräflerland may usefully be divided into three sections, the upper section, extending to near Schliengen; the middle region, between Schliengen and Staufen; and the lower section, from Staufen to near Freiburg. The best wines in the upper section grow on the south slopes of the Efringen hills and on the Isteiner Klotz ("Istein Block"), a stupendous rounded rock rising from the plain, in the past an important natural fortress covering the southwestern approaches, whose interior is riddled with embrasures and connecting corridors.

In the middle section we find the largest winegrowing communities, such as Auggen, with 383 acres, Schliengen, with 222, and Britzingen, with 198. The town of Müllheim, the wine-trading center of the whole Markgräflerland, is also located here. The best-known local and site names are Auggen, with its Letten and Schäf; Schliengen, with Ölacker and Langrain; Müllheim with Reggenhag; Hügelheim, with Pflanzer; Brit-zingen, with Sonnhohle; and Lerchenhühl and Laufen, with Altenberg. Zunzingen, halfway between Hügelheim and Brit-zingen, has the double distinction of being the last in the alphabet and of being, with 180 inhabitants, the smallest village in Baden. The wines of the middle section, which include Spätburgunder, Ruländer, and Traminer, tend to be a little more expensive than those of the rest of the area.

The lower section, beginning at Staufen, with its sites of Schlossberg and Heitersheim, is smaller, but also produces good wines. In Staufen's oldest inn can be seen the room in which the notorious magician, Johannes Faustus, departed this life. The Devil, in his avatar as Mephistopheles, to whom Faustus had sold his soul in return for supernatural powers, is said to have paid him a final visit to claim his part of the compact, wrung his neck, and carried his soul off to Hell. Farther north we come to Ehrenstetten, with its Ölberg; Ebringen, with Sommerberg and Klämmle; and Wolfenweiler, with Leutersberg. The five villages of Kirchhofen, Pfaffenweiler, Norsingen, Scherzingen, and Schallstadt share parts of the Batzenberg, the largest vineyard site of the Markgräflerland. Batzenberg is an elongated hill with a road on its crest, whose wines enjoy a reputation equal to those of the middle section. Pfaffenweiler is worth a visit because of its four-hundred-year-old inn Zur Stube, and Kirchhofen has an inn named Lazarus Schwendi Stube, named after the half-legendary sixteenth-century hero of the Upper Rhine. Merzhausen, immediately adjoining Freiburg, is reckoned as belonging to the Breisgau area.

The Kaiserstuhl, to the northwest of Freiburg, is an island of low hills rising from the middle of the Upper Rhine plain. Its area is very small; the greatest distance, a straight diametrical line from Ihringen in the southwest to Riegel in the northeast, is no more than ten miles. Yet the area's total output of grapes is very large, due to the fact that it has a much higher ratio of viticulture in relation to other forms of cultivation than any other winegrowing part of Baden; probably in the neighborhood of 30 percent. Its highest points are the wooded twin hills of the Totenkopf, 1,836 feet, and the Neunlindenberg, 1,833 feet, which afford splendid views across the Rhine plain, eastward to the southern Black Forest and westward to the Vosges.

The Kaiserstuhl is an isolated massif of volcanic rock, most of it black tephrite, which comes to the surface particularly on the steep western slopes between Ihringen and Sasbach. Near the latter place, the remains of Limburg Castle stand on a basalt hill. The eastern part of the massif, geologically younger, is formed of Tertiary chalk and marl; while the Tuniberg range, a southeastern appendage, has, in addition to limestone, Jurassic rock, shell lime, and red marl. The hills are covered with a coat of loess at least three times as thick as in other winegrowing areas, in places reaching a depth of nearly seventy feet. The innumerable loess terraces and the deep sunken paths through them give the countryside its characteristic impression of one formed more by the human hand than by nature. In the 1930s the head of the Viticultural Institute in Freiburg calculated that if one could join together all the Kaiserstuhl terraces in one row, one would get a length of five hundred miles. Looking at all the additional terracing being carried out with mechanical excavators today, forty years later, one may wonder whether it would not come nearer to double that length.

Until the beginning of the nineteenth century, only Elbling and Räuschling vines were planted on the loess. A change came about in 1815, when a physician named Lydtin, a retired army surgeon in the service of Napoleon, entered upon the scene. Inspired by his observation of the cultivation of Lacrimae Christi vines on the slopes of Vesuvius, he started a vineyard on a piece of rocky wasteland on Ihringen's Winklerberg, planting it with better varieties of vine. They took root in the black volcanic rock, which retains the heat of the day overnight, and produced superior wines. Today, a considerable and increasing proportion of vineyards, especially on the south and southwest slopes of the Kaiserstuhl, are planted on the bare, dark, hot, and very nutritive tephrite rock.

The hot, dry, subtropical climate, too, is favorable. The average annual rainfall is 656 millimeters (26 inches); the mean annual overall temperature is 50.2°F (10.1°C), and Ihringen, with 53.2°F (11.3°C) is Germany's warmest town. The Kaiserstuhl is still little touched by tourism because of its summer heat; vacationers prefer the cool Black Forest nearby. This is all right with the wine lover, and with the flower fancier, to whom the upper reaches of the hills, with about thirty varieties of wild orchids, are a veritable floral Eldorado.

Some of the Kaiserstuhl communities own the largest viticultural acreages of Baden. Ihringen, with its best-known sites of Winklerberg, Fohrenberg, and Schlossberg, owns 1,260 acres; Oberrotweil, in the west-central part, with Henkenberg, Käsleberg, Mondhalde, and others, 692 acres; Endingen, in the northeast, with Engelsberg, Steingrube, and others, 677 acres.

Besides Ihringen and Oberrotweil, there is Achkarren, with its Schlossberg, on which the best Ruländer grows; Bickensohl, with its Herrenstück; Bishoffingen, with its Steinbuck; Burkheim, with its Schlossgarten; Leiselheim, with its Gestühl; and Sasbach, with its Limburg. Nor should Breisach, with its Eckartsberg, be forgotten, although its vine-planted surface is minute, no more than 19 acres. These communities are all in the more favored southern and western part of the hills.

In the north, east, and southeast, Endingen, Bahlingen, Eichstetten, and Bötzingen are less favored by nature, as are the Tuniberg communities of Gottenheim, Merdingen, Rimsingen, Munzingen, and others, though there are, of course, exceptions. Wasenweiler, halfway between Bötzingen and Ihringen, comes close to the latter's quality. On the whole, the Kaiserstuhl produces the most full-bodied and fiery Ruländer to be found anywhere in Germany, very fruity Spätburgunder red and Weissherbst wines, as well as smaller quantities of Weissburgunder, Riesling, Traminer, and Gewürztraminer, all belonging to the best category of German wines. No wonder the Kaiserstuhl is so often called the "Kitchen of Bacchus."

One finds an attractive approach to the Kaiserstuhl hills by leaving the Autobahn at Riegel, passing through the old town of Endingen, and going on as far as Königschaffhausen. From here a new road leads up to Kichlinsbergen, and even higher, where one gets a first impression of the depth of the loess cover beside the road, and from the saddle of the hill a most enchanting view of the central and southern Kaiserstuhl, after which one goes down steeply, negotiating narrow hairpin bends to Oberbergen and Oberrotweil. A visit to Burkheim, on the western edge of the hills, is also worthwhile. It is one of the smallest walled towns, a picturesque place with a handsome town gate, half-timbered houses, and a town hall with a Renaissance facade. At the western end, what remains of old Lazarus von Schwendi's castle, a burned-out square shell overlooking the Rhine plain, qualifies for the title of Germany's ugliest ruin.

Historically and geographically, the Breisgau extends from

the foothills of the Black Forest, north and south of Freiburg, as far as the Rhine. It takes its name from the town of Breisach, the earlier form of which was Breisachgau. Thus, it includes not only the northern part of the Markgräflerland about as far as Heitersheim, but also the whole of the Kaiserstuhl hills. In the viticultural sense, the Breisgau and Kaiserstuhl, or the Breisgau and Markgräflerland, are separate and quite different areas. Viticulturally, then, the Breisgau extends from Freiburg as far as about five miles beyond the town of Lahr. Freiburg itself, most attractively situated in a large bay of the Rhine plain and surrounded by wooded hills on the east, is the main gateway to the southern Black Forest, the higher part of the range. It is a cathedral city; its red-sandstone minster, built between the thirteenth and fifteenth centuries, is, with its famous spire, one of the most remarkable religious edifices of the Gothic period in Germany. Freiburg is also one of the older German seats of science and learning, with a university founded in 1457. Its Augustinermuseum is dedicated to the art of the Upper Rhine valley, on both sides of the river. Its State Viticultural Research Institute has already been mentioned.

On the whole, the Breisgau, as a viticultural area, cannot compete with the Kaiserstuhl. The prevailing soils of most of the winegrowing areas to the north of Freiburg, such as Emmendingen, Mundingen, Köndringen, Malterdingen, Kenzingen, and others, are largely composed of loess, marl, and calcareous loam; warm and nutritive stony soils are comparatively rare. In addition, local growers have also been more conservative than those of other areas, in the 1950s still growing mostly Elbling and Räuschling wines, of which nothing good can be said. The result was some degree of viticultural recession in these parts, vineyard labor leaving for the industries of Freiburg and other larger towns. With these handicaps, although the cultivation of Elbling and Räuschling is no longer permitted, the bulk of production is still in light wines, mostly for local consumption.

There are, of course, exceptions. On favorable soils and

southerly slopes, some good wines are grown; notably on Hecklingen's Schlossberg, which produces Ruländer, Riesling, Gewürztraminer, Muskateller, and Spätburgunder. Good wines are also grown on the Schutterlindenberg above the town of Lahr. Northward, Lahr shares the long site of Kronenbühl with a number of villages, including Oberschopfheim, five miles away, the northernmost winegrowing village of the Breisgau.

Good-quality wines also come from the gneiss soil of the Glottertal valley north of Freiburg, as well as from Freiburg itself. The typical Glottertäler, a Weissherbst made from Spätburgunder grapes, is highly popular with Freiburg's students, and not only with them. The Glottertal valley runs from east to west and has perfect southerly slopes, on which, besides Spätburgunder, Ruländer is also grown. The valley is famous for its natural scenery, its warm climate and fertility, and has some of the highest vineyards of Germany, climbing up to 1,810 feet. Some of the best Breisgau wines also come from within the municipality of Freiburg itself, which is situated for the most part on gneiss soils. Freiburg produces Riesling and Traminer from the Schlossberg in the northern part of the city, and Ruländer, Spätburgunder, and Gutedel from the Lorettsberg and the Jesuitenschloss, which it shares with adjoining Merzhausen at its southern end.

The Breisgau changes over into the Ortenau without any noticeable natural boundary. Oberschopfheim, the northernmost winegrowing village of the Breisgau, is only about two miles west of Diersburg, one of the southernmost villages of the Ortenau. And yet, what a difference between these two areas! The Ortenau, extending as far as Baden-Baden in the foothills of the northern Black Forest, one of the most beautiful countrysides of southern Germany, has fertile soils of weathered granite, and in the north also red argillaceous slate, the so-called red lier, which, toward the plain, change over into loess and loam soils. Its very warm, well-protected slopes afford the best natural conditions for vine cultivation. The Ortenau is traversed by the Badische Weinstrasse, which begins at the attractive little town of Gengenbach, still quite medieval in appearance, situated in the valley of the Kinzig River, follows the river to Ortenberg and Offenburg, the economic and administrative center of the area, then twists in and out through most of the winegrowing localities until it reaches Baden-Baden. (The name of this route, which actually connects only the winegrowing communities of the Ortenau, is a little more modest than that of its counterpart in the Palatinate, which claims to be the Deutsche Weinstrasse.)

The town of Offenburg holds an annual wine market in the month of May. The town is surrounded by a semicircle of winegrowing communities, of which Ortenberg and Zell-Weierbach, the latter now incorporated into Offenburg, are the most important. The wine route now turns northeast to Durbach, only two and a half miles from Offenburg, which, with about five hundred acres of vineyard land, is the largest winegrowing community of the Ortenau, and also, after some of the still larger ones of the Kaiserstuhl, the largest of the whole of Baden. Durbach is surrounded by three hills with a number of steep southerly slopes. Climbing up on a vineyard path above the village, one receives an overwhelming impression of the vast Staufenberg site, with vineyards reaching up to Staufenberg Castle, built in the eleventh century by Otto von Hohenstaufen, bishop of Strasbourg, and now owned by the margrave of Baden. From here, or one of the other hilltops above the village, the Vosges and Strasbourg's minster can be seen on a clear day. Apart from its extensive aristocratic properties, Durbach has a State Domain and one of the largest winegrowers' cooperatives of Baden.

Continuing northward, the wine route crosses the Rench River at the town of Oberkirch, then proceeds to Waldulm and Kappelrodek, where it crosses the Acher River, bypassing pretty Sasbachwalden, now a little spoiled by a large sanatorium on its heights, then circles the neighborhood of Bühl (*Bühler Gegend*), with Bühlertal, Altschweier, and the town of Bühl itself. From here it is a short distance to the twin communities of Eisental-Affental. The hump of the stretch between Eisental and Neuweier affords another fine view of the Ortenau countryside, the sweep of the large, unbroken vine-planted acreage that almost reaches the castle ruins of the Yburg, high up above Neuweier. The nearby town of Steinbach was the home of Master Erwin von Steinbach, one of the principal architects of the Strasbourg minster and the creator of its famous rose window. His monument stands in the town's main street, the Meister Erwin-Strasse. The route continues via Varnhalt and below the south slope of the Fremersberg, 1,740 feet high, eventually reaching fashionable Baden-Baden, the great Black Forest spa built by the Romans. The town of Sinzheim, on the western side of the Fremersberg, also with considerable vineyard property, is the northern limit of the Ortenau.

With few exceptions, notably the southern and southwestern Kaiserstuhl, no viticultural area of Baden exhibits such an abundance and diversity of high-quality wines as that between Gengenbach and Baden-Baden. Here Spätburgunder, used for both red wine and Weissherbst, Riesling (locally named Klingelberger), Ruländer, and Traminer (locally known as Clevner), together with its spicier variation, Gewürztraminer, both rarities among Germany's peak wines, are grown, to which are added, as lighter table wines, Müller-Thurgau and Freisamer.

The pattern of distribution varies. The most widespread variety is Spätburgunder, which virtually disappears only on the red lier soil of the northernmost part, where Riesling is grown almost exclusively. Ruländer is confined mainly to the southern Ortenau; it does not seem to go far beyond Oberkirch. Riesling is by no means confined to the north, but seems to become rare in the south—the Kinzig valley between Gengenbach and Offenburg, and in places to the south of it. Traminer and Gewürztraminer, the special pride of the Ortenau, are again found mainly in its southern half, but apparently extend a little farther north than Ruländer. They represent the highest proportion of the local total, about 30 percent, at Durbach, but also make up substantial percentages farther north, on both sides of the Rench valley, while the southern parts, the Kinzig valley and the neighborhood of Offenburg, appear to account for smaller quantities.

The best-known sites in the south are Ortenberg's Schlossberg and Andreasberg and Zell-Weierbach's Abtsberg. The village of Durbach is not only the largest winegrowing community of the area, but also the most outstanding in that it grows within its boundaries, and on a great number of vineyard sites, all the main varieties found in the Ortenau, all of high or the highest quality. From its steep slopes comes a full-bodied, velvety Spätburgunder red wine, together with a fresh, fruity Spätburgunder Weissherbst; an excellent Ruländer, fresh and pleasing, or broader and stronger, according to the situation of the vineyard; a racy, lively Riesling; a famous, full-bodied Traminer and Gewürztraminer with fragrant bouquet, more delicate in the former, stronger in the latter.

The best-known sites are the vast Staufenberg, below the castle, and the Steinberg, where most of these varieties may be found. Riesling was first planted, before the turn of the century, on Durbach's Klingelberg site, which is part of the Staufenberg, and has spread from there, together with the name Klingelberger, through the central Ortenau. Another site on which it is grown is the Mühlberg. Lighter Ruländer comes from the Schwarzloch site; the broader, heavier one from the sunny Stollenberg. On the Kochberg site, mainly Spätburgunder is grown. The large Plauelrain site, with its inner sanctum the Ölberg, produces Durbach's Traminer and the more spicy Gewürztraminer, which must be acknowledged as belonging to the peak wines of German viticulture and as being fully equivalent to the best of their kind grown in Alsace.

A little higher up the wine route, at neighboring Bottenau as well as on the northern side of the Rench valley, at Ringelbach and Tiergarten, more or less sizable proportions of Traminer are grown; but in the two last-named villages, as well as at Oberkirch on the Renz River, a still more substantial percentage of Riesling is added to the predominant variety, Spätburgunder. Waldulm, with its Altenberg and Pfarrberg sites, and neighboring Kappelrodek, with Hex vom Dasenstein and Kappelberg, enjoy a high reputation for the quality of their Spätburgunder, which constitutes about 90 percent or more of their production. Sassbachwalden, a little farther north, with the sites of Klostergut, Schelzberg, and Alter Gott, still grows about 80 percent Spätburgunder. At Bühl and Altschweier, which share the large Sternenberg site, and Bühlertal, with the Engelsberg and Klotzberg sites, all on red sandstone soil, Riesling and Spätburgunder are grown in more or less equal proportions.

A little farther on, the twin villages of Eisental-Affental, a mile apart, specialize in different wines. Eisental, with its sites of Sommerhalde and Betschgraben, produces almost exclusively a very good Riesling; while Affental bears off the palm for the very best Spätburgunder red wine to be found in the whole of Baden, deep red, full-bodied, velvety and at the same time fiery—one of the best grown in Germany. To be precise, Affentaler, grown here for six hundred years, is a more fertile mutant of Spätburgunder, known to ampelographers as Blue Arbst, producing a wine that differs somewhat from that of the ordinary Spätburgunder by its darker color. Affental decorates its bottles with a little plastic monkey (*Affe*). This may be good for sales, but reveals ignorance or disregard of the etymology of the local name. "Affental" has nothing to do with monkeys or apes, but is derived from Ave-Tal ("*Ave* Valley"), a local valley in which the convent of Lichtental, near Baden-Baden, once owned vineyard property and which was therefore piously named after the devotional prayer to the Virgin, *Ave Maria.*

In the northernmost part of the Ortenau—which is based on red argillaceous slate, the so-called red-Pier—at Neuweier, Steinbach, Varnhalt, and Sinzheim, Riesling is grown almost exclusively. Neuweier's Mauerberg site, a large southerly slope immediately above the village and actually enclosed by a stone wall *(Mauer)*, is generally acknowledged to produce the best Riesling of the Ortenau. It is put into Bocksbeutel flasks, the characteristic form of Franconian wine bottles, which is said to be a privilege owing to the fact that the site was once owned by a local monastery belonging to the diocese of Würzburg.

The neighboring town of Steinbach has a still higher proportion of Riesling. Its best-known site goes by the curious name of Stich den Buben (an imperative that on the face of it may be translated as "Stab the Lad," but really has the more harmless meaning of "Trump the Jack," the name of an old-fashioned card game). Varnhalt, which seems to grow only Riesling, has as its main sites Steingrüble, Sonnenberg, and Klosterberg. The last name (translated "Monastery Hill") refers to the former monastery of Fremersberg, situated on the hill of that name between Baden-Baden and Sinzheim. The latter town has a site with a similar name, Klostergut ("Monastery Estate"), and another named Fremersberger Feigenwäldchen ("Little Fig Wood").

Although less well known to outsiders than the Kaiserstuhl, the far-famed "Kitchen of Bacchus," the Ortenau is considered by Baden's wine experts to be the heart of their region's wine lands. It is no accident that large aristocratic estates are situated in this area. With its different soils and milder, more humid climate, the wines of the Ortenau are naturally bound to be different from those of the Kaiserstuhl. Where the Kaiserstuhl undoubtedly scores is in its highly alcoholic and rumbustious Ruländer, especially that grown on the naked volcanic rock, which the more subdued Rülander of the Ortenau cannot match, at least not in the qualities mentioned. It is more difficult to decide about the respective merits of the Spät-burgunders of the two areas, although to many wine lovers those of the Ortenau may seem to be more refined, and the Kaiserstuhl can offer nothing that equals Affental's Blue Arbst. As regards its Traminers and Gewürztraminers, especially those of Durbach, the Ortenau is unrivaled in Germany, reaching the quality of those of Alsace, which the same kinds of Kaiserstuhl wine do not. Lastly, the Ortenau clearly scores in its Rieslings, both in quantity and in quality. Very little Riesling is grown in the Kaiserstuhl; its sometimes almost torrid dry heat is simply not the suitable climate for this peak variety of German wines.

There is a short gap in the spread of vineyards north of the Ortenau and those of northern Baden. These may be sub-divided into five viticultural areas: The Pfinzgau-Enzgau extends from Karlsruhe southeastward to Pforzheim, where the little Pfinz River joins the Enz. The much larger Kraichgau extends from Durlach, the eastern suburb of Karlsruhe, north-ward to near Wiesloch and northeastward for some distance along the Württemberg border. The very small Neckar and Jagst area begins at the entry of the Neckar into Baden and extends for only a few miles, while its tributary the Jagst, which runs mainly through Württemberg, crosses over into Baden only for shorter distances. The valley of the lower Tauber River, also called Badisches Frankenland ("Baden-Franconia"), is the easternmost area, from Beckstein and Königshofen to Wertheim, where the Tauber joins the Main, and with the town of Tauberbischofsheim as its center. The largest of the five areas is that of the southern Bergstrasse. Geographically, the Bergstrasse is the stretch of country between Darmstadt and Heidelberg, hugging the foothills of the Odenwald. But politi-cal claims interfere with geographic reality. About halfway along its length, between Heppenheim and the village of Laudenbach, the Bergstrasse is crossed by the border between the federal states of Hesse and Baden-Württemberg, which makes the wines of its southern half Baden wines. Furthermore, the Bergstrasse has been artificially extended, purely in the viticultural sense, to the town of Wiesloch, about eight miles south of Heidelberg. Wiesloch has the largest vine-covered acreage and is the most important viticultural center of northern Baden.

On the whole, however, viticulture seems to be more or less on the way out in most parts of northern Baden. At the present time, only about five thousand acres of vine-covered surface are left; in the past, the Tauber valley alone had fifteen thousand acres. Viticulture is not so essential here as it is in the Ortenau, in parts of the Breisgau, in the Kaiserstuhl, and in the Markgräflerland, where on steep slopes nothing but the vine can be planted. Also, as in the High Rhine area, there are flourishing industries in northern Baden offering easier, safer, and more remunerative work than can be found in viticulture.

Again, northern Baden, on the whole, does not produce wines of any great distinction, although there are, of course, exceptions to the general rule. The predominant varieties grown in the Pfinzgau-Enzgau and Kraichgau areas, on soils of shell lime, red marl, loess, and loam, are Ruländer—which naturally is not so full-bodied and strong here as it is in the Kaiserstuhl—Silvaner, and Müller-Thurgau. On Durlach's hill, the Turmberg, which has a State Domain attached to the local viticultural institute, Riesling and Spätburgunder are grown. A modest Riesling is also grown in some other places, while Spätburgunder, again not comparable to that of southern Baden in fullness and strength, is also grown in such places as Weingarten and Sulzfeld, but seems elsewhwere to be less significant as a red-wine grape in comparison with Portugieser. Some red wines characteristic of Württemberg are also grown locally, such as Müllerrebe (misnamed Schwarzriesling), Lemberger, and Trollinger.

It is difficult to believe that the valley of the lower Tauber River was at one time one of the largest winegrowing areas of northern Baden; at the present time, with increased industrialization and urban development, it is one of the smallest. Tauberbischofsheim, its main town, had lost most of its former significance as a viticultural center, but in the last two decades has been built up again into one of the major wine-producing parts of the area. Königshofen, on the Tauber's bank opposite Beckstein and near the Württemberg border, is a railway junction with its vineyards rising steeply above the railroad tracks. A few miles lower down is another railway junction, Lauda. It has a State Domain, and it was recorded as a place of wine cultivation in Carolingian times. The town of Wertheim is situated at the junction of the Tauber with the Main. Local soils are made up of variegated sandstone, on which a good deal of Gutedel, the typical wine of the Markgräflerland, but here known as Junker, is grown, while Silvaner and Müller-Thurgau are mainly planted on limestone and red marl. All Tauber wines are put in Bocksbeutel bottles like those of Franconia.

Very few winegrowing places are left in the small Neckar and Jagst area, where most people content themselves with homemade cider. Viticulture begins immediately where the Neckar crosses over from Württemberg, where the ruins of Hornberg Castle frown over it. Hornberg was once the home of Götz von Berlichingen (1480–1562), the "Knight of the Iron Hand," hero of one of Goethe's plays and famous for coining the pithiest invective in the German language. Below the castle, the little town of Neckarzimmern grows Silvaner, Riesling, and Müller-Thurgau; and nearby Neckarmühlbach and Heinsheim grow red varieties in addition. Klepsau and Neudenau, on the Baden stretches of the Jagst River, cultivate the same varieties.

In romantic old Heidelberg, much celebrated in student song, we are in the middle of the viticultural area of the Bergstrasse, though at the southern end of the "real" Bergstrasse. On its variegated sandstone soil, the municipality still has some 170 acres under vines. The local wine is, of course, also celebrated in student song, but cannot be celebrated quite so much in the sober written word. If, as is likely, the visitor is not very impressed with its quality, he may console himself by walking up to the castle and admiring, in its cellar, jolly old "Heidelberger Fass," a giant cask with a capacity of nearly 50,000 gallons, as well as the effigy of the midget court jester Perkeo, secular patron of wine drinkers.

At the southern end of the "imaginary" Bergstrasse, the town of Wiesloch has, on red marl soil, the largest vine-planted surface of northern Baden, about 220 acres. On its vineyard sites, Ruländer, Riesling, Traminer, and Spätburgunder are grown—very fair wines, though none of them quite so good as those of southern Baden—as well as Silvaner, Müller-Thurgau, and Portugieser, and, as a very rare exception, the St. Laurent vine, a mutant of Spätburgunder, found elsewhere in Germany only sporadically in Württemberg. Wiesloch received market rights in 967 under the emperor Otto I, and still has its old town wall with fortified watchtowers. It also has the best winegrowers' cooperative of northern Baden, which shows some hankering after the past—though after the recent past, in the Palatine Electorate—calling itself the Kurpfälzische Winzergenossenschaft.

In the climatically very well favored "real" Bergstrasse, along the foothills of the Odenwald north of Heidelberg, some fair-to-good wines are found. The largest vine-planted surface, with about 135 acres, is that of Schriesheim, which produces, on variegated sandstone, a good Silvaner and an almost equally good Riesling. The small communities of Grosssachsen and Lützelsachsen, still on variegated sandstone, are best known for their Spätburgunder red wines. The town of Weinheim has a soil based on porphyry, and produces a very fair Riesling, as well as Ruländer, Silvaner, and Müller-Thurgau.

Baden has the southernmost vineyards of Germany, and speaks of its wines with pride as "cherished by the sun" (*Badischer Wein von der Sonne verwöhnt*). Their quality can be proved statistically. The highest prizes any German wine can receive are the prize medals for naturally pure wines awarded annually by the German Agricultural Society (Deutsche Landwirtschafts-Gesellschaft, or DLG), for which all the viticultural regions of the Federal Republic compete. It stands to reason that these awards are made on the basis of the stiffest tests; it also goes without saying that the decisions are reached by a panel of absolutely impartial judges. Moreover, their deliberations take place nowhere in Baden, but in Mainz. With a vine-planted surface constituting only 12.5 percent of the West German total, Baden's share of all prizes awarded has for many years been 30 percent and more; in 1964, it was nearly 40 percent. Baden's growers are justifiably proud of their record. Actually, however, it is only Alemannic southern Baden, with the smaller acreage, that carries off these prizes; and it is easy to see that it is largely the Ortenau and the Kaiserstuhl that have brought this about.

10. Württemberg

WÜRTTEMBERG, situated between Baden and Bavaria, has a vine-planted surface of about 6,500 hectares (16,255 acres). Because of its higher altitude—and also, in part, owing to its more easterly situation, approaching the continental weather zone—Württemberg's climate is somewhat harsher than that of Baden, but nevertheless offers favorable conditions for the vine. Viticulture has its greatest extension in the northern half of the region, especially in the river basins of the Neckar and its tributaries, the Enz and Zaber rivers coming from the west, and the Rems, Murr, and Bottwar, Schozach, Sulm, Kocher, and Jagst, all coming from the east. In addition it comprises, in its northeasternmost corner, a section of the Tauber valley belonging to the river basin of the Main, and, in the extreme south, a short stretch along the shore of Lake Constance. Both these latter areas account for probably less than 5 percent of the total production.

The predominant soils are heavy but easily weathering calcareous Keuper (red marl) and lighter and warmer shell lime. More sporadically, vines also stand on Jurassic variegated sandstone and loess, and, near Lake Constance, Molasse formations. The average annual precipitation and atmospheric humidity are somewhat higher here than in other viticultural regions.

Perhaps even more than Baden, Württemberg is a region of agricultural smallholders, with considerable fragmentation of viticultural property. More than half the wine growers work plots of less than 25 ar (0.7 acres); more than 40 percent own between 0.7 and 2.47 acres; and only 3 percent have more than 2.47 acres (1 hectare) of vine-planted surface. These statistics explain the need to unite into cooperatives. The ordinary winegrower usually has no properly equipped separate wine cellar and delivers his harvest to his cooperative for processing and storage.

The first Württemberg winegrowers' cooperative was founded at Asperg near Ludwigsburg in 1854; the second, at Neckarsulm in 1855. Today there are more than 140 in 360-odd winegrowing communities. Alongside the older, smaller local cooperatives, there are a number of larger, more up-to-date ones. Thus, Möglingen, near Asperg, has a very large modern central cooperative serving the whole of the Ludwigsburg district, and at Beutelsbach there is the equally large and modern central cellar of the Rems valley cooperatives. The largest and most modern of them all is that of the central cooperative for the whole region (with the somewhat cumbersome name Landeszentralgenossenschaft Württembergischer Weingärtnergenossenschaften), which operates a giant cellarage plant at Untertürkheim in the Stuttgart conurbation. This plant processes and stores not much less than all the individual cooperatives manage together, and in size and modern equipment it is a counterpart of the Baden central cellarage at Breisach.

Larger estates include the Herzoglich Württembergische Hofkammer ("Ducal Domain of Württemberg") with vineyard sites near Stuttgart, Untertürkheim, Stetten in the Rems valley, Mundelsheim on the Neckar, on Maulbronn's Eilfinger Berg at the western end, and at Hohenhaslach at the eastern end of the Stromberg range of hills—a nice selection of the choicest places. There are also a number of other large aristocratic estates, perhaps a dozen in all. The municipality of Stuttgart has large vineyard sites of its own; and the State Teaching and Research Institute at Weinsberg, near Heilbronn, has eighty-four acres of vineyard sites near Weinsberg itself and elsewhere in northern Württemberg.

Most of the region's wines are grown in the winding,

climatically favored valleys of the Neckar and its tributaries, on vineyards situated in well-protected nooks and crannies. Cultivation is carried on, virtually throughout, on steep, terraced slopes. More or less level surfaces, common enough in the Palatinate and Rheinhessen, are quite exceptional in Württemberg. The resulting technical difficulties of cultivation are considerable. The region's viticulture involves an average annual work load of 2,887 hours per hectare (1 hectare equals 2.47 acres), as compared with 1,609 in Rheinhessen, 1,804 in the Rheingau, and 1,809 in the Palatinate. It equals the work load of the Moselle region—2,889 working hours per year, per hectare—without, however, having the Moselle's advantage of a more equable maritime climate and a much greater yield.

Württemberg grows more red than white grapes, the proportions being 57 and 43 percent, respectively. Thus, it has the highest share of red varieties among German regions. Of the white varieties, Riesling predominates, with 22 percent of the total production. Silvaner contributes 10 percent, and Müller-Thurgau, 7 percent. More occasionally, and in small quantities, Ruländer, Traminer, Gutedel, and Muskateller may be planted. A promising recent crossbreed of Trollinger x Riesling has been developed under the name Kernerrebe by the viticultural institute at Weinsberg.

There is great variety in the assortment of red wines. Reds, which Württemberg shares with other regions, are Portugieser, with 9 percent of the total production, and Spätburgunder, which amounts to less than 4 percent. Most of the reds are virtually peculiar to Württemberg, and found outside it only sporadically in northern Baden near the Württemberg border. The most widespread, most typical, and most important red-wine variety, contributing 25 percent of the total production, is the late-ripening Trollinger vine, with grapes that may weigh more than two pounds. Its light-red wines, paler but more pungent than Spätburgunder, are hearty and pithy. The second red variety confined to Württemberg, and contributing about 6 percent of the total production, is the Lemberger. Comparatively late in ripening, it is darker in color than Trollinger, somewhat reminiscent of Burgundy in taste, but light as a Portugieser; it is often blended with Trollinger to produce a darker, less acid, more full-bodied wine. The third local red variety is the Müllerrebe (often misleadingly named Schwarz-riesling), which accounts for 10 percent of the total yield, is early in ripening, and produces a wine of medium quality, mild and aromatic but tending to be somewhat deficient in acidity. The fourth is a new variety, Samtrot, an artificial mutation from the Müllerrebe, developed at the Weinsberg institute, producing a ruby- to dark-red wine, velvety in taste, with a considerably higher "must" gravity, and generally a good deal better than its parent, the Müllerrebe. A fifth variety, Blue Saint Laurent, gives a good, dark-red wine, but is grown only sporadically and in small quantities. A sixth local red variety, becoming increasingly rare now, is the Blue Affentaler, unrelated to and much inferior to Spätburgunder, and therefore, despite the identical name, unrelated also to the Blue Arbst of Affental in Baden, which is a natural mutant of Spätburgunder. Also practically confined to Württemberg are the two red crossbreeds developed at the Weinsberg institute, the Herold-rebe (Portugieser x Lemberger) and Helfensteiner (Früh-burgunder x Trollinger).

There is another Württemberg specialty, namely its Schiller-wein. The name is not, as one might believe, a tribute to the poet Friedrich Schiller, Württemberg's most famous son, but is taken from the verb *schillern* ("to change in color," "to be iridescent"). The reason for this is that it is made from a mixture of red-wine and white-wine grapes planted on the same plot, ripening at the same time, and picked, pressed, and fermented together. Thus, what might at first sight appear to be a Weissherbst (Rosé) is something quite different. Schillerwein was once universally popular in Württemberg, but is now said to have become rare. The reason for its decline seems to be that "mixed settings," the planting of different vines on the same plot, which it presupposes, is officially frowned upon on principle.

To sum up, very broadly, the characteristics of Württemberg wines: They have a very individual, hearty, pithy taste, and an earthy, lingering "tail," of aftertaste, which is especially noticeable in wines grown on shell-lime soils.

Eight natural winegrowing areas may be distinguished, although most of them are only marginally more differentiated one from the other than are those of Baden: (1) the Upper Neckar valley along the slope of the Swabian Alb range from Rottenburg, where the river emerges from the foothills of the Black Forest and runs in a northeasterly direction as far as Plochingen, where it knocks against the barrier of the Schurwald hills and is deflected, in a sharp bend, in a northwesterly direction. (2) The Middle Neckar area, from the northwestern turn of the river to Stuttgart and from there northward in a series of tortuous bends to Gundelsheim; where it passes over from Württemberg into Baden. This is the largest area, including also the valleys of the Murr, Bottwar, Schozach, and Sulm rivers, all on the eastern side of the Neckar. In its course through the hill country, the Neckar valley becomes increasingly warmer and more fertile, so one may also distinguish climatically an upper and lower section of this area (*Oberland* and *Unterland*), with the town of Marbach as their approximate boundary. (Württembergers also speak of the former as the "Middle Neckar" and of the latter as the "Lower Neckar," ignoring the fact that the lower course of the river is in Baden.) (3) The Rems valley on the eastern side. (4) The Enz valley on the western side, including the southern slopes of the Stromberg range. (5) The Zabergäu, the wide valley of the Zaber River between the Heuchelberg and the Stromberg ranges. (6) The Kocher and Jagst river valleys on the eastern side of the Neckar. (7) The middle Tauber River valley above Mergentheim, in the northeastern corner of Württemberg. (8) The Lake Constance area. (The two last-named areas do not belong to the Neckar basin.)

There is a "Swabian wine route," largely confined to the Middle Neckar area, beginning at Gundelsheim in the north and ending at Esslingen in the south. From Neckarsulm it turns eastward to Erlenbach, then turns back to Heilbronn, Flein, and Talheim, crosses the river to Lauffen and Kirchheim, recrosses to Gemmrigheim, Hessigheim, and Mundelsheim, makes a detour to Grossbottwar and Kleinbottwar, returns to the Neckar at Marbach, swings across the hills to Neckarrems, makes another detour to Waiblingen on the Rems, goes back to Fellbach, halfway between Waiblingen and Cannstatt, crosses the hills to Untertürkheim, and proceeds along the Neckar to Uhlbach, Obertürkheim, Mettingen, and Esslingen.

The Upper Neckar valley, comprising brown Jurassic rock, grows mostly light and neutral Silvaner wines on the sunny southerly surfaces of the Swabian Alb slopes. The most important winegrowing communities are Neuffen, with its Täleswein (Talwein; that is, "Valley Wine"), and Metzingen, both someway up the Swabian Alb. The easternmost winetown on the slopes of the Alb is Kirchheim-Teck (to be distinguished from the Kirchheim on the wine route mentioned above). Higher up the Alb, the town of Reutlingen grows small quantities at an altitude of up to 1,900 feet. The towns situated on the Neckar itself, Rottenburg, Tübingen, and Nürttingen, have few vineyards in their vicinity. Between the Swabian Alb and the Upper Neckar, vineyards are nowadays isolated and far-between features. They do not give the landscape its typical stamp as they do from Esslingen northward.

The area of the Middle Neckar valley, together with the Murr and Bottwar, Schozach and Sulm valleys, is Württemberg's richest wine land. Wherever one turns, one looks at steep, terraced hills, towns and villages with half-timbered houses at the foot of castle ruins, a countryside saturated with history and lavished with natural beauty. On the right bank of the Neckar, the old town of Esslingen, with its fifteenth-century Liebfrauen church and many remains of medieval architecture, in the past an important wine-trading center, has as its best-known site the Schenkenberg. The string of winegrowing communities farther down the river, Mettingen, Obertürkheim, Uhlbach, Untertürkheim, and Cannstatt, are incorporated as suburbs of

Stuttgart, the city center being situated on the opposite side of the river. The viticultural complex of Stuttgart also includes Fellbach, an independent community to the east of Cannstatt, with a very large vineyard acreage.

Most of the Stuttgart complex is based on Keuper (red marl) soil; only Cannstatt's vines grow on shell lime and have a distinct character of their own. It produces mainly full-bodied red wines, Trollingers and other varieties, but also a great deal of Rieslings and other white wines. Every wine in this neighborhood has a high reputation. The highest-quality wines on the eastern side of the Neckar come from Untertürkheim's Dautenklinge, Gips, and Mönchberg sites, Cannstatt's Zuckerle and Halde, and Fellbach's Lämmler. Inner Stuttgart itself, on the opposite side of the Neckar, has in its Mönchberg one of the country's peak sites.

The center of Stuttgart lies in a bowl of hills, along which the vineyards creep up to the outskirts of the city, and, in the case of the Kriegsberg and Mönchberg sites, right up into the city's center. The capital of the federal state of Baden-Württemberg—"the big city between woods and vines," as it likes to call itself—has nearly a thousand acres of vineyard land, a sizable acreage for a modern large industrial city, and is second only to the much smaller town of Heilbronn as the largest winegrowing community in the country. In the sixteenth and seventeenth centuries Stuttgart had almost four times its present acreage of vineyard land and was widely famed as the richest German wine town. As a contemporary French nursery rhyme has it: *Si l'on ne cueilloit de Stuttgart le raisin, la ville iroit se noyer dans le vin* ("If one didn't pick Stuttgart's grapes, the town would drown in wine").

The attractive town of Ludwigsburg, to the north of Stuttgart, is the center of a rural district with a great number of winegrowing communities producing a large share of the country's total yield of grapes. On the opposite side of the Neckar lies the little town of Marbach, birthplace of Friedrich Schiller. From here the wine route leads into the valleys of the

Murr River and its tributary the Bottwar. In the latter valley, the communities of Kleinbottwar, Grossbottwar, Oberstenfeld, and Beilstein own some of the largest vineyard acreages of the region. Besides juicy Trollingers, a great deal of good Riesling and Silvaner is grown; a specialty of the valley is its Muskat-Trollinger, a red wine with a pleasant Muskateller aroma. The best-known sites are Kleinbottwar's Götzenberg, Grossbottwar's Harzberg, Oberstenfeld's Lichtenberg, and Beilstein's Wartenberg. The village of Oberstenfeld is well worth a visit, not only for its beautiful location but also for its treasures of medieval architecture, above all, its eleventh-century St. Peter's church.

Back along the winding Neckar valley, the wine route leads past steep terraces (on shell-lime soil, for a change), through the communities of Mundelsheim, Hessigheim, and Gemmrigheim, then crosses the river to Kirchheim and Lauffen, all of them owning extensive vineyard acreages, growing mainly Trollinger wines. Mundelsheim's Kašberg is one of Württemberg's peak sites. Hessigheim's Felsengarten ("Rock Garden") is named after its steep slope climbing up to high rock towers overlooking the Neckar valley, a stretch of the river often called the "Swabian Dolomites." At Lauffen, where the Zaber joins the Neckar, and, again on the other side, at Talheim on the Schozach, Müllerrebe predominates among the red-wine grapes, while Flein, nearer to Heilbronn, grows an excellent Riesling. Here we are again on the Keuper soil of the Heibronn neighborhood. Flein's best sites are Sonnenberg and Staufenberg.

The town of Heilbronn, situated in a large circular valley, is the center of the wine trade of northern Württemberg, and at the same time the largest winegrowing community of the whole region, with nearly eleven hundred acres of vineyard land, planted mostly with red varieties—Trollinger, Spätburgunder, Müllerrebe, and Samtrot. The town's best sites are the Wartberg, Staufenberg, and Stiftsberg. Like the Heilbronn environment, the Sulm valley is also based on Keuper soils. Neckarsulm, where the Sulm joins the Neckar, has the Scheuerberg site, worked by the members of Württemberg's second-oldest cooperative, founded in 1855. Up the Sulm, there are more than a dozen winegrowing communties, some of them with vineyard acreages of considerable size. Erlenbach-Bin-swangen, with one of the largest, leads to the town of Weinsberg (the valley is often called the Weinsberg valley).

The town of Weinsberg leans against a hill of perfectly conical shape, ringed with wine terraces and surmounted by a ruined castle rejoicing in the name of Weibertreu ("Wives' Loyalty"). The castle's name recalls a legend telling how, in 1140, when the Hohenstaufen king Conrad III, in his war against the Guelfs, had already taken the fortress, he magnan-imously allowed the good women of Weinsberg to save whatever was most precious to them before the surrender of the town, whereupon they saved their husbands' lives by carrying them out piggyback. Weinsberg has not only one of the largest vineyard acreages but also produces some of the best wines, especially Trollinger and Lemberger from the Schemelsberg, and Riesling from the Ranzenberg, its two main sites. A State Teaching and Research Institute, which has produced the improved red-wine grape Samtrot, the red-wine crossings Heroldrebe and Helfensteiner, and the white-wine crossing Kernerrebe, is also located here.

Generally speaking, in the Weinsberg valley on both sides of the Sulm, red and white wines are grown in more or less equal proportions. A short distance to the north of Weinsberg, Eberstadt belongs to the large-acreage communities; eastward, the village of Grantschen produces a good Lemberger on its Wildenberg site; in the upper part of the valley, between Willsbach and Löwenstein, Silvaner predominates. Back on the Neckar, the little town of Gundelsheim, lying below the ruined castle of Horneck, once the stronghold of the Teutonic Knights, and with the large, promisingly named vineyard site of Him-melreich ("Kingdom of Heaven"), forms the northern end of the chain of middle Neckar winegrowing communities.

The Rems River joins the Neckar at Neckarrems. In the very beautiful lower part of its valley, on both sides of the river and up as far as Schorndorf, there are more than twenty communities growing both red and white wines—predominantly Trollinger and Portugieser, and Riesling and Silvaner, respectively—on steep Keuper terraces. The best-known places, most of them with picturesque half-timbered buildings, are Grossheppach and Kleinheppach, Geradstetten (higher up, on the north side of the river), and, with the largest viticultural acreages, Stetten, Beutelsbach, Strümpfelbach, and Schnait (on the south side). The last two are situated in a parallel side valley accessible from Beutelsbach. The outstanding sites are Stetten's Brotwasser and Pulvermächer, Grossheppach's Wanne, Kleinheppach's Greiner, and Schnait's Halde. The best Reislings are grown by Stetten and Schnait. Beutelsbach houses a large modern central cooperative serving the whole Rems valley.

The Enz River comes from the Black Forest and joins the Neckar just below Besigheim, one of Württemberg's most picturesque medieval towns, built high above the river. Some of its most rewarding sights are the twelfth-century twin towers flanking the gate of the town wall; the half-timbered town hall, built in 1459; and an exquisite wood carving, the altar of the old town church, forty-six feet high and dated about 1515. The wines of the Enz valley, and, to the north of it, those on the south slope of the Stromberg range, are grown on shell-lime terraces. Besigheim's main vineyard site is the large Wurmberg, nearly 150 acres in size, which produces one of Württemberg's best Trollingers as well as an excellent Lemberger. A few miles higher up the Enz, the town of Bietigheim also grows mainly Trollinger. The market town of Vaihingen and, to the west, the beautifully situated village of Rosswag, with its best site, Halde, are the other main winegrowing communities on the banks of the river.

There is a greater number farther north, on the south slopes of the Stromberg hills. Bönnigheim owns 300 acres of vineyards, growing red and white wines in more or less equal proportions. Farther west, Hohenhaslach, with its main site of Kirchberg, grows one of the best Trollingers. Ochsenbach, Häfnerhaslach, Gündelbach, and other towns also produce good Trollingers,

Lembergers, and Spätburgunders. Near the western end of the Stromberg range, the beautifully situated town of Maulbronn and the neighboring town of Knittlingen are especially remarkable. Maulbronn contains a former Cistercian Abbey, founded in 1147, its buildings still well preserved. Before it was closed during the Reformation, it was Württemberg's richest monastery. Maulbronn's Eilfingerberg is one of the country's peak sites for Riesling. In the Middle Ages, this hillside belonged to the abbey, and there is a local anecdote to account for its name, which is claimed to be a corruption of "Elffinger Berg" ("Eleven Fingers' Hill"). During Lent, the brother cellar master is said to have asked the abbot for permission to test the wines for their development and was told that he was allowed to stick his finger into the bungholes and lick it. When the abbot later asked how the wine was coming along, the cellar master answered: "One really ought to have eleven fingers." Nearby Knittlingen, whose Reichshalde site immediately adjoins Maulbronn's Eilfingerberg, also grows an excellent Riesling. Knittlingen prides itself on being the birthplace of no less a personage than the much-fabled magician Johannes Faustus, born in 1480, and has duly set up a monument to his memory.

The fertile Zabergäu, traversed by the little Zaber River, which joints the Neckar at Lauffen, is a broad valley extending between the Stromberg and Heuchelberg ranges, which run almost parallel to each other. The sheltered south slopes of the Heuchelberg are dotted with little towns and villages lying below castle ruins, and abound in vineyards on red Keuper soil. The main town is Brackenheim, on the Zaber, among whose sites the Zweifelsberg is remarkable for one of the country's most excellent Lembergers. Nearer to the Heuchelberg slopes is Neipperg, whose Schlossberg is a peak site for Riesling. Good Riesling is also grown by the town of Schwaigern, actually situated in the little Lein valley on the north side of the Heuchelberg, but having its vineyards, among them the Grafenberg, on the south slopes of the hill range. The other communities at the foot fo the Heuchelberg, Nordheim,

Dürrenzimmern, Haberschlacht, and others, and those on the banks of the Zaber from Güglingen up to Zaberfeld, grow mostly red wines, especially Trollinger and Lemberger.

The eastern tributaries of Kocher and Jagst, which join the Neckar a few miles above Gundelsheim, traverse the Hohenlohe plateau. The best-known winegrowing communities on the Kocher, with vineyards situated on steep, shell-lime terraces, are Forchtenberg, Niedernhall, Grisbach, and Ingelfingen, and, at some distance south of the river, Cleversulzbach, Pfedelbach, and Michelbach. Winegrowing towns on the Jagst are Möckmühl and, higher up, Dörzbach. The wines grown are predominantly Silvaner and Müller-Thurgau.

The Tauber River, whose middle course runs through the northeasternmost corner of Württemberg above the spa town of Mergentheim, belongs to the basin of the Main River. The area includes the small Vorbach River, a tributary of the Tauber. The soils are made up of shell lime, as are those of the Kocher and Jagst valleys, and the wines grown are again predominantly Silvaner and Müller-Thurgau. The main winegrowing communities are Laudenbach, Weikersheim, Elpersheim, and Markelsheim, the last-named with the largest vine-planted acreage.

In the extreme south, Württemberg covers a stretch of the shore of Lake Constance, on both sides of the industrial town of Friedrichshafen, the whole area annexed to it under Napoleon in 1806.

The names of Württemberg's wines are only extremely rarely found decorating wine lists in other parts of Germany, let alone abroad. The Swabians have a reputation of being Germany's most enthusiastic wine drinkers; they are said to drink, annually and per capita, three times as much as the average citizen of the Federal Republic. Like that of Baden, Württemberg's total production does not suffice to satisfy local demands. For one thing, there is limited space for suitable vineyard land in valleys often hemmed in by large chunks of wooded hill country; for another, the cost of production on steep slopes is high. At any rate, considerable quantities of wine have to be imported from other German regions as well as from abroad. The result is that in both southern regions prices of local wines are somewhat higher than in regions that have to export their wines. But the Swabians like their own wines best and are cheerfully prepared to pay more for the home product. For the outsider, therefore, the best way to become acquainted with Württemberg's wines is to go and drink them where they are at home.

11. Nahe

THE NAHE region has a total vine-planted surface of nearly 3,280 hectares (about 8,102 acres); thus, its acreage is only slightly more than half the size of that of Wüttemberg. There are eighty-odd winegrowing communities. The little Nahe River, only 81 miles in length, rises on the southern slopes of the Hunsrück range, runs in a generally northeasterly direction through Bad Kreuznach, and turns northward at some distance beyond this spa town to join the Rhine between Bingen and Bingerbrück.

The upper limit of Nahe viticulture is marked by the vineyards of the villages of Hochstetten and Martinstein, where the river valley widens out. Winegrowing communities are found on both sides of the river, with the exception of its lower course, north of Kreuznach, where they are confined to its left side. The Nahe receives two tributaries on its right-hand side, the Glan and the Alsenz, which come down from the northwest corner of the Palatinate, but viticulturally form part of the Nahe region. To the west of Kreuznach and the lower course of the river, winegrowing communities are settled along, and in side valleys between, a number of larger streams—the Ellerbach, which is joined by the Gräfenbach, the Guldenbach, and the Trollbach. These western tributaries of the river come down from the Soonwald, an eastern extension of the Hunsrück, which shelters the whole winegrowing region against north winds. A great many smaller pieces of woodland reach down toward the main valley alongside the tributaries, alternating with fields and meadows and vineyard slopes.

The valley of the lower Nahe forms the western margin of the Mainz basin. Like its eastern neighbors, Rheinhessen and the Palatinate, the Nahe region enjoys very favorable natural conditions, with a minimum of rainfall. Very warm, sunny, dry weather gives the vines an equable, mild climate favoring their growth, and, with an early spring and long autumn, allowing the grapes an ample ripening period to bring about their fullest development. By contrast with those of the Moselle, the soils of the Nahe region are extremely variable, including weathered slate and volcanic porphyry, red sandstone, marl, heavy potter's clay and light loam, loess, and calcareous sand. The diversity of the region's soils and its slopes with gradients varying between gentle and steep account for an extraordinary variability in the distinctive local character of its wines, ranging from lighter, naturally sparkling, fragrant types reminiscent of Moselles to full-bodied, fiery, powerful ones more comparable to Rhine wines. Nahe wines are often characterized—in a very broad sense but with some justification—as a kind of blend between Moselle and Rhine wines.

According to the latest official statistics, for the 1971 vintage, white-wine varieties constitute 99 percent and red wine 1 percent of the total yield. Among the white wines, Silvaner contributes 32 percent, Müller-Thurgau 30 percent, and Riesling 27 percent. One may reasonably assume that among the 10 percent of white wines not accounted for statistically, Ruländer represents the major share, that Scheurebe, perhaps the most successful among the new crossbreeds (Silvaner x Riesling), follows, and that the third and fourth places are occupied by Weissburgunder and Traminer, respectively. Of the 1 percent minority of red wines, Spätburgunder is grown sporadically on a few especially favored sites, and a small amount of Portugieser is also grown locally.

In the systematic development of its old-established viticulture into a modern one aiming at quality production, the Nahe has been lagging behind Rheinhessen, the Rheingau, and the Moselle; in fact, modernization dates back only to the turn of the present century. However, in the meantime the region has very successfully caught up with its neighbors. At the present time, it is highly thought of among professionals for its modern vineyard layout and intensive cultivation, as well as for its modern cellar technology. Its wines are well cared for and clean-tasting, they have collected a considerable crop of prize medals and indeed gained some international prestige. Much of this improvement is due to the labors of the State Viticultural Domain of Niederhausen-Schlossböckelheim, founded in 1902, which has gained for itself a record of outstanding achievement. Its main seat is between the two villages from which it takes its name, on the most favored stretch of the Middle Nahe, but it also owns and controls two outlying estates, the Münster-Sarmsheim Domain on the Lower Nahe and the Altenbamberg Domain on the lower course of the Alsenz River. From their foundation the mandate of the united domains has been to raise the general quality of Nahe wines, to advertise them by their own superior quality production, and at the same time to serve as a model in vineyard and cellar work to local wine-growers.

Viticulturally, the Nahe region may be roughly divided into three main areas: the upper course of the river, including its tributary the Glan, the middle course, including the Alsenz, the spa town of Kreuznach and communities to the west of it, and the lower course, including the Guldenbach and Trollbach valleys.

The Nahe's upper course has a good deal of slate and nutritive igneous rock on which fresh, lively Rieslings, somewhat reminiscent of Saar wines, and other good table wines grow. The main winegrowing communities are Monzingen on the left and Merxheim and Meddersheim on the right bank of the Nahe; further Odernheim, at the mouth of the Glan; and Meisenheim, higher up that tributary. Monzingen, with its extensive south slopes, is especially known for its racy and earthy-steely Rieslings.

The middle course of the river is the main area of

cultivation, with soils of weathered porphyry and slate, red sandstone, loam, and sand. The reputation of Nahe wines is chiefly based on the high quality of the wines of this area. The best-known sites on the steep south slopes of the village of Schlossböckelheim, on porphyry rock, are Königsfels, Mühlberg, Felsenberg, and Kupfergrube, the last two largely owned—and, indeed, first planted—by the State Domain. It may seem strange that the viticultural potential of these slopes, on heat-storing porphyry, with minimal rainfall and a generally ideal microclimate, was recognized only seventy-odd years ago. Yet, in the nineteenth century the Kupfergrube ("Copper pit") site, now covered with carefully terraced and beautifully tended vineyards, was nothing but a dismal wasteland of scrub and rocks surrounding an old copper mine; it was cleared for viticulture by convict labor as recently as the turn of the present century. Rieslings from Schlossböckelheim's Kupfergrube are today undoubtedly the most celebrated wines of the whole Nahe region. The adjacent village of Niederhausen, with its main sites of Hermannsberg, Steinberg, and Hermannshöhle, partly owned by the State Domain, also produces, mainly on slate soil, excellent Rieslings with great bouquet; and, beyond a bend in the river, so does Norheim, with its peak sites of Dellchen, Kafels, and Kirschheck.

A short distance downstream we reach Bad Münster am Stein-Ebernburg. The latter place, where the Alsenz joins the Nahe near a northward bend, has only recently been incorporated as part of the former municipality, a spa with radium brine baths on the opposite side of the river. The town is flanked by two huge red porphyry rocks, Rotenfels and Rheingrafenstein, the former a stunning, near-vertical precipice 1,080 feet high, Germany's steepest cliff face. At its foot there is a thickly planted vineyard on a kind of ledge, facing due south, the Rotenfals Bastei. The site is within the boundary of the nearby village of Traisen, but part of it is owned by the Niederhausen-Schlossböckelheim State Domain. All the neighboring places, Münster am Stein, Ebernburg, and Altenbamberg, the latter a short distance up the Alsenz, have extensive vineyard sites producing wines of high quality. The community of Ebernburg lies at the foot of the castle of the same name, the most famous one of the Nahe countryside.

Bad Kreuznach is not only an important spa with radium brine baths, but also by far the largest winegrowing community of the region, as well as the center of its wine trade. Moreover, it is the seat of a State Teaching and Research Institute. Most of its vineyard soil is based on red sandstone. Some of its best sites are the Kauzenberg, immediately overlooking the river and town and topped by Kauzenburg Castle, now serving as a restaurant with a pleasant terrace; Brückes; Krötenpfuhl; St. Martin; Mönchberg; Narrenkappe; and Hinkelstein. The main emphasis is on Riesling of high quality, though perhaps not quite reaching that of the best Norheim, Niederhausen, and Schlossböckelheim sites; in addition, smaller quantities of Silvaner, Ruländer, Scheurebe, Weissburgunder, and even a little Traminer are grown. The main local industrial works produce a great deal of cellar machinery—particularly, modern sterilizing filters, a most important invention of cellar technology, serving to remove yeast bacteria and other microorganisms from the wine already cleared by other preliminary treatment.

Winzenheim, situated north of Bad Kreuznach and now incorporated as its suburb, produces Rieslings and other wines equal in quality to those of Kreuznach itself from its sites of Berg, Honigberg, and Rosenheck. A number of communities in or near the Gräfenbach and Ellerbach valleys to the west of Kreuznach, some of them producing quite impressive, vigorous wines, should also be included in the Middle Nahe area; among them are Hargesheim, with its sites of Mollenbrunnen and Straussberg; Roxheim, with Hüttenberg, Mühlenberg, Höllenpfad, and other sites; Rüdesheim (not to be confused with the far more important Rheingau town of the same name), with Goldgrube and Wiesberg; Weinsheim, with Kellerberg and other sites; Hüffelsheim, with Gutenhölle, Mönchberg, and other sites; and Waldböckelheim, near Schlossböckelheim, with

Drachenbrunnen, Römerberg, Johannesberg, and other sites.

The soil of the Lower Nahe is based mainly on Rhenish slate, as is that of the western part of the Rheingau, and many experts recognize a similarity between its wines and those of the Rheingau. On the other hand, the predominant direction of the river is northward, which, unlike the greater part of the Rheingau, allows only a limited southerly exposure of the vineyards in its immediate vicinity, although those of the lateral valleys of the Guldenbach and Trollbach, more or less far away from the main valley, are a good deal more open to the south. The bulk of the wines grown are Silvaners, Rieslings being reserved for the most favored sites. The wines are mostly full-bodied, smooth, and with an earthy aftertaste, and may on the whole be described as table wines of fair to good quality. The main winegrowing communities on the river bank are Bretzenheim, Langenlonsheim, Laubenheim (no connection with the place of the same name in Rheinhessen), Münster-Sarmsheim, and Bingerbrück; higher up in the Guldenbach valley, Heddesheim and Windesheim; in the Trollbach valley, Dorsheim, Burg Layen, and Rümmelsheim.

12. Rheingau

THE RHEINGAU, with a total vine-planted surface of about 3,070 hectares (7,583 acres), is the seventh in size among German viticultural regions. It extends along the right bank of the Rhine from Hochheim, near its junction with the Main, to Lorchhausen, a distance of about twenty-six miles. Just north of Mainz the Rhine, coming from the south, runs against the barrier of the Taunus range, an eastern extension of the Rhenish Slate Hills complex, and is deflected for about eighteen miles in a westerly direction until it resumes its northwesterly course after passing Rüdesheim. Hochheim's vineyards form an isolated complex above the first bend of the river; they do not belong to the Rheingau either geographically or politically but only viticulturally, that is, their wines are sufficiently similar to those of the Rheingau proper to qualify for inclusion within that category. The so-called Lower Rheingau—the stretch of the river from its northwestern bend at the Bingen gorge as far as Lorchhausen—belongs to the Rheingau mainly on historical and political grounds, having been part of it for nearly a thousand years. Geographically it resembles the characteristic picture of the Middle Rhine; steep slopes with a predominantly westerly exposure and partitioned into walled vineyard terraces are found only in this area, while to the east of Rüdesheim, on the east–west course of the river, gently inclined slopes with an almost invariable southern aspect predominate. As a consequence of this geographical difference, the wines of the Lower Rheingau—at any rate, its white wines—

are in character transitional to those of the Middle Rhine region. The northern boundary of the Rheingau is formed by the heights of the Rheingaugebirge, the foothills of the western Taunus range. Of the total surface, 60 percent is densely wooded, and 12 percent, or 30 percent of the cultivated surface, is planted with vines. Vineyard slopes climb up to a maximum altitude of 1,000 feet above sea level. Generally, the Rheingau presents one of the most charming and harmonious landscapes of Germany.

There is geologic evidence that in the Tertiary period most of what are now the Rheingau vineyards were covered by a sheet of water, the northern rim of the Mainz basin. At the present time the winegrower may still find shells and ammonites when working his ground. And today every Rheingau wine carries with it as its characteristic feature the unmistakable heritage of its native earth. In the Lower Rheingau the vines grow mostly on argillaceous slate, graywacke, and quartzite, elsewhere predominantly on deep fertile loam and loess soil shot through with slate and quartz covering potter's clay, marl, and conglomerates, and at the bottom level, gravel and alluvial sand—at any rate, a mixture that varies in almost every site and determines a wide range and a great play of nuances in the taste and flavor ingredients of local wines.

In conjunction with a favorable composition of soils, the region is blessed with a lavish environment comprising all the prerequisites for the growing of great wines. The climate is warm and dry, with a mean annual temperature of 50.9°F (9.9°C) and a mean annual precipitation of between 450 and 500 millimeters (18 to 20 inches). With almonds, figs, and lemons ripening in the open, it conveys a more "southern" impression than the Fiftieth Parallel that runs through it would seem to suggest. The heavily wooded hills above the vineyards shelter them from storms and rain; the north winds, thrown upward by the Taunus heights, clear the sky above the valley but do not touch the valley itself and its vineyard slopes.

On its east-west run, the Rhine widens out to an almost

lakelike expanse, more than a third of a mile wide, partly divided into branches by a succession of long, narrow islands. The broad water surface reflects the sunlight, thereby increasing the irradiation of the vineyards, equalizes the temperature by returning the warmth of the day overnight, and increases the moisture of the air by evaporation, upcurrent winds pervading the slopes with warm humidity. The autumn mists rising from the river, known as *Traubendrücker* ("grape pressers"), favor the ripening of the grapes and the development of the *Botrytis cinerea*, the "noble mold" fungus, the precondition for the success of the precious Beerenauslese and Trockenbeerenauslese wines. In the winter the watery vapors spread over the slopes, protecting them from frost hazards.

These ideal natural conditions make the little Rheingau Germany's most valuable winegrowing region, indeed the culmination of her viticulture. They are especially suited—one might almost say tailor-made—for the growing of her most valuable grape, the Riesling. Contrary to the development in other German regions, the Riesling's share of the total Rheingau yield is increasing (1962, 70 percent; 1964, 77 percent; 1971, 79 percent; at the present time, probably 80 percent or more). The last statistics published, for the 1971 vintage, show a share of 11 percent for Müller-Thurgau, 6 percent for Silvaner—both less than in earlier statistics—and a stationary 2 percent for Spätburgunder.

Rheingau Riesling is decidedly in a class by itself. It has less of the flowery character of Moselle Riesling but a greater roundness, depth, and intensity; some connoisseurs even speak of its more "spiritual" character. Of course there are here, as everywhere else, differences in quality from one vintage to another; there is an enormous difference between grapes picked at the normal harvesting time and the late-picked ones; there may also be a considerable difference between Rieslings grown on vineyards down by the river and those from farther away and higher up the hills, from where the river can be seen only as a distant glitter. The former may be full-bodied, juicy, and smooth, but less racy and fruity, less distinguished by a harmony of fine acidity and sweetness, or, to use a somewhat overworked attribute, less elegant than those from higher up and a few miles away. Even the prestigious Marcobrunn Riesling, grown on a large site down by the bank of the Rhine, is, in the opinion of some connoisseurs, not all that it's cracked up to be.

However, considering all these limitations, Rheingau Riesling remains one of the greatest white wines of the world. Many German wine lovers consider it absolutely unrivaled among white wines. They can refer to a witness who is above suspicion of local or national prejudice, the American Frank Schoonmaker, who in his book on German wines writes, in a happily chosen phrase: "This seems to be one of those rare corners of the earth that rank as a sort of vintner's Mother Lode, where sun and soil and one special variety of grape combine with man's help to produce a miracle which cannot be performed or repeated elsewhere." It may be added that Schoonmaker has also written books and articles on the wines of other countries, is by profession an importer of European wines, and is generally a highly respected member of the international wine trade.

Roughly one-quarter of the vine-planted acreage is owned by the Hesse State Winegrowing Domains (Rheingauer Staatsweingüter) and a few great landed proprietors, mostly aristocratic. The State Domains, whose central administration and main cellarage are at Eltville, are Germany's largest viticultural management, working a total of 470 acres, of which, however, about 25 are at Bensheim in the Hessische Bergstrasse region, included as a kind of appendage. The State Domains are the owners of the beautiful former Cistercian Abbey of Eberbach, where every year internationally attended and highly prestigious wine auctions are held. The famous and very large Steinberg estate of Eberbach is exclusively owned by the State Domains as well. Its remaining holdings are dispersed over the finest sites elsewhere, for example, Hochheim's Domdechaney, Rauenthal's Baiken and Gehrn, Erbach's Marcobrunn, Hattenheim's

Mannberg, Kiedrich's Gräfenberg, Rüdesheim's Schlossberg and Berg Rottland, Assmannshausen's Höllenberg, and others. Of the large aristocratic estates, the best-known are those of Johannisberg Castle, Vollrads Castle, and Reichartshausen Castle. The State Teaching and Research Institute at Geisenheim, founded in 1872 and today the most important of its kind in Germany, holds a large estate of 124 acres. In addition to the large estates, there are many smaller holdings and a number of local growers' cooperatives—in one village, Hallgarten, there are three.

Documentary evidence of viticulture in the Rheingau is late compared to that for other parts of Germany. This is also true of the monastic foundations and their systematic expansion of the hitherto apparently rather sporadic winegrowing in the region. Of nearly a dozen monastic settlements founded under the auspices of the archbishops of Mainz, two leading ones, Johannisberg and Eberbach, have left their special stamp on Rheingau viticulture.

Johannisberg's most important contribution was made in the eighteenth century, namely, the chance discovery of the "noble mold" and generally of the beneficial possibilities of late gathering. Up to that time, the prospect of the grapes beginning to rot on the vine was greatly feared; consequently, the general practice was to begin picking on St. Michael's day (September 29) and to complete the harvest on St. Gallus's day (October 16). Every autumn, Johannisberg, because it was under the jurisdiction of the Benedictine Abbey of Fulda, which is nearly a hundred miles away as the crow flies, had to send a mounted courier carrying a sample of the grapes to obtain the superior prelate's official permission to begin the picking. However, on one occasion the courier failed to return in time. The Johannisberg monks, watching their grapes getting moldier and moldier, became more and more despondent, and by the time the courier had at last returned with the official permission, two weeks late, everybody expected a miserable vintage. Naturally they were astonished when it turned out to be the best in living memory. The story has long been relegated to the folklore category, but its essential historicity, including the fact that it refers to the year 1775, has since been confirmed by documentary evidence. Only the cause of the courier's delay cannot be verified, and explanatory tales are still being told with variable embellishments, especially of an amatory kind.

The town of Hochheim, on the lower Main (already referred to as giving its name to the English term "Hock") has a number of notable sites, of which Domdechaney, Kirchenstück, and Rauchloch may be specially mentioned. Its Königin Viktoriaberg, so named in honor of Queen Victoria's visit in 1850, is not exactly in the local top bracket. With some practice, Hochheim wines can easily be distinguished from other Rheingau wines by a peculiar "smokiness" of taste. Around the bend of the Rhine, Niederwalluf, historically the gateway to the Rheingau, has the Walkenberg as its main site. The town of Eltville is the first of the more widely known winegrowing communities. Its wines, from such sites as Sonnenberg, Langenstück, Taubenberg, and others, are pleasing enough but not superlative in quality. A few miles higher up, the village of Martinsthal is best known for its Wildsau site. Eltville's neighbor to the west, Erbach, is most widely known for its internationally famous Marcobrunn site, which extends as far as Hattenheim and has a special landmark in the Marcobrunn spring. Less well known sites, such as Steinmorgen, Michelmark, Hohenrain, and others, are situated higher up within Erbach's boundaries. Hattenheim has a number of very good sites, including Mannberg, Wisselbrunn, Heiligenberg, Engelmannsberg, Bergweg, and Boxberg; higher up within its boundaries is the Steinberg, the exclusive property of the State Domain and too exalted to display the name of Hattenheim on its wine labels.

The landmark of Oestrich is an old crane that must have loaded a good many wine barrels on board ship in its working days starting in the year 1652. The main sites of the village are Doosberg and the very popular Lenchen. The little village of

Mittelheim is distinguished by the oldest Romanesque church of the Rheingau, St. Aegidius's (St. Giles's) Basilica, which contains a painted wood sculpture of St. Urban, the patron saint of winegrowing, dating from the early fifteenth century. He does not seem to have been extremely successful with the local wines, mainly from the Edelmann, Sonnenberg, and Honigberg sites, which are of only modest quality. Immediately adjacent is the larger village of Winkel, which produces some excellent wines from its sites of Hasensprung and, higher up, Dachsberg. The town of Geisenheim is, apart from its important viticultural institute, best known for its sites of Rothenberg, Hinkelstein, Morschberg, and others, all producing good-quality wines, the first perhaps the best. Geisenheim is the oldest community in the Rheingau; its name, together with the oldest mention of the region, figures in a document issued under the rule of Charlemagne in 772: "*in Rinechgôwe in villa que dicitur Gisenheim.*"

Rüdesheim, with the now incorporated Eibingen, is the administrative center of the Rheingau, and its largest winegrowing community. It is also the main gate for the Rheingau tourist traffic; of the four million or so annual visitors, the great majority, fortunately, do not get far beyond it and its winy and noisy delights. The town's chief popular attraction is the Drosselgasse ("Thrush Lane"), said to be Germany's most expensive piece of real estate, a thoroughfare no more than seven feet wide, always crammed full of bustling crowds of honeymooners and merrymakers inside and outside the wine taverns that line it, as one might say, in an uninterrupted pair of strings. This is *emphatically not* the place where the cognoscenti drink their wine, and the more discerning wine lovers may be glad to give it a wide berth. The old Brömserburg Castle down by the river houses a wine museum offering a historical survey of all the paraphernalia connected with winegrowing, wine making, and wine consuming.

To the west of Rüdesheim and around the northwest bend of the Rhine, the more gently inclined vineyard hills give way to steep, terraced slopes, which remain the characteristic feature of the Lower Rheingau, the Rüdesheimer Berg itself being the steepest section, and the Schlossberg, above the Bingen gorge and extending to the neighborhood of Assmannshausen, being the steepest part of the whole Rüdesheimer Berg. On it, just opposite Bingen's Mäuseturm, stand the ruin of Ehrenfels Castle, in the past one of the two Rheingau strongholds of the archbishop of Mainz. The town commands a great number of vineyard sites producing excellent wines, some of them among the greatest of the region. Those situated on the face of the Rüdesheimer Berg carry the word *Berg* preceding their name; hence, Berg-Roseneck, Berg-Rottland, and Berg-Schlossberg. The sites behind the town are more gently inclined; among them are Bischofsberg, Magdalenenkreuz, Kirchenpfad, and, the highest, Klosterlay, just below St. Hildegardis's Abbey. For a fine view of the bend in the Rhine and the vineyards, one may walk up, or get oneself hoisted by chair lift, to the top of the Rüdesheimer Berg, the Niederwald, unfortunately made ugly by the outsize Germania monument, a monstrosity of the Wilhelminian era.

Around the bend, where the Rhine resumes its normal width, we come to the pretty little town of Assmannshausen. None of its white wines is of any great interest; its specialty is red wine, made exclusively from the Spätburgunder (Pinot noir) grape, grown on a total of eighty-five acres. By far the most important site is the Höllenberg with its purplish Taunus phyllite slate, the largest part of it, fifty acres, owned by the State Domains. The Höllenberg valley, well above Assmannshausen, extends in a west-to-east direction, providing steep vineyard slopes facing due south. The Höllenberg Spätburgunder is a full and vigorous dry red wine, velvety and aromatic, and with a light almond taste, in good vintages considered the equivalent of good French Burgundies and most often compared to Chambertin—at any rate, widely appreciated as the unsurpassed German red wine. In past centuries, Spätburgunder was more generally grown in the Rheingau; up to the beginning of the present century it was locally known, in variant spellings, as Klebrot. It appears under that name in Eberbach inventories as early as the late fifteenth century; its earliest mention, 1470, occurs in the records of the Hattenheim draymen's guild. Assmannshausen appears to have recognized its specific suitability for the cultivation of Klebrot only in the middle of the eighteenth century.

Between Assmannshausen and Lorchhausen, the geography of the region changes. The Rieslings grown on the steep, slaty slopes of this stretch, often facing southwest, are lighter than those grown on the east-to-west run of the river and almost sparkling; in general character they may be described as transitional between Rheingau and Middle Rhine wines. The old town of Lorch, with many medieval remains, is a most attractive place. Its parish church, St. Martin's, contains a famous carved altar, dated 1480. The top of Nollig hill, which extends northward to Lorchhausen, affords a fine view over the town, its terraced vineyards, the Rhine, which here widens out again for two or three miles, and the Lorcher Werth, a large island curiously shaped like a flattened club with a long handle.

Rauenthal, very misleadingly named (literally, "Rough Valley"), is the easternmost of the hillside villages and the farthest away from the Rhine. It sits on top of its vineyard sites, a little out of the way, reached after steep, hairpin bends by a road branching off just north of Martinsthal from the main road leading from Eltville to the Taunus spas. A short walk from the village southward takes one to the Bubenhäuser Höhe, which offers a grand view of the Rhine valley from Mainz to Bingen. This is the upper limit of the vineyard sites on the south slopes of the Rauenthaler Berg. The best sites, Baiken, Gehrn, Wülfen, Nonnenberg, Rothenberg, Langenstück, and Wieshell, are in the top bracket of Rheingau wines; even the more humble Siebenmorgen and Kilbitzberg are still of very good quality. The local parish church contains as its most valuable treasure a fourteenth-century sculpture of the Virgin and Child holding out his hand for the grape.

Kiedrich, somewhat lower than Rauenthal, is situated about two miles from the Rhine. Its main sites are Gräfenberg, Sandgrub, Wasserros, Heiligenstock, and Turmberg. The first of these has on various occasions produced unsurpassed peak wines, but the following two come close to it in quality. The Turmberg carries the keep of the ruined castle of Scharfenstein, built about 1215 and formerly one of the two Rheingau fortresses of the archbishop-electors of Mainz.

Kiedrich is often called "the Gothic wine village." Its St. Valentine's church, built in the fourteenth and fifteenth centuries, is the most impressive monument of late Gothic architecture in the Rheingau. It seems to be too large for the needs of a comparatively small village, and to have been designed originally as the place of worship of an important center for pilgrimages. Another attraction of St. Valentine's is the choir school for young boys and men, which sings, at Mass every Sunday and on all holidays, the Latin liturgical hymns linked to wine and the labors of winegrowing throughout the year. This choir, one of the best in Germany, continues a six-hundred-year tradition of Gregorian choral singing in the "Germanic" variant associated with Mainz (cantus Gregoriano Moguntinus). Kiedrich is unique in preserving this form of liturgy, common in the past to all Rheingau parishes within the former archbishopric of Mainz but gradually discontinued elsewhere since the early nineteenth century. There can be no more evocative representation of the ritual implications of viticulture and the sacred function of wine than in this liturgical music.

The former abbey of Eberbach with its famous Steinberg is situated about two miles west of Kiedrich. The refectory of the lay brothers now serves as a museum of antique wooden winepresses and vats. The cellar vaults, like those of all old wine cellars, are covered with a black mold, the fungus Cladosporium cellare, usually known as Kellertuch ("cellar cloth"), which has a useful function in regulating the humidity content of the cellar. The historic Cabinet Cellar with its Gothic vaults has been well maintained in its original form.

Not far from Eberbach's Steinberg site, the village of Hallgarten lies below the Hallgartener Zange ("Hallgarten Pincers"), a wooded hilltop 1,914 feet above sea level, with a belvedere tower providing distant views of the Rhine valley and the Taunus hills. From among its surrounding vineyard area, the sites of Jungfer ("Virgin"; probably indicating a convent as the former owner) and Hendelberg, the latter rising to a height of 1,000 feet, merit special mention as producing some of the finest Rieslings of the region. The parish church contains a beautiful fifteenth-century terra-cotta statue known as the *Madonna with the Shard*, a Virgin and Child, the Virgin holding a little wine jar (the "shard") in her right hand and a grape in her left.

Vollrads Castle, an attractive ancient manor house, home of one of the Rheingau's most important landed proprietors, is situated some distance inland from Winkel and Mittelheim. Its great wines have the privilege of being exempted from showing on their labels the name of Mittelheim, the community to which the castle actually belongs. In its most valuable vineyard, Schlossberg Marienberg, stands a stone statue of the Virgin and Child with the grape, blessing the vines.

The most impressive vineyard site of the Rheingau, that of Johannisberg Castle, occupies a large conical hillside about a mile back from the Rhine, with the castle itself standing 610 feet above sea level. The vineyards of Johannisberg village are situated behind and on both sides of the castle. The Rieslings of Johannisberg Castle are peak products of German viticulture with a worldwide reputation. In its extensive cellars its wines improve for a long time in wooden casks, as in the olden days, and mature to their optimal condition in bottle storage for several years. Their lasting power is quite extraordinary. In the eighteenth century, the monks used a recess in the vaults as a cellar museum, naming it their "Bibliotheca Subterranea"

("Vinotheca" might have been more appropriate). This carefully barred and locked holy of holies still contains two bottles of the 1748 vintage and, in addition, specimens of all good vintages from 1842 to the present day. They are expertly tested once every twenty years.

All wines sold by the castle are naturally pure, never artificially sweetened. In bad vintages, any part of the yield that is below the necessary "must" weight, that is, having an insufficient amount of natural grape sugar, has to be sold to a firm producing sparkling wine, so-called Sekt (the German equivalent of champagne), by a contract going back to the year 1865. The castle indicates the grades of its products by the differing enamel colors of its cork capsules, which have now been adapted to the requirements of the new wine law. The capsules of plain Quality Wines, or Qualitätswein (which by the terms of the new law, though not by the statutes of the castle, may be sugared), are colored yellow. Of the specially graded Quality Wines, or Qualitätswein mit Prädikat, Kabinett comes in red and orange, according to quality, Spätlese in green and white, Auslese in pink and sky-blue, while both Beerenauslese and Trockenbeerenauslese share gold.

Like Eberbach, Johannisberg Castle also claims a historic right to the title "Cabinet wine"—an even older claim—though it does not have a cellar known as the "Cabinet cellar." Its claim is based on the fact that during the eighteenth century its best wines went into a separate cellar in the palace of the prince-abbot, later prince-bishop, of Fulda. The contents of this cellar were under a strictly separate management, known as the "Secret Cabinet"; hence, these wines came to be known as "Cabinet wines," a name that was later adopted more widely as a general quality description, often in addition to Spätlese or Auslese, an inflationary proliferation that the original claimants could do nothing about. Nevertheless, both Johannisberg and Eberbach share a rueful dismay that a designation that once stood for the perfection of their wines should now, by the new wine law, have been demoted to the bottom of the specially graded list—what is more, that in the German spelling Kabinett, it should be considered a little plebeian.

The reputation of the wines of Johannisberg Castle is apt to eclipse that of the produce of the rest of the local sites. The Johannisberg vineyards cover a total of 445 acres, of which only 82 belong to the castle. The remaining acreage belongs to several proprietors of large estates and medium-sized holdings, as well as a considerable number of small growers united in a cooperative. Among the sites of Johannisberg village, Hölle, Goldatzel, Vogelsang, and others produce highly distinguished wines. The best-known local name, Erntebringer, in the past that of a site to the east of the castle, is now a so-called *Gattungsname* ("generic name") that may be applied to wines grown within a wider radius.

13. Franken (Franconia)

THE FRANCONIAN region has a total vine-planted surface of 2,750 hectares (6,693 acres). It extends alongside and near the Main River and its tributaries from about halfway between Bamberg and Schweinfurt in the east to about halfway between Aschaffenburg and Hanau in the west. Within these limits, the river deviates from its general east-west direction in a series of erratic turns and bulges. At Schweinfurt it takes a southward plunge, skirting the western slopes of the Steigerwald range. At Ochsenfurt it describes the Main Triangle by turning northwest and flowing past Würzburg, the capital of the region. At the apex of this northwesterly run, after receiving the Wern and Franconian Saale rivers—the latter its main northern tributary—it begins the Main Quadrangle around the heavily wooded Spessart hills, first turning south again, then changing to west, taking up the Tauber, its main tributary, at Wertheim, and, shortly after, the smaller Erf, then turning north at Miltenberg, now forming the divide between the Spessart and the equally densely wooded Odenwald hills, and finally flowing northwest after passing Aschaffenburg.

It is a discontinuous viticultural region, with many longer or shorter stretches bare of vineyard land. It is estimated that during the Middle Ages Franconian viticulture covered a surface of about 40,000 hectares (98,800 acres), the same size as that of Württemberg before the Thirty Years' War; that is, an acreage fourteen and a half times larger than the present one. This medieval viticultural region is said to have been contained within little more than the geographical limits of the present day, but it was continuous, with none of the present gaps. Warlike devastations, vine pests, bad harvests, exhausted soils, and so forth can be only part of the explanation of the decline because medieval viticulture covered tracts that at the present time would be considered entirely unsuitable for winegrowing. On the other hand, there are indications that the climate of the region was milder before the fifteenth century than it is today.

Official statistics for the 1971 vintage record 98 percent white and 2 percent red varieties as constituting the total yield. Among the white wines, Silvaner contributed 43 percent, having dropped from the 1964 yield of 55 percent; Müller-Thurgau also contributed 43 percent, having risen from 32 percent in 1964; and Riesling's share was 4 percent, the same as in 1964. Despite its considerable reduction, Silvaner still maintains the highest percentages in all German regions.

For the proportions of varieties not accounted for by official statistics, one has to fall back on data supplied in the late 1960s by the Bavarian State Domain. According to these figures—which are probably more in the nature of estimates—Rieslaner, a Silvaner x Riesling crossing, contributes 3 percent of the total; Perle, a frost-resistant crossing of Gewürztraminer x Müller-Thurgau, between 4 and 5 percent; Spätburgunder, 1 percent; and Portugieser 2 percent. Scheurebe, another Silvaner x Riesling crossing, is said to occupy about 25 acres; Ruländer, about 8.5 acres; Frühburgunder, about 16 acres. Traminer is said to be rare. To these estimated figures must be added the (probably minimal) percentages of four other recent crossings which, like Rieslaner and Perle, are products of the Bavarian State Viticultural Institute. These are Ortega (a Müller-Thurgau x Siegerrebe crossing; the latter a crossing of Madeleine angevine x Gewürztraminer), Mariensteiner (Silvaner x Rieslaner), Osiris (Riesling x Rieslaner), and Albalonga (Rieslaner x Silvaner).

Franconian wines, except the red ones, are traditionally bottled in glass flasks of a distinctive shape known as

Bocksbeutels. Against all attempts, mostly inspired by prudery, to explain the name differently, it must be maintained that it means, literally, "he-goat scrotum." This bottle shape is supposed to be a privilege, and Franconian wines are prepared to share it only with those of the Tauber valley and those of a few localities in the northern Ortenau. Attempts by growers of other German regions to sell their wines in flasks of this shape have been blocked by a decision of a Würzburg court and the final judgment of a superior court in Bamberg, which found that Franconia is the Bocksbeutel's fatherland and has an ancestral exclusive right to it. This, of course, does not prevent non-German producers from copying the shape of the bottle; one of many examples of pseudo-Bocksbeutels is the flask of the Portuguese Mateus Rosé.

Most of the soils of the Franconian region are rather heavy. The formation occupying the widest area is shell lime, which covers the whole of the inside of the Main Triangle, together with some areas on the left bank of the southward run of the river, the whole of the left bank on the northward run, the valley of the Franconian Saale, and the left bank of the southward run past the Main Quadrangle. The soil on the inside of the Main Quadrangle is made up of the somewhat lighter variegated sandstone of the Spessart hills.

The Franconian region is the only one in the Federal Republic—indeed in the whole EEC—that in its main west–east direction extends from the maritime climatic zone into one already increasingly affected by continental influences. To the west of the Spessart hills, a maritime climate prevails; to the east, in the larger part of the region, continental conditions are already very perceptible. Winters may be severe, with temperatures going down to -13°F (-25°C). Springs are generally short, with frosts recurring in mid-May (the so-called ice saints). Summers are long, hot, and mostly dry, but there may be early frosts in October. The mean annual temperature for the whole region is 47.8°F (8.8°C) (as compared with 49.8°F (9.9°C) in the Rheingau and 50.2°F (10.1°C) in the Kaiserstuhl). However, because the river does not traverse the region in the shortest east–west direction, but in manifold turns and loops, it manages to divide up the total regional climate, in spite of its near-continental general character, into niches with more favorable microclimates, thus securing adequate living conditions for the vines.

Particular local soils may further or hinder the growth of the vines and influence both the quantity and the quality of the yield either positively or negatively, depending on whether or not a particular variety is suited to the individual soil type. For instance, Keuper soils are favorable to Müller-Thurgau; shell-lime soils, less favorable. Silvaner generally produces better results from shell-lime than from Keuper soils; its wines from variegated sandstone tend to be of inferior quality, and poorer still from soils on primary rock.

Riesling vines seem to be on the whole more adaptable to different soils. Indeed, they are planted only in the very best places, for example, on the most favored sites of Würzburg, Randersacker, Escherndorf, and Homburg, all of these on shell-lime soils, but also on the gypsum-Keuper soil of Iphofen. To be sure, in accordance with the heavier soils on which they are grown, they share the typical dry, earthy character of other Franconian wines, although they are richer in bouquet; and it is also said that, because of the less favorable climate, and because they are a late-ripening variety, they reach full maturity only once in about five years. These disadvantages are not, however, shared by the excellent Rieslings grown on the primary rock soils of Hörstein, Wasserlos, and Michelbach in the extreme northwest of the region, in the maritime climatic zone, well protected from north and east winds by the Spessart hills and on the whole more favored climatically than most other parts of the region.

Like Riesling, the Rieslaner and Perle crossbreeds, both developed by the State Viticultural Institute, as well as Scheurebe, can be planted successfully on different kinds of soil. Rieslaner ripens earlier than Riesling and therefore produces excellent results almost every year. The Perle vine is the hardiest against frost, said to withstand winter cold of -31°F (-35°C); moreover, it has the advantage of a short period of vegetation, sprouting only when the dreaded "ice saints" are safely over.

The variegated sandstone soils of the Main Quadrangle are primarily red-wine soils. Between Kreuzwertheim and Aschaffenburg, Spätburgunder and Portugieser form the bulk of the Franconian red varieties, with Frühburgunder, velvety and aromatic, the best. White varieties, except Silvaner, are also grown in the Main Quadrangle, and probably in greater quantities than red ones; on the other hand, red varieties grown on shell-lime and Keuper soils produce disappointing results.

Franconian viticulture is almost exclusively confined to slopes, mostly rather steep ones. Valuable top soil is lost every year, washed down by rain or blown away by the wind. Worst affected by exhaustion for more than a century have been the lighter variegated sandstone soils of the red-wine-producing area in the Main Quadrangle. The building of terraces held by supporting walls has delayed erosion but has not prevented it. Moreover, in a technological era, terracing is, of course, an impediment to economic mechanical working of the soil. In the last decades, red-wine cultivation has recovered to some extent through the initiative of individual communities and the larger wine estates, especially the State Domain, which are restoring the topsoil by an intensive application of organic stable and compost manure.

If in the red-wine area of the lower course of the river geologic factors are chiefly responsible for the decline of winegrowing, east of the Spessart hills climatic factors are the main determinants. Shell lime makes heavy soils. Steep slopes with a southern aspect are subject to the hazard of desiccation, especially when the soils are exposed to sun and wind without tree shelter. As the capacity of these soils to store up humidity is very low, they need permanent water storage always supplying them with necessary humidity below ground. Such underground water storage could be provided by woods. On the other hand, woods also shelter the vines from wind and frost. But woods are scarce in the upper shell-lime area, above Würzburg and as far as Schweinfurt. In general the steep slopes change over into level ground at the top, which is mostly covered with a thin, fertile layer of loess. This level ground is being used for the cultivation of wheat, barley, and sugar beets. As for barley, it seems to be grown predominantly for the benefit of Franconia's southern neighbors, the genuine Bavarians, who are among the world's most insatiable beer swillers. (The statistical Bavarian, though including considerable minorities of wine-drinking Franconians and Swabians, drinks about a third more beer than the statistical general German and about twice as much as the statistical Briton.)

Understandably, on good agricultural land, woods have to give way to agriculture. In locations that are poor in woodland, wind shelter is usually formed by stone banks; indeed, the whole riparian stretch above Würzburg is often called the "landscape of the vineyard walls." But stone walls do not shelter the vineyards from dangerous spring frosts. This kind of protection is provided by means of fixed spraying installations or by heating, either with little heaps of briquettes or with portable stoves. In many communities heating is preferred to spraying. On cold May nights vineyards of such towns are aglow with red fires.

In contrast to the upper shell-lime area, the vineyards of the Keuper zone, on the slopes of the Steigerwald range, between Hassfurt in the north and Uffenheim in the south, are amply protected—and supplied with underground sources of humidity—by extensive oak and beech forests covering the heights.

With its various handicaps—a near-continental climate with a low mean annual temperature and frequent May frosts, a predominance of heavy soils, the exhaustion of soils in the red-wine area, the steepness of the vineyard slopes, creating the hazard of erosion, a scarcity of woodland, and altogether too great a reliance on Silvaner in the past—Franconian viticulture is up against greater odds than any other German region. Indeed, it had already entered a critical phase about the middle of the nineteenth century when chemical fertilizers were still unknown. The situation deteriorated still more with the arrival of the fungoid vine pests *Oidium* and *Peronospora*, followed by the parasite *Phylloxera*; and around the turn of the present century it seemed that wine cultivation on the Main River was virtually on the point of extinction. By the beginning of World War I its acreage had been red·iced to about a quarter of what it had been in the middle of the previous century. It is not a coincidence that of all German wine regions Franconia shows the greatest increase in industrialization; there are works of some kind or another in almost every town and village—though, thank goodness, plonk-factories are not among them.

Scientific viticultural research began in the early twentieth century. There has been no attempt to enlarge the size of the Franconian region again; instead, all attention has been focused on the quantitative and qualitative raising of yields on the climatically best favored vineyard sites. The State Viticultural Institute in Würzburg, always in the forefront of viticultural research in Germany, has been very successful in combating local disadvantages. In cooperation with the State Geological Office in Munich, the institute has mapped the entire Franconian region geologically and ascertained the vine varieties most suitable to the respective soil formations so that they may be recommended in its recurrent publications to the grower before he begins planting. Moreover, the institute has developed a series of remarkable new breeds, six white and two red crossings, of which Rieslaner and Perle are already successfully and widely grown.

There are three large estates. The first is that of the Bavarian State Domain. (The State Domain is under the same administration as the State Viticultural Institute and the Vine-Breeding Institute—all three centered in Würzburg—and the Teaching Institute, located at nearby Veitshöchheim. The nucleus of the State Domain's vineyard property consists of that of the former prince-bishops in various localities and sites of their territory, which fell to the Bavarian crown in 1814. At the present time, the state-owned vineyard land consists of a total of 445 acres distributed over fourteen estates of varying sizes, situated on all four geologically different soils of the region. The two other large estates, similarly dispersed, are those of two old charitable foundations, the Bürgerspital zum Heiligen Geist, founded as a home for aged and indigent citizens by wealthy patricians in 1319, and the Juliusspital, founded by Prince-Bishop Julius Echter von Mespelbrunn in 1576. The Bürgerspital owns a total of 865 acres, almost twice as many as the State Domain, while the Juliusspital owns about 310 acres.

The villages of Ebelsbach and Eltmann, on opposite sides of the river, are the uppermost winegrowing communities of the region. From here the wooded Steigerwald range with its Keuper soils swings in a gentle arc southwestward about as far as the village of Uffenheim, always at some distance from the river. The best-known winegrowing communities of the Keuper zone are in the southern half of the Steigerwald, namely, the attractive little town of Iphofen with its Zehntkeller ("tithe cellar"), once belonging to Würzburg's Juliusspital, today one of the most popular hostelries in Franconia; the nearby village of Rödelsee; and Castell, situated at the foot of a large castle. Iphofen's Julius Echterberg and Kammer sites are especially known for their elegant Rieslings; Rödelsee produces excellent wines from its sites of Küchenmeister and Schwanleite; and Castell, from its Schlossberg. Not far north of Castell are the villages of Greuth and Abtswind, the latter's main site being Altenberg, part of which belongs to the State Domain. Other estates of the State Domain in the Keuper zone are on Handthal's Stollberg site, in the northern part of the Steigerwald, and on Ippesheim's Herrschaftsberg site, below Frankenberg Castle, near the southern end of the hill range.

Following the course of the river, we enter the shell-lime zone near Mainberg, at the foot of its old castle, only a mile or two above the industrial town of Schweinfurt, which is, however, also well known for its trade in Franconian wines. Here the river takes its southward turn, the eastern side of the Main Triangle. There is quite a long gap in vineyard land until Wipfeld, Obereisenheim, and Untereisenheim on the right bank are reached. On the opposite side, at Fahr, begins the narrow "Main Loop," also known locally as the "Wine Loop" because it is literally ringed with vineyards both outside and inside. At its apex lies Volkach, one of oldest and most engaging towns of Franconia, with its main sites of Ratsherr and Kirchberg. At the end of the loop lies Nordheim, with its sites of Vögelein and Kreuzberg.

The stretch from Volkach to Sommerach, which lies at another, though broader, loop is now usually known as the "Wine Isle." It is actually an island, created by the building, in 1956, of the Rhine–Main–Danube Canal, which leaves the river below Volkach and rejoins it below Sommerach. The whole of the Wine Isle has nearly 620 vineyard acres, including the Sommerach sites of Katzenkopf and Rosenberg, those of Nordheim named above, and a smaller acreage belonging to Halburg Castle. Opposite Volkach lies Astheim, with its Karthäuser site, so named after a former Carthusian monastery.

From Astheim a road leads up to the top of the ridge within the Main Loop, the Vogelsburg. Its steep south slope, falling down to the village of Escherndorf, forms a magnificent amphitheater of vineyards nearly 250 acres in size, among them the famous sites of Lump, Eulengrube, and Hengstberg, which are especially known for their superior Rieslings. A few miles south of Escherndorf lies the old town of Dettelbach at the foot of a hill surmounted by a monastery and a place of pilgrimage, Sancta Maria in Vineis, embedded in a luxuriant wreath of vineyards.

Kitzingen is another old town, founded, according to local tradition, by Adeloga, sister of the Frankish king Pepin, Charlemagne's father, and still revered in Franconia as St. Adelheid. She is believed to have taken the veil and to have founded a convent in the neighborhood of the town. The same story also connects her with the planting of the first vines in the region. While this seems to be no more than a legend, a local Benedictine convent supported by considerable vineyard property actually existed throughout the Middle Ages. Kitzingen is no longer a winegrowing community; instead, it has become a manufacturing center for vineyard and cellar work, supplying growers and cellarmen with all their needs, from tractors and other machinery, through fertilizers and means of pest control, down to Bocksbeutel flasks, corks, and caps.

The walled and turreted town of Sulzfeld, a few miles farther downstream, is one of the most pleasant winegrowing communities on the banks of the Main. On the opposite side of the river, the two Old World towns of Marktbreit and Ochsenfurt mark the southernmost extent of its course. In between, but again on the inside of the triangle, the charming old village of Frickenhausen grows remarkably good wines on its southerly vineyard slopes, especially on its Kapellenberg site.

On the northwest run of the river, the winegrowing communities of Sommerhausen and Eibelstadt are followed by the large village of Randersacker, situated in a circular valley, which grows some of the peak wines of the region, especially from its famous Pfülben, Hohbug, and Spielberg sites, which also produce some excellent Rieslings. In the past, Randersacker was the favorite village of the prince-bishops of Würzburg; their vineyards were inherited by the Bavarian crown and now form the Randersacker estate of the State Domain.

From here it is only about three miles to Würzburg, one of Germany's handsomest towns, the center and great climax of the region, enjoying the blessed harmony of beautiful scenery, impressive buildings, and great wines. The city, one of Germany's most outstanding centers of late Baroque architecture, was almost completely wiped out by the RAF on the night of March 16, 1945, more than a month after Dresden, when twenty minutes of horror sufficed to lay waste what thirteen centuries had built up. However, Würzburg has been rebuilt from the rubble to its old spendor as faithfully as was humanly possible.

A visit to the Mainfränkisches Museum, established in the

Feste Marienberg since 1946, is a rewarding experience. Its most important collections include some of the works of Franconia's greatest artist, Tilman Riemenschneider (1455–1531), a sculptor in wood and stone, who spent most of his working life, and died, in Würzburg. A separate hall of the museum contains the Franconian wine museum, with a collection of huge oaken winepresses of the Baroque period, many old, picturesquely carved cask bottoms and bolts, goblets, tankards, and jugs once used by prelates, noblemen, and master craftsmen, skillfully forged inn signs, banners of Würzburg guilds and societies connected with the wine trade, coats of arms of leading Franconian winegrowers' families, and so forth.

Würzburg has a great number of vineyard sites. The best known, and also the most outstanding in quality, are the sites of Stein and Leiste. The former, situated to the north of the city, a long limestone ridge with sun-drenched slopes facing south, is an unbroken, 272-acre complex of vineyards, the largest continuous vineyard site in Germany. It is subdivided into individually named sections, such as Stein-Harfe and Stein-Schalksberg. The height of the ridge provides the most comprehensive view of the city, including the Feste Marienberg. The name Steinwein, properly applicable only to the wines of this complex, is often wrongly extended to the wines of the whole region, making Steinwein synonymous with Frankenwein. Apart from a few privately owned vineyards, the three great Würzburg-based estates of the State Domain, the Bürgerspital, and the Juliusspital are the main sharers of this property. Stein wines, which include a considerable proportion of Riesling, are among the best of Franconia.

The eastern side of the Marienberg, sloping down to St. Burkhard's and facing the river and the city, is the Schlossberg site. The southern slope is the Leiste, subdivided into the Innere Leiste, its western continuation the Äussere Leiste, and the Felsenleiste at the bottom of the valley. The Innere Leiste is owned exclusively by the State Domain, while the Äussere Leiste is shared by the State Domain, the Juliusspital, and the

Bürgerspital. The predominant varieties of the Innere Leiste are Riesling and Rieslaner, whose wines reach a very high quality in good years. Leiste wines are generally milder, more delicate, and more fragrant than those of the Stein.

From the Käppele, a pilgrimage church on an equally steep hill a short distance upstream, one has a view of the city and the Stein beyond it, as well as the Feste Marienberg on its steep, long slope with the Leiste vineyards. The Käppele, with its graceful, onion-domed spires, a work of Balthasar Neumann, is being looked after by a local Capuchin monastery.

Back in the city again, the administrative headquarters and drinking rooms of the State Domain are in a separate wing of the Residenz, the former palace of the diplomatic envoys to the prince-bishops. Its wine cellars, the Hofkellerei, architecturally the most beautiful anywhere, extend below the whole of the Residenz and under part of the large square in front. Here its wines are processed and mature only in wooden casks; the Hofkellerei is conservative and has only limited respect for the latest technical equipment. The bottle cellar contains about 400,000 bottles. The Bürgerspital and Juliusspital each have enormous drinking halls partitioned off in niches, and in addition to these establishments there are any number of jolly small wine taverns in Würzburg.

Veitshöchheim, about three miles below Würzburg, was chosen as a summer residence by one of the last prince-bishops; it still has a "Cavaliers' Building" surrounded by a splendid park embellished with gardens and lakes. Here the State Viticultural Institute maintains its teaching department, connected with the small vineyard site of Wölflein behind it. Thüngersheim, two or three miles farther down the river, is one of the larger winegrowing communities. Its wines, mostly grown on steep, stony slopes, are vigorous and of great character. The second-largest estate of the State Domain, consisting of the sites of Scharlach, Neuberg, and Ravensberg, is located here. A mile or two farther north, a tiny tributary, the Retz, joining the Main at Retzbach, forms a short but charmingly green east–west valley producing wines of distinctive character and flavor. The principal winegrowing communities on the opposite side of the Main are Erlabrunn, Himmelstadt, and Laudenbach. On the right bank of the river are Stetten, with a good growers' cooperative, and the attractive old town of Karlstadt, with its medieval town wall.

Beyond Gambach, the valley of the Main becomes narrower, leaving little room for vineyards. Instead, two tributaries take over as providers of wine, the little Wern River, which meanders through the widest northern part, the hypotenuse, of the Main Triangle, and, more important, the Franconian Saale, the main northern tributary, which joins the Main at Gemünden. The chief winegrowing center on this river is the small town of Hammelburg, lying below the old castle of Saaleck, whose south slope, the Schlossberg, is its most valuable site. The vineyards of this town are among the oldest known in the history of Franconian viticulture—Charlemagne made over his royal estate of Hammelburg to the Benedictine Abbey of Fulda in the year 777. The State Domain has another of its estates, with the sites of Trautlestal and Übersaal, at Hammelburg, where it has replaced the traditional Silvaner, which is too sensitive to frost, with the hardier Müller-Thurgau and Perle varieties. Higher up the Franconian Saale, a string of winegrowing villages stretches as far as the neighborhood of the spa town of Kissingen.

Below the southward bend of the Main, where it begins the Main Quadrangle around the wooded Spessart hills, there is a long gap in the distribution of vineyards. They reappear only at Erlenbach, a mile or so off the left bank. Now the river describes a number of loops before turning westward. At the apex of the first of these lies Homburg, which produces some of the greatest wines of Franconia, including Riesling, from its large site of Kallmuth.

For a stretch below Homburg, as far as Freudenberg, the Main forms the boundary between Bavaria and Baden. Halfway along this stretch, the picturesque old town of Wertheim lies at the junction with the Main Tauber, its main southern tributary. The name Badisches Frankenland (Baden-Franconia), the land of the lower Tauber, is more than a geographical designation. Although its wines are classified as Baden, and not Franconian wines, they are similar to those of the Main, as is the general character of the countryside and its communities, which are united by a common history.

Opposite Wertheim, on the Bavarian side, lies Kreuzwertheim. Here, on the steep, variegated sandstone slopes of the Spessart hills, the cultivation of red-wine grapes begins. The State Domain has a small estate on the Kreuzwertheim site of Kaffelstein and on the Stockmeister site of the neighboring village of Hasloch, which produces mainly Spätburgunder. Below Hasloch, Dorfprozelten produces both white and red wines. Here again the State Domain is represented by one of its estates, forty-seven acres in size, on the Höhberg site. Farther down and on the opposite side of the river, Bürgstadt is well known for its red wines, especially its velvety, fragrant Frühburgunder, which grows on the lighter sandy soil of the valley of the Erf, a small southern tributary, as far up as the village of Eichenbühl.

At the beautiful medieval town of Miltenberg, practically next door to Bürgstadt, the Main turns north again. On its right bank, Grossheubach cultivates predominantly red wines, particularly Spätburgunder on its Bischofsberg site, part of which is an estate of the State Domain. The best-known and largest redwine community, producing an excellent Spätburgunder, is the picturesque little town of Klingenberg, mentioned as a winegrowing place in the records of the Abbey of Fulda as early as 776. Its main sites are the steep Schlossberg, which climbs to the ruin of the Klingenberg, and, higher up still, the Hochberg. Klingenberg's red-wine cultivation is continued at Erlenbach, farther down, and at Gosswallstadt, on the left bank of the river.

Below the larger town of Aschaffenburg, the Main turns northwest, the valley widens out, and the variegated sandstone of the Spessart hills gives way to primitive rock, which provides an ideal soil for Riesling on this last stretch of Franconian viticulture. The most important community is Hörstein, with its Abtsberg and Reuschberg sites. The former, as its name ("Abbot's Hill") indicates, was originally monastic property, owned by the Benedictine Abbey of Seligenstadt on the other side of the Main. The Abbey was founded in 815, a year after Charlemagne's death, by Einhard, a member of the circle of scholars at the emperor's court, his secretary, and author of his biography, the *Vita Caroli Magni*. After secularization, the vineyard site of the abbey was inherited by the Bavarian crown, and now forms an estate of the State Domain, thirty-five acres in size. There are two more Riesling-growing villages in the neighborhood, Wasserlos and Michelbach; the latter, situated in the extreme northwest corner of Bavaria, is the last of the Franconian winegrowing communities. All the wines of the State Domain grown on its estates at the foot of the Spessart hills from Kreuzwertheim to Hörstein mature in oaken casks in the cellars of the state-owned Johannisburg Palace of Aschaffenburg.

Lists enumerating Franconian winegrowing localities and sites sometimes append a very small area that is not Franconian at all, but, like Franconia, is included in the state of Bavaria. It is situated in the easternmost German sector of Lake Constance, which is Bavarian. The main winegrowing village, only a mile or two from the Württemberg village of Kressbronn, is Nonnenhorn. Its Seehalde and Sonnenbüchel sites produce much the same kinds of mainly red wines as those of Württemberg and Baden on the shore of Lake Constance.

For those who did not, like the natives, grow up imbibing Franconian wines, their full enjoyment may require some apprenticeship. Franconian Silvaner is the driest of all German white wines, often even somewhat hard, quite unlike the pleasing, slightly sweet wines from other regions. Because of its dryness it is often likened to the Chablis of Burgundy. It also has a markedly earthy taste, which it shares with the dry Italian

Frascati. It is full-bodied, pithy, and vigorous, with a slightly higher alcohol content than most other German wines, and with an agreeable lingering aftertaste. Most wine lovers would probably claim that Silvaner is not the top-ranking German variety. The Franconian locals would probably answer that they prefer a solid, dry, earthy Silvaner to the airy-fairy fragrance of a Riesling—and good luck to them.

At any rate, Franconian wine generally has the reputation of being the most natural among German wines. The hardness often mentioned is simply the result of their growers' worthy resistance to the temptation of tampering with their product, either by prematurely stopping fermentation or by sugaring. Even small table wines can usually be relied upon to be *naturrein* ("naturally pure") and *durchgegoren* ("fermented right through"). The big estates set a good example to the smaller growers and cooperatives by keeping Franconian wine the way it is. For example, in the cellars of the State Domain, peculiarities depending on variety, soil, or climate are never modified or equalized by cellar techniques.

Local wine parochialism exists in all winegrowing regions. For instance, to order a bottle of, say, Moselle in a Rheingau restaurant would be regarded as something very near blasphemy, or at least an obscenity. But Franconia seems to have received a double dose of wine jingoism. Nowhere do people seem to be more touchy about their wines, or to protest so much. Indeed, local wine propaganda showering paeans of praise, in speech and print, upon the "honest" home product sometimes gets a little tiresome. After all, it seems to be so very unnecessary. Franconian wine is good wine—and from the best sites very good wine—if not the *ne plus ultra* among German wines, as the locals apparently want to make it. It cannot be, in view of its natural handicaps of soil and climate.

14. Mittelrhein

THE TOTAL vine-planted surface of the Middle Rhine region, according to official statistics referring to the year 1971, measures 864 hectares (2,134 acres), while according to statistics for 1968 it included 976 hectares (2,429 acres); thus, a considerable reduction has been taking place. The region extends along the Rhine from Bingerbrück, at the Rhine's junction with the Nahe River, to Oberdollendorf, north of the Siebengebirge, the Seven Hills group, for a length of eighty-four miles. It is the stretch of the Rhine valley where the river, in a series of bends, forces its way through the Rhenish Slate Hills complex. With its northern limit at about latitude 50° 40', it is the northernmost winegrowing region of the Federal Republic. It may be divided into a southern and a northern section, about equal in length, with the junction of the Moselle at Koblenz in the middle.

There are, however, two qualifications to be made concerning the total extent of the region. The southern section begins at Bingerbrück only on the left bank; on the right it begins between Lorchhausen and Kaub, about nine or ten miles farther down. As has already been pointed out (see page 207), the reason for this inequality and apparent oddity is historical rather than geographical and viticultural.

The principal vine varieties grown in this region, according to the statistics for the 1971 vintage, are 84 percent Riesling (a drop of four percentage points since 1964), 9 percent Müller-Thurgau (an increase of three points), and 4 percent Silvaner (the same as in 1964). The rest, not accounted for statistically, would seem to be made up largely of the two red-wine varieties Spätburgunder and Portugieser, which represent a specialty in several places. However, in general, the growing of red-wine grapes is decreasing. Efforts of growers to plant other varieties, especially those with lower acidity and good bouquet, have not been entirely unsuccessful in spite of setbacks with some of them. But, considering the nature of the soil, it is difficult to replace Riesling with other varieties.

By and large, Middle Rhine Rieslings are not in the same class as those of the Rheingau. They are fresh, vigorous, pithy table wines of medium quality; some are better than that, but none is of exactly overwhelming quality. Even from the best sites and the best vintages, there is nothing that can be compared with a really good Rheingau wine. They are grown mostly for local consumption; what is left over is often not enough to quench the thirst of the tourist hordes. To come upon a wine bottle with a Middle Rhine label anywhere outside Germany would be a most unlikely happening; even within Germany, outside the region itself, it would be surprising enough.

The somewhat "underprivileged" character of Middle Rhine wines is often attributed to the fact that the river here follows a predominantly northerly course, in contrast to its direction through the Rheingau, and therefore the Middle Rhine comprises, in general, climatically less favorable east- and west-facing sites. This is only partly true. There are several loops and bends bearing slopes with a perfect southerly exposure. Moreover, a good many Middle Rhine wines are grown on sheltered south slopes of narrow side valleys at some distance from the Rhine. On the whole, climatic conditions are favorable. Early springs and long, sunny autumns are characteristic of the region; frost damage in spring and autumn is relatively rare; the large water surface of the river provides a beneficial storage of warmth and protection against frosts.

The main natural handicap of the Middle Rhine is the

poverty of its soils. They are predominantly clay, slate, and graywacke, only occasionally with loess deposits, and with gradients of up to sixty degrees. Partly because of this steepness they are mostly deficient in good topsoil, and because of this limited capacity for storing water they tend to suffer from aridity. Thus, here, in contrast to other regions, it is not the dry, hot summers that bring the good wines, but rather the vintages with warm but slightly rainy summers. Even moderately warm but rather wet summers will produce wines of acceptable medium quality on these quickly warming, permeable soils. Only at the northern end of the region, in the Siebengebirge, do we find soils based on volcanic rock, which seem to be a little better.

Because of the predominant steepness of the slopes, the vines are generally trained on high, individual stakes—as on the Moselle and its tributaries—not on frames connected by wires. *Flurbereinigung* or *Umlegung,* as the regrouping and reconsolidation of scattered holdings is called, would be of decisive significance for the preservation of viticulture in the Middle Rhine, but obviously this cannot be thoroughly undertaken because of the region's very difficult terrain, with vineyards often terraced high up on breakneck slopes.

The spectacular beauty of this part of the Rhine valley, and especially of its upper half, is well known. It is the "romantic Rhine," much celebrated in poetry and song, bordered by attractive old towns and surmounted on steep heights by medieval castles, most of them picturesque ruins. The southernmost of these, opposite the Rheingau town of Assmannshausen, is handsome Rheinstein Castle, which has been restored and is now being used as a museum. A short distance farther down, Trechtingshausen is the southernmost winegrowing village of the region. It is followed by Niederheimbach, from which a side valley leads to Oberheimbach, and by Rheindiebach, which gives access to a longer side valley with good south-facing vineyard slopes at Oberdiebach and Manubach. After another mile or two we reach the old town of Bacharach, below the ruin of Stahleck Castle, with Posten and Wolfshöhle as its best-known vineyard sites. (Bacharach, in the mutilated form of "Backrag," once gave its name to all German wines imported into England, before the similarly mutilated "Hock" came into fashion. Three hundred years ago the town was, indeed, widely famed for its wines, although it is questionable whether the wines going under its name were of local growth or even from anywhere nearby. It seems more likely that the town was merely—or mainly—the distribution center for wines coming from higher up the river. Nevertheless, the wines from the Middle Rhine were highly appreciated, certainly until the end of the seventeenth century, when they were surpassed, in the general opinion, by better ones.) From Bacharach a narrow valley leads to the village of Steeg, about a mile to the west, which grows good Rieslings on its south slopes, St. Jost being perhaps the best of its sites.

From here on, both banks of the river belong to the Middle Rhine region. The old town of Kaub, first mentioned in 983 as *Cuba villula* ("little country house"), lies on the eastern side, surmounted by its castle ruin of Gutenfels. But it has a more picturesque medieval edifice built in front of it on a rocky island in the middle of the Rhine—indeed, one of the most famous monuments of the whole Rhine valley—the Pfalz. The name is a popular short form for Pfalzgrafenstein; built in the fourteenth century, at a time when the unity of the empire was crumbling away and every separate ruler protected his territory with military might and customs barriers, it is an outer fort, customs, and pilot station of the Palatine Electorate, a counterpart of the so-called Mäuseturm, the toll tower of the archbishop-elector of Mainz at Bingen. Pfalzgrafenstein is also the name of one of Kaub's wines, although Backofen is the better-known site.

The next stop downstream, but again on the left bank, is Oberwesel, the Roman Vosolvia, overshadowed by the Schönburg, one of the most picturesque of the Rhine castle ruins, in which a small hotel has been created. The town's Liebfrauenkirche contains a beautiful sculpture of the Virgin and Child with the grape. In the Middle Ages Oberwesel was part of the territory of the archbishop-elector of Trier, who appears to have raised his own profitable share of river tolls here. The best-known local sites are the Ölsberg and the Engehöll, the latter situated in a side valley with good south-facing slopes.

A bend in the river leads, on the right bank, to the almost vertical, 440-foot-high Lorelei rock, according to legend, haunted by a siren who by her beauty and singing lures mariners to their death on the perilous reefs below. Here the Rhine, normally about 550 yards across, narrows down to a width of only 132 yards.

No more than a mile below the Lorelei, the sister towns of St. Goar and St. Goarshausen face each other on opposite banks. St. Goar, on the left, received its name from a sixth-century Aquitanian missionary around whose hermitage the little town grew up. Rheinfels Castle above the town has the distinction of surviving all the wars of the Middle Ages unscathed and then being turned into a ruin by the French, who blew it up in 1797. St. Goar's wines come mainly from the south slopes of a side valley leading to the neighboring community of Werlau. St. Goarshausen lies below the ruins of two castles, Katz and Maus ("Cat" and "Mouse"), the south slopes of each, as well as part of the Lorelei's flanks, being the principal local sites. On the heights above St. Goarshausen lies the community of Patersberg, noted for the red wine from its Teufelstein site.

Boppard, the ancient Celtic Baudobriga, lies at the beginning of a narrow loop of the Rhine; its main site, the large Hamm, a short distance down the river, is three miles long and faces perfectly southward. Like Oberwesel, in the Middle Ages Boppard was part of the territories of the archbishop-elector of Trier, who probably raised another toll from passing vessels here.

Below the great loop of the river, on the left side, lies the old walled town of Rhens, earlier known as Rhense, a name probably derived from Rhenus, the Latin name of the Rhine. Starting in the thirteenth century, the little town was the meeting place of the German electors who gathered here to nominate the Holy Roman Emperor. Just outside its walls, Emperor Charles IV (1355–87) erected the Königsstuhl ("king's chair"), an octagonal monument which the German kings ascended after their election. On the opposite bank lies the town of Braubach; towering nearly five hundred feet above it is the Marksburg, the only one of the many medieval Rhine castles to escape destruction. The town's best-known vineyard site is the Mühlberg. A few miles farther down, the Lahn River joins the Rhine between the sister towns of Oberlahnstein and Niederlahnstein. Viticulture on this tributary is included within that of the Middle Rhine region, but has only limited significance. There are sporadic vineyards at the village of Fassbach, the neighboring spa town of Ems, the town of Nassau, and two or three villages in between and beyond.

After receiving the Moselle at Koblenz, the Rhine leaves its narrow valley to enter the more level and open northern section of the region, where the vineyard slopes are on the whole a little less steep. Leutesdorf, Hammerstein, Rheinbrohl, and Unkel, the last-named producing red wines from its Sonnenberg site, are the best-known winegrowing communities of this stretch, before the Rhine reaches the Siebengebirge. Here Rhöndorf's Domlay vineyard overlooks the graveyard in which Konrad Adenauer, the first chancellor of the Federal Republic, is buried. Königswinter produces the red Drachenblut ("Dragon's Blood") from the Drachenlay site on the flanks of the steep Drachenfels rock, apparently for the benefit of a multitude of tourists. The vineyards of Niederdollendorf and Oberdollendorf, in a valley north of Königswinter, mark the northern end of the Middle Rhine region.

It is hardly surprising that nowadays tourists descend on the "romantic Rhine" in droves, especially in the summer holiday season. Alas, the halcyon days when Lord Byron, traveling by stagecoach, had it all to himself, are over. It is also obvious that the riverside roads, the B9 on the left and the B42 on the right bank, are bound to carry very heavy motor traffic. However, at least in the upper part of the valley, one can escape the worst of the traffic by taking to the hill roads running parallel to the main roads. The one on the left side is the Rheingoldstrasse, beginning at Rheindiebach in the south and running, via Bacharach, Oberwesel, St. Goar, and Boppard, as far as Rhens. The road on the right, the Loreley-Burgenstrasse, is shorter, only about twelve and a half miles long; it begins at Kaub and runs, via the top of the Lorelei, through Patersberg, St. Goarshausen, and past the Liebenstein and Sterrenberg ruins, to Kemp-Bornhofen. Both hill routes lead to places revealing magnificent views of the Rhine valley. They have the additional advantage of taking the traveler to places he does not see from the bottom of the valley, namely, the winegrowing communities situated high above their vineyards.

꧁꧂

15. Ahr

THE LITTLE Ahr River rises in the Eifel hills and joins the Rhine between the towns of Sinzig and Remagen, both ancient Gallo-Roman settlements, Sentiacum and Rigomagus ("King's Field"), respectively. The Ahr viticultural region extends from west to east along the lower course of the river for about fifteen and a half miles between Altenahr and Heimersheim. In the past it stretched farther in both directions, above Altenahr to Kreuzberg, and in the Middle Ages even as high up as the village of Dümpelfeld and, in a side valley, to the village of Kesseling, while to the east it included Bodendorf, Sinzig, and Remagen as late as the first half of the twentieth century. The valley vies with that of the Middle Rhine in claiming to be the northernmost winegrowing region of the Federal Republic. Both claims are justified up to a point: the Ahr region lies north of latitude 50° 30′ in its entirety, while the Middle Rhine stretches from latitude 50° 40′, extending beyond the mouth of the Ahr for a distance of only ten or twelve miles.

According to official statistics covering the 1971 vintage, the total cultivated surface of the region amounted to 495 hectares (about 1,223 acres); according to statistics for 1968, it covered 531 hectares (about 1,312 acres). The main varieties planted were Portugieser, contributing 30 percent (as against 33 percent in 1964); Spätburgunder, 24 percent (as against 23 percent in 1964); Riesling, 23 percent (the same as in 1964); and Müller-Thurgau, 17 percent (as against 16 percent in 1964). Because of the high percentage of red-wine production, the Ahr is popularly styled "the German red-wine paradise." Indeed, in spite of its small size, the region is the largest *continuous* red-wine-producing tract; everywhere else, red-wine production is more sporadic. Nevertheless—and paradoxically—the Ahr contributes only between 2 and 3 percent of the total of the Federal Republic's red-wine production, which in itself is small enough, amounting to only 15 percent of the total of all German wines.

Red-wine cultivation on the Ahr dates back only to the end of the seventeenth century, when for the first time red varieties, especially the Pinot noir of Burgundy, were planted. Within a century the red-wine varieties had almost completely ousted the earlier white wines. However, it would seem that initially the blue grapes were used mainly to produce the pinkish Weiss-herbst (Rosé), in order to obtain a wine poorer in tannin; that is, a somewhat sweeter one.

The Ahr region owes the fact that Spätburgunder thrives in it despite its northerly latitude—and that in good vintages it may even attain very good quality—to its warmth-storing soils—loess at the valley bottom, weathered slate and volcanic rock on the slopes—and especially to the concerted action of river and rock in the almost gorgelike narrowness of its upper section. The river traverses this stretch in many bends and twists between Altenahr and Walporzheim, where a fantastic jumble of Cyclopean rock, known by the homely name of "die bunte Kuh" ("The Spotted Cow") forms its boundary. This section is characterized by microclimatic shelters screened off by natural windbreaks, wherein the sun heats rocks and air so effectively that, as the local saying has it, "the grapes are being boiled in August and broiled in September."

Between Ahrweiler and its junction with the Rhine, the river assumes a fairly straight course, and the valley bottom opens to a width of about a third of a mile. The slate layers are softer than those of the upper section; both the sand and gravel layers of the valley bottom and the higher terraces are covered with deposits of fertile loess. Wines grown on a base of volcanic rock, as on the basalt cone of the Landskrone at Heimersheim, the eastern end of the region, have a characteristic taste all their own.

The region is as much favored climatically as it is geologically. Sheltered on both sides by the Eifel plateau, it has an overall average annual precipitation of 560 millimeters (22 inches).

Until the middle of the present century, about two-thirds of the vine-planted surface was still planted with red-wine grapes, mostly Spätburgunder. Since then the ratio has markedly changed in favor of Portugieser, and especially of the white varieties, Riesling and Müller-Thurgau. This change has partly viticultural and partly marketing reasons: an increasing exhaustion of the soil with regard to Burgundy vines; a higher yield potential of other varieties by means of modern soil treatment and vine cultivation; a general preference of consumers for sweeter wines; and, lastly, increased competition in the Common Market. The best Spätburgunder is ruby-red in color, has a fine bouquet, a piquant spiciness, and a dry, yet very pleasing, fire. The Portugieser vine makes much fewer demands on soil and climate; its wines are lighter in color, sweeter, and fresher in acidity. The white wines of the Ahr are also relatively light and naturally sparkling.

In spite of the natural advantages of the valley, there can be few places where the grower's labor is as arduous as in the Ahr region, especially in its upper part. Because of the steepness of the slopes, vines generally have to be trained on separate, unconnected stakes. They have to be most carefully nursed, even if there are only five or six of them on the smallest *Stuhl* ("chair" or "stool"), as the tiny terraced plots high up in some rocky nook are locally called. To reach such a diminutive vineyard patch, entirely out of reach of any kind of viticultural machinery, the grower may have to climb eight hundred feet or more above the valley, carrying his tools in his hands and a basket containing stable manure on his back, or he might have to carry black, broken-up slate to provide a heat-absorbing top layer for the soil.

From west to east, the main winegrowing communities and best-known sites are the town of Altenahr with its Eck site below the ruin of Are Castle; Mayschoss, with Mönchberg and Scheiferley; Rech, with Hardtberg and Herrenberg; Dernau, with another Hardtberg and another Schieferley; and Marienthal, whose sites include Klostergarten and Trotzenberg. Marienthal is the locale of a former convent, which owned large vineyard property; the property now belongs to the State Domain, which is closely allied with the State Viticultural Research and Teaching Institute at Ahrweiler. Walporzheim's best-known sites are Domlay and Kräuterberg. The town of Ahrweiler, with its main sites of Daubhaus, Rosenthal, and Ursulinengarten, is the largest producer of the region. The small village of Bachem, with Karlskopf and Steinkaul, produces, in addition to the more common red varieties, a quantity of very good Frühburgunder, an early-ripening and lighter-colored natural mutant of Spätburgunder. The spa town of Bad Neuenahr is better known for its Apollinaris mineral spring than for its viticulture, which, indeed, contributes the smallest share of the total harvest in the region; its main sites are Schieferley and Sonnenberg. Heppingen, with Berg, and Heimersheim, with Kapellenberg and Landskrone, are at the end of the string of winegrowing communities along the Ahr.

The great majority of growers in the region own as an average only about one and a quarter acres of vineyard land each, and that, more often than not, is fragmented in scattered plots. It is obvious that the smallholder cannot afford a cellar of his own with a modern winepress and other complicated and costly equipment, and that he has to join a cooperative. The first Ahr cooperative was founded in 1868 by the growers of Mayschoss, following the earliest Württemberg cooperatives of Asperg (1854) and Neckarsulm (1855). Today about 90 percent of the Ahr's growers are organized in fifteen cooperatives, which work with up-to-date machinery and steel fermentation tanks, and develop about 80 percent of the total harvest. Together with Baden and Württemberg, the Ahr region has the highest density of cooperatives per square mile.

Although at the present time it contributes less than a quarter of the Ahr's total production, Spätburgunder is the basis of the region's reputation. A great deal of praise is showered on it; admittedly, in great vintages it certainly has very good quality and may be both fiery and velvety. But the assertion, frequently heard, that it can bear comparison with the Pinot noir of Burgundy, or even the recurring story that wily French connoisseurs often cannot tell Ahr Spätburgunder from their own Burgundies, really seems to be going just a little too far. Probably a great number of German red-wine lovers would consider the Ahr Spätburgunder a smaller wine than that of Assmannshausen or that from some especially favored place in Baden.

The visitor who wishes to use his own judgment in the rating of German Spätburgunder wines may be well advised to give the Ahr a wide berth in the holiday season, and especially on weekends, when noisy hordes of motorized humanity from the cities of the lower Rhine and the Ruhr descend upon the area. But he may also spare a kindly thought for the plight of the local smallholders who have to struggle hard for their existence and who are likely to have different views of these bibulous invasions into the "German red-wine paradise," no matter how cacophonous.

16. Hessische Bergstrasse

THE BERGSTRASSE is the stretch of country between the western slopes of the Odenwald hills and the wide Rhine plain. In a narrower sense, the name is also used to denote the thirty-three-mile-long road that runs from Darmstadt to Heidelberg through the Odenwald foothills. It is an extremely fertile belt of country, popularly known as "Germany's spring road," blessed with the mildest climate found anywhere in Germany, a mean annual temperature of 50°F (10°C), with figs and almonds ripening under the open sky. Springtime, with its splendor of blossoming peach and almond trees, comes to the Bergstrasse even earlier than to Rheinhessen and the Palatinate on the opposite bank of the Rhine, often as early as the end of February. It is sheltered from north and east winds by the broad slopes of the densely wooded Odenwald. On the other hand, the hills are also repsonsible for a higher average annual rainfall than that of the regions on the other side of the plain. Bensheim, the main center of the Bergstrasse, has an average of 710 millimeters (28 inches) per year, as against the 520 millimeters (20.8 inches) of Mainz and Oppenheim. Nevertheless, the climate of the Bergstrasse is, on the whole, favorable for the cultivation of the vine. Picturesque old towns and villages situated along the main road and nestling in side valleys contribute to the charm of the countryside.

The Bergstrasse, though a geographical unit, has by the vagaries of history been divided into a northern half, belonging to Hesse, and a southern one, belonging to Baden; the former situated opposite Rheinhessen, the latter opposite the Palatinate. A separate appendage of the Bergstrasse is the "Odenwald

Wine Island," situated some distance east of Darmstadt and with Gross-Umstadt as its center.

The viticultural region, extending in its main range from Zwingenberg in the north to just beyond Heppenheim in the south, is by far the smallest of all the eleven German regions, covering, according to official 1971 statistics, a total vine-planted surface of only 291 hectares (about 719 acres). According to the same statistics, Riesling contributes 52 percent of the vines planted (as against 46 percent in 1964); Müller-Thurgau, 20 percent (as against 21 percent in 1964); and Silvaner, 20 percent (as against 29 percent in 1964). The total contribution of red-wine varieties—Spätburgunder and Portugieser—is 1 percent. The remaining 7 percent appears to be shared mainly by Ruländer, Traminer, and Gutedel.

Because of the small extent of the Bergstrasse's viticultural region, its soils are less diverse than those of Rheinhessen, on the other side of the plain. The bases of the hills are covered with loess and blown sand, which in places extend high up the slopes. The higher slopes comprise granite and diorite rocks. Consequently, the vineyards on the lower sites are planted mainly on loess and blown sand, while those on the higher sites are rooted in weathered granite and diorite rock. It is chiefly on these nutritive soils that the wines of Zwingenberg, Auerbach, Bensheim, and Schönberg, the latter in a side valley, are grown. Farther south, the sites of Heppenheim, extending in three lateral valleys to Hambach, the ruin of Starkenburg Castle, and Erbach, are based on variegated sandstone, which, owing to its high shale content, provides a favorable soil for the cultivation of the vine.

Viticulture at Jugenheim, in the past the most northerly winegrowing community, mentioned in the medieval *Codex Laureshamensis*, appears to have come to an end before or during World War II. At the present time the little town of Zwingenberg is the northernmost winegrowing locality of the Bergstrasse. Most of its vineyards are situated on the steep slopes of the Melibokus, one of the highest elevations of the Odenwald hills; they are difficult to work and yield wines of only modest quality. Auerbach, below its castle, one of the largest and most picturesque medieval ruins, has now been incorporated as part of Bensheim. Its main site, Rott, produces one of the best wines of the region.

Bensheim is the largest town of the region. Its most important sites are Kalkgasse, Paulus, and Hemsberg. In a side valley opening from Bensheim, the village of Schönberg—now, like Auerbach, incorporated into the town—owns the very good site of Herrnwingert. Heppenheim, close to the Baden boundary, with an attractive market square, a town hall dated 1551, pretty half-timbered houses in the old town center, and dominated by the ruin of Starkenburg Castle, includes within its boundaries the winegrowing villages of Hambach and Erbach in different side valleys. Its chief sites are Steinkopf, Maiberg, and Schlossberg. The "Odenwald Wine Island," situated in a lower part of the hills, is not geographically part of the Bergstrasse, but its wines are classified with those of the rest of the region and are, indeed, similar in character. Apart from Gross-Umstadt and Klein-Umstadt, with the best-known site of Stachelberg between them, the "island" includes the winegrowing villages of Dietzenbach and Rossdorf.

Bensheim has a small State Domain of approximately twenty-five acres, which is administered by the Rheingau State Domain at Eltville. Of the total vine-covered acreage of the region, 80 percent is worked by spare-time winegrowers, each owning an average of about three-quarters of an acre of vineyard land, who obviously cannot process and market their wines on their own. There used to be three cooperatives—at Auerbach, Bensheim, and Heppenheim—which since 1969–70 have been amalgamated with the enlarged Regional Winegrowers' Cooperative at Heppenheim. The "Wine island" has its own Odenwald Cooperative at Gross-Umstadt.

The Hessische Bergstrasse—like the Baden section—cannot be said to produce *great* wines. They are, in general, lighter, less full-bodied, and with less bouquet than those of the Rheingau or of Rheinhessen. They are dry, vigorous, occasionally even quite heady, and pleasantly fresh, especially when drunk young.

Appendix
The New German Wine Law:
Synopsis and Brief Commentary

A GOOD many provisions of the new German wine law have already been touched upon in previous chapters, particularly in Chapter 3, "Grape Growing and Wine Making." The law was promulgated on July 17, 1969, and came into force on the same date two years later. It is the fifth in the series of German wine laws, its predecessors dating from 1892, 1901, 1909, and 1930. The new law is generally considered—not only by German experts—to be the most stringent and thoroughgoing of its kind the world over; a sign of this is the fact that the number of articles contained in successive laws has increased from thirteen in the first to ninety-seven in the last.

The present law is distinguished by a unique precision and guarantees a maximum of safety when purchasing German wine. The supply is more easily surveyed, the choice made simpler, the risk lessened. Thus, it serves the consumer primarily, protecting him against amateur misjudgment or deception. But, beyond this, it also has the task and aim of preserving the special nature of German wines, of improving their chance in the market—they are faced with the competition of southern wines produced in far greater quantities and under much more favorable climatic and labor conditions—and of stimulating an increase in efficiency on the part of the grower and cellarman. The widely shared belief that the Germans are not entirely devoid of thoroughness seems to be amply borne out by the new law.

There was a great deal of wrangling in the Federal Parliament on particular points of the proposed new law years before the Treaty of Rome came into existence, and thereafter it did not have an easy passage within the EEC. However, eventually it was recognized that the special climatic conditions of a northern country require special considerations; and, finally, Germany's particular demands largely overcame French and Italian objections, while the general and paramount EEC rules remained more in the nature of a legal framework.

The touchstone of the German position is the notion of "quality in the glass." By contrast, the French and Italian systems emphasize the recognition of certain vineyard sites judged suitable for the production of quality or ordinary wines. In the German opinion, this division between those alleged to produce table wines only and those fit for the lower and upper grades of quality wines springs rather more from the idea of quantitative regulation and inhibits the grower's individual efficiency effort. After all, the quality of a wine does not depend exclusively on the site, but on attention to the vines, a careful grape harvesting, and skillful cellar treatment, as well as the weather of the vintage season. Therefore, German experts tend to label this system as one of permanent privilege, within which the wine grown often has only a kind of quality presumption in its favor. If, for instance, a French *vigneron* owns a vineyard officially classified as producing Vin de Table (or Vin de Consommation Courante), he is stuck with this rating more or less permanently, however good the vintage year or however much effort he has put into his vineyard and cellar work. Even trying to have a really good site belonging to the intermediate category of vin Delimité de Qualité Supérieure upgraded to the top category of Appellation d'Origine Contrôlée seems to meet with considerable bureaucratic objections. This would never do under German law.

It is one of the Common Market agreements that wines are graded in three quality classes, or categories. The difference is the question of how this is done. The core of the new German law is the classification of German wine in the three categories of Deutscher Tafelwein (German Table Wine), Qualitätswein (Quality Wine of specified—in the sense of precisely demarcated—cultivation regions), and Qualitätswein mit Prädikat (that is, specially graded Quality Wine, the highest category). There are six grades of specially graded wine: Kabinett, Spätlese, Auslese, Beerenauslese, Trockenbeerenauslese, and Eiswein. The grade is shown on the label of every bottle of German wine.

Every German grower, living in whatever region and cultivating whatever kind of vine, may apply for a higher rating of his product if he wishes. Prerequisites for the recognition of quality wine are:

1. Public control of the choice of plot and corresponding kinds of vine.

2. Observance of the approved cultivation methods.

3. Observance of the officially permitted early, main, and late gathering periods.

4. Processing of the wine only within the boundaries of the respective cultivation region.

5. Attainment of minimum "must" weight, varying according to quality class, vine variety, and cultivation region.

6. Increasing the natural sugar content only in accordance with prescribed rules.

7. Being limited to the approved procedures and substances of cellar treatment.

8. Observance of the prescribed storing time and of various registration and cellar bookkeeping duties.

9. Passing the official quality test successfully. This means that a definite judgment as to whether a wine is a quality wine in the meaning of the law can be passed only after the "degustation," or sensory appraisal, within the scope of the quality testing, if and when it has previously complied with all objective legal requirements.

This unique system of testing and quality control is indeed difficult and time-consuming, but it conforms best to the natural, economic, and legal conditions in the Federal Republic.

An official test number is conferred only to wines that have passed the following triple-graded test:

1. The harvesting test begins in autumn in the vineyard, when the applicant has to report a particular harvest, for example, his Spätlese, at the local mayor's office, whereupon the supervising officials inspect his vineyard and cellar.

2. The analysis test follows when the wine has been developed and bottled in the cellar. The producer has to submit to the testing authority a testimonial of analysis prepared by a specially licensed laboratory. In addition, he has to submit three bottles of the particular wine as samples.

3. The sensory testing takes place under official supervision. (The Germans have a quaint predilection for the word *organoleptic* instead of *sensory*.) A panel of experts "degustate," that is, appraise, the wine and evaluate it in accordance with a twenty-point system. The features of color, clarity, bouquet, and taste are marked separately, and only after the wine has received a prescribed minimum number of points in all categories will the official testing authority return the test results, in which it may give its assent to the application, or grant a lesser designation, for instance, a Kabinett instead of the hoped-for Spätlese, or even only a Qualitätswein, or it may reject the application altogether. Incidentally, the professionals performing the sensory test are known as "consultants" (no joke, that's what independent but sworn-in appraisers are called in Germany). Two thousand years ago, good old Horace admonished novices to judge a wine *colore, odore, sapore* (often shortened to the COS rule by modern writers), meaning "by color, smell, and taste," in that sequence. His advice falls a bit short of modern testing standards: he forgot to insist on *claritate*, the second requirement in modern testing, "by clarity."

Anyway, to come back to our own times, whether he tried for a particular grade of the specially graded Quality Wine list (Qualitätswein mit Prädikat) or only for a Quality Wine (Qualitätswein) designation, the successful applicant is given an official test number, which he is obliged to display on his labels. The official test number (*amtliche Prüfungsnummer*; A.P.Nr. for short) is composed of the following digits, the total longer or shorter according to circumstances, and best read from back to front. The last two digits refer to the year of submission of the application (not to the vintage year). Thus, if the grapes were harvested in the first year in which the law came into force, 1971, the last two digits will be 72; more rarely, when the application has been delayed, 73. The next-to-last set of digits, varying in length according to the time when the application was submitted, or considered, refers to the serial number of the application. The preceding set is the code number of the producer. The first individual number or group of digits represents the code number of the testing office. To give two examples:

1. Administration of the Hessian State Wine Domains: A.P.Nr. 3305001572 = 72 (year of application); 015 (serial number of the application; that is, the fifteenth application submitted to the office in that year); 050 (code number of the administration of the Domains); 33 (code number of the locality of the Domains: Eltville).

2. Weingut Louis Guntrum, Nierstein am Rhein: A.P.Nr. 490718710172 = 72 (year of application); 101 (serial number of the application); 187 (code number of the estate); 907 (code number of the locality of the estate: Nierstein); 4 (code number of the testing office: Nierstein).

There is a difference between the two examples—that is, there is an additional number (4) in the second example—because until 1973 the use of a code number for the testing office had not been uniformly regulated; the Eltville office will hence-forward use the code number 6.

The governments of the wine-cultivating states of the Federal Republic have by legal decrees fixed minimum natural "must" weights which the Quality classes must attain. These are graded, according to kinds of vine and cultivation regions, between 57 and 72 Öchsle degrees (see above, page 71), thus considerably above the EEC value of 50 Öchsle degrees. German Quality Wine may have been sugared before fermentation, if need be, just like top-quality French wines. The sugaring or, as EEC law prefers to call it, the increasing of the natural alcohol content, is, contrary to the EEC limit, restricted as regards the maximum volume of total alcohol content. As to the old bone of contention, the German practice of wet sugaring, allowable until 1979, that of ordinary Quality Wine may increase the total volume up to 10 percent at the most, that of Table Wine up to 15 percent. For the rest, sugaring is, in correspondence with EEC law, precisely prescribed in all details. Measures of cellar treatment have also been standardized by the EEC.

Quality wines of the highest category, Qualitätswein mit Prädikat, have to satisfy additional requirements beyond those applicable to ordinary Quality Wines. All of them, from Kabinett to Trockenbeerenauslese and Eiswein, must fulfill the following requirements:

1. As a matter of course, they must meet all the conditions necessary to receive an official test number.

2. The grapes used must be harvested not within a single region but within a single area (Bereich); that is, a demarcated part of a region—a newly introduced concept.

3. The addition of extraneous sugar is not permitted. The spread of the minimum content of natural sugar from Kabinett to Trockenbeerenauslese ranges between 70 and 150 Öchsle degrees. Under certain conditions, the French permit the sugaring even of their Appellation d'Origine Contrôlée wines. This means that they will always have these top wines, however

poor the vintage year. The Germans will not always have Qualitätswein mit Prädikat.

The indication of origin, thus of the site (Lage), is of special importance in the case of German wine, since the microclimate from valley bottom to hillcrest often varies considerably in accordance with differences in slope inclination, soil composition, exposure to solar radiation, exposure to wind, and other factors. The establishment of a vineyard roll is another innovation of the law; it is an official register with a description and cartographical mapping of all sites, grand sites, and areas admitted for the declaration of origin of German wines. As before the introduction of the new law, the site is the most narrow indication of origin; it usually bears the name common to a whole complex of individually owned plots from the surface of which wines of the same quality and value are gained. This site, as a group of adjacent vineyard plots, may be situated in one single community or in several communities of the same cultivation region. A site can henceforth be registered only if it has a minimum size of 5 hectares (12.35 acres) of vine-planted surface.

There are, however, a few exceptions to this latter rule. There are some considerably smaller sites whose names have, over the last hundred or more years, helped to build up the international reputation of German wines. To give only three examples, the famous Bernkastel Doctor comes from a site measuring only 1⅓ hectares. Nierstein's Glöck does not seem to extend to a much larger acreage. On the Ahr River, Walporzheim's Gärkammer, one of the best Spätburgunder sites, measures no more than half a hectare. Such cases are being taken care of by a clause to the general provision admitting exceptions from the 5-hectare rule "if the formation of a larger site is not possible because of the topographical conditions of utilization or because of the special quality of the wines gained from the surface." So one might have hoped that the really outstanding site names might have been saved from oblivion.

Unfortunately, this is not always the case (see below). On the other hand, there seems to be no upper limit set for the size of a single site (*Einzellage*). To give one example, the Achkarren Schlossberg in the Kaiserstuhl hills, with an ideal southerly aspect one of Germany's most famous sites for Ruländer wines, used to comprise 14 hectares, surely enough to comply with the law. Now a great many other local sites at the Schlossberg's flanks—but by no means all of them on impeccable south slopes—have been amalgamated with it, bringing it up to the mammoth size of 91 hectares. All these additions now share the prestige of the original Schlossberg, and their wines, of course, fetch the same prices. There now remains only one other Achkarren site, the Castellberg.

The limitation to a minimum size of 5 hectares has been accompanied by the abolition of a vast number of names of former single sites—as well as of names given to so-called *Gattungslagen* ("generic sites"), that is, names that could be used for any wine grown within a radius of fifteen kilometers (five miles) of the locality indicated. The first example that comes to mind is Nierstein's well-known Domtal ("Cathedral Valley"). But there is no valley of that name anywhere near Nierstein; moreover, the town has no church that can aspire to the dignity of a cathedral. Hence, the abolition of this latter type of name can only be greeted with a sigh of relief.

It is rather different with the relegation of a legion of old single-site names to limbo. There are pros and cons to it. The pros put forth the practical reason that their multiplicity was a nuisance to business. The vast clutter of baffling site names was entirely superfluous and merely bewildering to the consumer, as well as a handicap to the export of German wines; so, they thought, good riddance to them. The cons, on the other hand, were in a weak position from the beginning. They comprised the romantically and poetically inclined, and especially those interested in folklore and the history of religion. A good half of the Moselle site names are of Gallo-Roman origin but transformed into a quasi-German appearance. In most other regions, the greatest number of deformed names include *Hölle*, either by itself or in combination, but these names have nothing to do with the Devil's home premises, being deformed from *Halde*, an obsolescent word for a hillside or slope. It is only in Baden and Württemberg that *Halde* has not been transmogrified into *Hölle*. The universally known Liebfraumilch has nothing to do with Our Lady's milk but is possibly derived from *minch*, a medieval word for the present *Mönch*, thus describing a monk of Our Lady's Church. In the Palatinate, Gimmeldingen's old-time Meerspinne has nothing to do with an imaginary sea spider, but is a transformed *Mehrgespann*, a vehicle drawn by two or more draft animals. Also in the Palatinate, Wachenheim's still-existing Gerümpel is not the word with the English equivalent of "junk"; it is a deformation of the name of a former proprietor, a man with the alien and perhaps somewhat sinister-sounding name of baron von Grympl. There is quite a respectable mental leap from Gerümpel to Kröv's Nacktarsch ("Bare Bottom") on the Moselle; it is said to be derived from an original *Nektar* (though not everyone would be easily convinced of the suitability of the alleged old name). And so forth, almost ad infinitum.

Some claim that the number of old site names was around 20,000; more often, it is said to have been 30,000 or more. In fact, nobody seems to have bothered to count them. But it is possible that the large discrepancy in numbers given is at least partly accounted for by the fact that certain communities realized the advantage of reducing the multiplicity of site names earlier on, and did so voluntarily before the new law came into force. An example is the Rheingau village of Kiedrich, which in 1952 reduced thirty-five old site names to seven: Gräfenberg, Klosterberg, Wasserros, Sandgrub, Heiligenstock, Turmberg, and Scharfenstein. The new law only completed the job by amalgamating the last two with the first four as single-site names, but leaving Heiligenstock as that of a grand site. It is likely that other communities came to the same insight and acted in the same way.

The new law has drastically slashed the old site names to about one-tenth of their former number—a great advantage, all things considered. However, the question is whether it is always the right names that have been saved from oblivion and retained for future use. For instance, it comes as both a puzzle and a shock to find that Oppenheim's Reisekahr, one of Germany's most superb Rieslings, has been wiped off the map completely, while the names of much lesser local growths have been retained. Again, Boppard's Hamm, while not in the same class, was widely recognized as one of the best Middle Rhine Rieslings; furthermore, it came from a site of several miles' length, all with impeccable southerly aspect. It has been relegated to limbo, too; but only officially. The abolition of the name Hamm has not yet percolated to the Bopparders themselves, who stubbornly refer to any local wine by that name. There is also a local restaurant named Bopparder Hamm.

In other cases, names that hitherto had been regarded as those of the best of a place have been "elevated" to the status of a grand-site name. An example is Nierstein's Auflangen. This seems to be a nominal upgrading, but is an actual downgrading, as a bottle of "Auflangen" bought since 1971 no longer contains the same wine that it did before. Again, a lesser example of the same sort: Auerbach's Rott once ranked among the best wines of Hessische Bergstrasse, known to everyone as the foremost, if not the only, wine of the place. Now it has become the local grand site, having to take a number of inferior single sites under the mantle of its prestige.

Among its many innovations, the new law has piled up, on top of the remaining single-site names, a little pyramid of *Grosslagen* ("grand sites") and *Bereiche* (subdivisions of a region, most conveniently translated as "areas"); both concepts are, perhaps, a little controversial. The grand site is a composite unit of single sites, legally demarcated as part of an area, producing, or supposed to produce, wines of the same general character and equivalent quality. Its purpose may be explained in the following, perhaps somewhat roundabout, way. In a year that is good in both quality and quantity, the discriminating wine drinker who selects a Qualitätswein mit Prädikat according to his preference in sites will have no difficulty in securing an adequate supply. But even in middling years it may happen that the particular single site of his choice does not have a sufficient amount of, say, Spätlese grapes fully maturing on it. In that case, the Spätlese grapes of several equivalent single sites will be pressed and developed together and sold under the name of the superimposed grand site.

The demarcation of grand sites is often a matter of perplexing intricacy. They may be in, or partly in, one locality; for instance, Nierstein has no less than four, some of them spilling over into adjacent villages. On the other hand, the whole of the Kaiserstuhl hills is one large grand site, containing a great number of local single sites; they are not all, by any means, in close proximity, nor do they produce wines of exactly similar character. The next higher unit, the area, is Kaiserstuhl-Tuniberg, the latter the name of a limestone range extending southeast from the volcanic Kaiserstuhl group. The highest unit, the region, is Baden, which has the greatest number of areas—namely, seven. As a region, Baden is not geographically demarcated—it is politically demarcated—and the wines of most of its areas are more diverse in character than those of other regions.

As far as grand sites in general are concerned, one particular objection may be leveled at the diversity of the types of their names. In some cases the name is that of one of their former single sites, often the most prominent one (for example, Nierstein's Auflangen), in others, the name of a hill or group of hills, of a river valley, a castle, or some other feature of the countryside may be used; but unfortunately there is also a residual category of fancy names, mostly plain kitsch, reminiscent of nothing so much as of those dreamed up by the plonk merchants.

The eleven designated wine regions are divided into the following thirty-one areas. The Ahr has only one: Walporzheim-

Ahr; the Middle Rhine has two: Rheinburgengau in the north and Bacharach in the south; the Rheingau has two: Johannisberg from Lorchhausen to Walluf and including Wiesbaden, and Hochheim at the eastern end; the Nahe two: Kreuznach in the north and Schloss Böckelheim in the south; the Moselle-Saar-Ruwer four: Obermosel, Saar-Ruwer (including Trier), Bernkastel, and Zell; Rheinhessen three: Bingen, Nierstein, and Wonnegau; Hessische Bergstrasse two: Starkenburg and Umstadt; the Palatinate two: Südliche Weinstrasse and Mittelhaardt-Deutsche Weinstrasse; Franconia three: (from east to west) Steigerwald, Maindreieck, and Mainviereck; Baden seven: Lake Constance, Markgräflerland, Kaiserstuhl-Tuniberg, Breisgau, Ortenau, Badische Bergstrasse-Kraichgau, and Badisches Frankenland; Württemberg three: Remstal-Stuttgart, Württembergisches Unterland, and Kocher-Jagst-Tauber. Most of these areas show the heavy hand of bureaucracy. The experienced wine lover would have reached more differentiated divisions.

To turn to a more positive innovation of the modern law: the substitution of Kabinett for the old "Cabinet." The latter term was a somewhat vague indication of more than ordinary quality, more often than not added to Spätlese or Auslese, and, moreover, largely confined to the Rheingau region. It has been banished from labels and revived, in the Germanized form of Kabinett, as a precisely defined indication of quality, the bottom rung of the Qualitätswein mit Prädikat ladder, never to be joined to other specially graded Quality Wine designations, and available as a possible goal for all German wines. One often hears that the present designation Kabinett is nothing more than the banished old term *Natur*. This is nonsense. Apart from being unsugared, the "must" used for Kabinett has to have reached a minimum weight of between 70 and 81 Öchsle degrees—the difference depending on cultivation region and vine variety; the grapes must have been harvested 100 percent not only within the region but within the area enclosing the indicated origin (locality and site or simply locality); after bottling, the wine must, in the sensory testing forming part of the official testing procedure, show that it is fully typical of its origin and of the kind of vine indicated on the label, and that it has reached the required minimum number of points for color, clearness, smell, and taste.

A still more important advance was the absolute and general prohibition of any reference to "naturalness." It was to the shocked surprise of many that the terms *Natur, Naturwein,* or *naturrein,* meaning that the "must" had not been treated with extraneous sugar, had to disappear from wine labels in accordance with the new law. The notion of "naturalness" used to be an absolute cornerstone of German enological nomenclature, but it was also peculiar to it; and it was only after lengthy and heated debate that it was dropped. The objection to it raised by the French within the Common Market legislation has already been mentioned. But there is more to it. According to the general German food act, any reference or allusion to naturalness is permitted only if the respective food stuff is absolutely free of extraneous additions, is marketed year after year with the same composition, with the same quality, and at the same price (subject, of course, to inflationary rises). But wine is not, and never can be, entirely free of additives. For its preservation it needs the addition of a very slight dosage of sulfurous acid, practiced by the ancients and still true for all wines the world over. Thus, according to the definition of the food law, wine can never be a natural product. So say the chemists and jurists. Against this, the enologist would object that in the old wine law there existed no absolutely safe quality standard, and that, therefore, *Natur* had to serve as a kind of emergency index of quality in the absence of some better term. This it did indeed, serving for a long time as a distinctive mark of fully matured quality. However, this recognized quality standard has been increasingly abused. At first, certain irresponsible German growers, tempted by the prestige value of the term *Natur,* started to put it on labels of miserably thin, acid stuff that should have been properly sugared, and that in due course became known as *gequälte* ("tormented") *Naturweine*. This was only the beginning of the *Naturwein* inflation. By the time that the snob value of this kind of stuff had begun to level off, importers, too, had begun to realize the profitmaking value of the term, putting it on labels of cheap wines imported from southern Europe, northern Africa, and other subtropical countries. These so-called *Naturweine* were indeed "natural" in the sense that they were in no need of additional sugaring, but otherwise had nothing in common with the genuine German product called by that name. The old law could do nothing about such practices.

When the new law prohibited the concept of naturalness, it established in its place the new value category Qualitätswein mit Prädikat, introducing a genuine controlled quality guarantee. There are, of course, exceptional years when virtually no wine is in any need of extraneous sugaring—1971 was the last of them. But, generally, if the consumer wants to be absolutely certain of an unsugared wine, all he has to do is to buy a bottle marked Qualitätswein mit Prädikat, with the additional designation Kabinett, Spätlese, Auslese, Beerenauslese, Trockenbeerenauslese, or Eiswein, the choice among the last six being determined by his personal taste and how much he cares to spend.

The grower who is content to produce simple table wines need not bother with all the bureaucratic vexations mentioned; he needs no official test number. All he has to do is to put the official declaration Deutscher Tafelwein on his labels and remember carefully that German Table Wine has to be prepared exclusively from German grapes. (There is no such thing as EEC wine.) However, in contrast to producers of Quality and specially graded Quality Wines, his choice of blending is interregional; for example, he may blend a Moselle wine with one from the Palatinate, and so forth.

Moreover, in order to avoid confusion with the higher quality classes, five new and larger winegrowing regions, named after rivers, have been introduced specifically for the benefit of the Table Wine category: Rhein, Mosel, Oberrhein, Neckar, and Main. Unfortunately, they are a bit lopsided, for while the last four correspond simply to Moselle-Saar-Ruwer, Baden, Württemberg, and Franconia, respectively, Rhein includes the Ahr, Middle Rhine, Rheingau, Nahe, Rheinhessen, and the Palatinate, a rather motley collection.

In the absence of a regional designation on the label, it may be assumed that the wine is a blend made up of the product of two or more regions and that none of the parts contributed by a single region reaches 75 percent or more of the total. The label will give a fancy name, the choice of which must not, however, be suggestive or reminiscent of any real site name.

If in the interregional blend one particular region, that is, one of the five specifically designated for the Table Wines category, has contributed 75 percent or more, the wine is one rung higher up and may go under the name of that region, for instance, Rhein. However, it will still be known by a fancy name. If, in additon to the regional name, the label bears a local designation after the word *Bereich* ("area"), at least 75 percent of the blend must come from the named area.

Lastly, if the label bears the name of a village or town, at least 75 percent of the contents must come from within the boundaries of that particular local community. It is important to note that on this highest step of the Table Wine category interregional blending is no longer allowed; that is, the rest of the blend must come from the same Table Wine region. Site names are not permitted within the whole of the Table Wine category. Thus, if one sees a site name following that of a locality on the label, it indicates that the wine is at least in the Quality Wine category, which, incidentally, is also made explicit on the label.

Briefly, the regulations applying to the two upper Quality classes, both Qualitätswein and Qualitätswein mit Prädikat have to bear the name of the cultivation region (in their case, of course, that of one of the original eleven) on the label, meaning, for instance, that in the case of the former all portions of a blend must originate from that same region. The widest possible characterization of a Qualitätswein will still have a fancy name, the intermediate one that of an area (e.g., Bereich Bernkastel), the narrowest one that of a locality followed by that of the particular vineyard site. The widest possible characterization of a Qualitätswein mit Prädikat bears the name of an area; meaning that if there is any blending, all parts must come from the same area, while the narrowest one indicates that of a locality followed by that of a vineyard site. As the narrowest geographical designation, the names of sites are strictly reserved for Qualitätswein and Qualitätswein mit Prädikat only. Thus it can be seen that in the regulations of geographical designation there is an overlap among the three categories.

As regards color, the new law distinguishes the five main kinds by the name Weisswein, Rotwein, Roseewein (not Rosé), Rotling, and Perlwein. In the case of the higher-quality grades, the designation Roseewein may be replaced by the traditional name Weissherbst, and that of Rotling by the equally traditional one of Schillerwein (see pages 45 and 191). Perlwein is a simple but refreshing table wine containing natural or added carbonic acid. Aside from the particular preparation of Rotling, in which white and red grapes are grown, pressed, and fermented together, any so-called red-white blending, meaning the blending of ready-made red and white wines, is prohibited.

What is not indicated on the label, nor otherwise excessively advertised, is the fact that every wine sold is a blend of 75 percent of its own vintage with 25 percent of a previous one. Thus, a wine of the last of the much-cited "vintages of the century," 1971, has a quota of 25 percent of the far more plentiful and much cheaper 1970 wine. In this case, it cannot have done great harm to the famous 1971 vintage, since that of 1970 was, fortunately, also of a pretty high quality. But one wonders how this rule will work out in the long run. At any rate, the law does not say that the added 25 percent should be of the immediately preceding vintage, but only of a previous one.

Just a few more gratulations and grumbles about old designations which have disappeared from labels since 1971 and partly been replaced by others. There are, in the first place, the old indications *Wachstrum*, or *Kreszenz* (both meaning "growth"), followed by the name of the producer, replaced by that of *Aus eigenem Lesegut* ("of own vintage property"), followed by the producer's name; also, the old indication *Originalabfüllung* is replaced by the new *Erzeugerabfüllung* ("producer's bottling"). In both cases the difference is purely verbal; the respective words mean exactly the same. The words *eigen* and *Erzeuger*, incidentally, also cover corporate bodies like winegrowers' cooperatives. As far as mere embellishing frills like *bestes Fass* ("best cask"), *echt* ("genuine"), and *garantiert* ("guaranteed") are concerned, good riddance. However, the elimination of the adjectives *feine* and *feinste* ("fine," "finest") to emphasize the heightened quality of a Spätlese or Auslese is controversial. They seem to have been regarded as mere eyewash. This they may have been often enough, but by no means invariably. One may often find old bottles marked by these adjectives where they indicate a considerable difference in quality. And what about the phraseology of the law itself? Is not the substitution of the term *anreichern* ("enriching") for the old *verbessern* ("improving") in the official jargon anything more than a bit of eyewash? Would a term suggesting plain sugaring have sounded too indecent?

Surprising as it may seem, "brand" wines are not entirely excluded from the higher-quality classes, although they are subject to a special regulation within the framework of official testing. A brand wine is, of course, a proprietary article, well known in the market, unchangeable in character and quality, standarized in display and packaging, and offered everywhere at the same (and permanent) price (disregarding inflationary changes, of course). The modern concept of wine marketing, assuring large numbers of consumers and a steady consumption, meets the wishes of an increasing number of wine drinkers, especially of young people who are just starting to buy wine and to whom the notions familiar to the old expert are still a sealed book. Depending on its quality, a brand wine may be an ordinary Table Wine, a Quality Wine or even a specially graded Quality Wine. Since, however, it is characterized by unchangeable quality and taste, it is subject to separate provisions in the testing procedure. According to these, a brand wine may receive a test number only for the duration of one single year.

To sum up: Most criticisms raised against particular provisions of the new law are in the nature of objections to supposed superficialities or minor blemishes. Taken as a whole, it is of an unrivaled standard. It is designed to promote quality consciousness in German wine cultivation, thereby to serve the interests of the consumer and at the same time to improve the market chances of German wine. German viticulture can cope with the overwhelming competition from outside only if by steadily striving for quality it nurtures and maintains the unique character of its product. The law encourages this quality consciousness through the requirement of individual quality testing, at which time the classification of a wine is determined by its quality in the glass—undoubtedly the best place where it can be evaluated. Thus, it is up to every individual producer to raise the quality of his product by the proper choice of vine variety, improved cultivation methods, and special care so as to obtain the official test number that explicitly informs the consumer of the quality of the wine offered.

Index

Abtswind, 227
Achkarren, 175, 258
Additives, 263
Affentaler, 181, 182, 191
Aging wine, 79-80
Ahr region, 243-47; areas of, 261-62; climate of, 245; Roman remains in, 89-90; size of, 243; soils of, 244-45; Spätburgunder of, 247; wines of, 247
Ahrweiler, 246
Albalonga, 59
Alben, 41
Alcoholic content of wine, 70, 71, 72, 77
Alemannians, 90-92, 94, 95
Alf, 160-61
Alken, 164
Altenahr, 246
Altenbamberg, 204
Altitude, 20, 33
Altschweier, 181
Alzey, 148; State Research Institute at, 52, 53-55
Analysis test of wine, 254
Anreichern, 72
A.P.Nr. (test number), 255
Aris, 56
Assmannshausen, 211, 214-15, 247
Astheim, 228
Auerbach, 249, 250, 260
Auflangen site (Nierstein), 143, 260
Auggen, 172
Ausbau, 79
Aus eigenem Lesegut, 267
Auslese, 69, 70, 80, 218, 253; meaning of, 68-69
Auxerrois, 36
Avelsbach, 156
Ayl, 154

Bacchus, 55
Bacharach, 238-39, 262
Bachem, 246
Bad Dürkheim, 133
Baden-Baden, 179
Baden-Franconia area, 167, 183, 233
Baden region, 165-187; areas of, 261, 262; climate of, 167; cooperatives of, 167; size of, 165; soils of, 167; subregions of, 166; wines of, 167, 169, 171, 175, 177, 182, 186-87
Baden Winegrowers Association, 81
Badische Bergstrasse area, 166, 183, 185-86, 262
Badisches Frankenland area, 262

Badische Weinstrasse, 177-78
Bad Kreuznach, 205
Bad Münster am Stein, 204
Bad Neuenahr, 246
Batzenberg, 173
Bavaria, 226, 234
Bavarians, 225
Beerenauslese, 80, 209, 218, 253; meaning of, 69
Beilstein, 163, 195
Benedictines, 112
Bensheim, 113, 210, 248, 250
Bergstrasse area of Baden. See Badische Bergstrasse area
Bergstrasse region. See Hessische Bergstrasse region
Bernkastel, 157-58, 262
Bernkasteler Doctor, 158, 257
Bernkasteler Riesling, 139-40, 153
Besigheim, 197
Beutelsbach, 197
Bickensohl, 175
Bietigheim, 197
Bingen, 139, 145-46
Bingen area, 136, 145-46, 262
Bingerbrück, 206
Binger Rosengarten, 140
Bishoffingen, 175
Black Forest, 166, 177
Blauer Burgunder, 35
Blauer Malvasier, 46
Blauer Spätburgunder, 43-46. See also Spätburgunder
Blends, 73-75; cover wine for, 60; Müller-Thurgau, 51; red wine, 49; regulations concerning, 74-75, 265; white wine, 139
Blue Arbst, 181, 182, 191
"Blue fining," 78
Bockenheim, 134
Bocksbeutel bottle, 81, 182, 185, 222-23
Bodenheim, 143-44
Bonnigheim, 197
Boppard, 240, 260
Botrytis cinerea fungus, 45, 69, 70, 209
Bottenau, 180
Bottles, 81. See also Bocksbeutel bottle
Brackenheim, 198
Brand wines, 139-40, 153, 267-68
Braubach, 241
Brauneberg, 101, 157
Breisach, 167, 175
Breisgau area, 166, 175-77, 262
Bremm, 41
Bretzenheim, 206

Britzingen, 172
Brömserburg Castle, 213
Bubenhäuser Höhe, 215
Büdesheim, 146
Bühl, 181
Bühlertal, 181
Bürgerspital, 227, 230, 231
Burg Layen, 206
Bürgstadt, 233
"Burgundian Gate," 86
Burgundy, 43–46
Burkheim, 175

"Cabinet." See Kabinett
Cabinet Cellar, 217, 218
Calmont site, 101, 162–63
Camina, 59
Casks, fermentation, 76–78
Castell, 227
Cellar technique, 68, 72–75
Cellar treatment, 75–80
Celts, 83, 84, 86, 93
Charlemagne, 101–3, 112, 114, 115
Chasselas Napoléon, 58
Christianity and wine: Biblical references, 110–11, 119–23; Christ in the winepress, 121–23; missionary labors, 109; monasteries, 112–15; patron saints, 116–19; sacramental wine, 124–25; site names, 119
Cladosporium cellare fungus, 216–17
Clarifying wine, 78
Claudius, Matthias, 117
Cleversulzbach, 199
Clevner, 43
Climate, 17, 19–23
Codex Laureshamensis, 113–15, 129, 249
Color of wine, 125, 266
Common Market agreements, 252–53
Cooperatives, winegrowers', 147, 167, 189, 246–47
COS rule, 254
Courtillier musqué, 54
Cover wine, 60
Cramunt site, 101
Crossbreeds, 49–60, 226; red wine, 59–60; white wine, 49–59

Dalsheim, 114
Deckrot, 60
Deidesheim, 132
Dernau, 246
Deutsche Landwirtschafts-Gesellschaft (DLG), 81, 186
Deutsches Weinsiegel seal, 81
Deutsches Weintor, 128
Deutschler Tafelwein. See Table wine
Dhron, 157
Diabetiker Weinsiegel seal, 81

Dienheim, 86, 89, 114, 140–41
Dietzenbach, 250
"Doctor's" wine, 158, 257
Domina, 59
Dorfprozelten, 233
Dorsheim, 206
Dörzbach, 199
Dreikonigswein, 70, 71
Durbach, 178, 180, 182

Ebelsbach, 227
Eberbach, 106, 210, 211, 216
Ebernburg, 204–5
Eberstadt, 196
Ebringen, 173
Edlfäule, 69
Edenkoben, 129
Ediger, 163
Ehrenfelser, 57
Ehrenstetten, 173
Eibelstadt, 229
Eisental, 181
Eiswein, 71, 253
Eitelsbach, 156
Elbling, 40–42, 150, 151
Elpersheim, 199
Eltmann, 227
Eltville, 210, 212, 250
Endingen, 174
Enkirch, 160
Enz valley, 192, 197–198
Erbach, 210, 212, 250
Erden, 159
Erlabrunn, 232
Erntebringer site, 219
Erzeugerabfüllung, 267
Escherndorf, 223, 228
Esslingen, 193
Eucharist, celebration of, 109, 121, 125
European Economic Community (E.E.C.), 27, 252, 256

Faber, 54
Färbertraube, 60
Faustus, Johannes, 173, 198
Federweisser, 77
Fellbach, 194
Fermentation, 73, 76–77
"Fining," 78
Firne, 80
Flein, 195
Flurbereinigung, 64–65
Forchtenberg, 199
Forst, 132–133
Forta, 56
Franconia region, 220–35; areas of, 262; Bocksbeutel bottles of, 81, 221–22; climate of, 222–23, 224; Keuper zone, 225, 227; Main Quadrangle, 224, 232; Main

Triangle, 228, 232; in Middle Ages, 106, 229; patron saint of, 117; size of, 220; soils of, 222, 223, 224; "Wine Isle," 228; wines of, 221–22, 223–24, 235
Frankenberg, 227
Frankentaler, 46
Franks, 90–91, 94–95, 96
Frauenberg site, 161–62
Freiburg, 176, 177; State Viticultural Institute at, 52, 57, 60, 168
Freinsheim, 133–34
Freisamer, 52
Frickenhausen, 229
Frosts, protecting vines from, 63
Frühburgunder, 46, 60, 138, 145, 224, 246

Gamay, 55, 56
Gärkammer site, 246, 257
Gau-Algesheim, 145
Gau-Bickelheim, 147
Gaul, 83, 85, 86, 90–91, 94
Geilweilerhof, Federal Research Institute at, 51, 55–56, 59, 128
Geisenheim, 213; State Teaching and Research Institute at, 50, 57–58, 60, 211
Gengenbach, 179
Geradstetten, 197
German Winegrowing Institute, 144
German Wine Information bureau, 144
German wine law. See Law
German wines: characteristics of, 16–17; reputation of, 17, 28
German words derived from Latin, 96–101
Germany, East, viticulture in, 15, 104
Germany, West (Federal Republic): climate of, 17; history of viticulture in, 83–108; latitudes of vineyards in, 15; size of vine-planted surface in, 16; soils of, 17; winegrowing areas of, 261–62; winegrowing regions of, 17–18, 261–62, 264–65
Gerümpel site, 133, 259
Gewürztraminer, 32–34; blending of, 75; crossbreeds of, 53–54, 55
Gimmeldingen, 131, 259
Glöck, 143, 257
Gloria, 56
Glottertäler, 177
Goldener Oktober, 153
Graach, 158
Grand-sites, 260–61
Grantschen, 196
Grape "mash," 68, 71
Grape "must," 68, 71–72
Grapes: crushing of, 68, 101–2; harvesting of, 67; pressing, 75–76; ripeness of, 77; ripening of, 66–67
"Grapevine Madonna, The," 124

Grauer Burgunder, 34, 35
Greuth, 227
Grisbach, 199
Grossbottwar, 195
Grossheppach, 197
Grossheubach, 233
Grosssachsen, 186
Gross-Umstadt, 250
Gross-Vernatseh, 46
Gundelsheim, 196
Gundersheim, 148
Guntersblum, 140–41
Gutedel, 39–40, 171–72; crossbreeds of, 54, 57
Gutenborner, 58
Gütezeichen, 81

Haardt, 131
Haardt area, 126–27; Lower, 127, 128, 133–34; Middle, 127, 128, 130–33; Upper, 127, 128–30
Hagnau, 168
Hallgarten, 211, 217
Hambach, 250
Hamm, 240, 260
Hammelburg, 232
Hammerstein, 241
Handthal, 227
Hargesheim, 205
Harvesting test of wine, 254
Hasloch, 233
Hattenheim, 210, 212
Heckenwirtschaften, 102
Hecklingen, 177
Heddesheim, 206
Hegau, 169–70
Heidelberg, 185
Heilbronn, 195
Heinsheim, 185
Heitersheim, 114–15
Helfensteiner, 60, 191
Heppenheim, 114, 249, 250
Heppingen, 246
Herbst, meaning of, 100
Heroldrebe, 60, 191
Hessigheim, 195
Hessische Bergstrasse region, 248–50; areas of, 262; early viticulture in, 113; size of, 249; soils of, 249; wines of, 250
High Rhine area of Baden, 166, 170
Himmelstadt, 232
Himmlisches Moseltröpfchen, 153
Hochheim, 18, 207, 210, 212, 262
Hochrhein. See High Rhine area of Baden
"Hocks," 18
Hohenhaslach, 197
Hohentwiel area, 166, 170
Höllenberg valley, 214
Homburg, 223, 232

Hörstein, 223, 234
Hüffelsheim, 205
Hügelheim, 172
Humidity, 21
Huxelrebe, 54

Ihringen, 174
Ingelfingen, 199
Ingelheim, 145
Ingelheim area, 136, 143, 145
Iphofen, 227
Italian Riesling vine, 30–31

Jagst River, 167, 183, 185, 192, 199
Johannisberg area, 262
Johannisberg Castle, 211–12, 217–19
Jugenheim, 249
Juliusspital, 230–31

Kabinett, 70, 80, 218–19, 253, 262–63
Kaiserstuhl area, 64–65, 166, 173–75, 187, 261, 262
Kallstadt, 133
Kanzem, 154
Kanzler, 54
Kappelrodek, 181
Kasel, 156
Kaub, 239
Kellertuch, 216–17
Kellerweg, 141
Kerner, 57
Kernerrebe, 190
Kiedrich, 211, 216, 259
Kinheim, 160
Kirchheim-Teck, 193
Kitzingen, 228–29
Klävner, 43
Klebrot, 42–43, 215
Kleinberger, 41
Kleinbottwar, 195
Kleinheppach, 197
Klein-Umstadt, 250
Klepsau, 185
Klettgau, 170
Klingenberg, 233
Klingenmünster, 128
Klüsserath, 156
Knittlingen, 198
Kobern, 164
Kocher-Jagst-Tauber area, 262
Kocher valley, 192, 199
Kolor, 60
Königsbach, 131
Königshoten, 184
Königswinter, 241
Kraichgau area, 166, 183, 184
Kreszenz, 267
Kreuznach area, 262
Kreuzwertheim, 233

Kronenbühl site, 177
Kröv, 160, 259
Kues, 157
Kupfergrube site, 204

Labels: of blends, 74–75, 265; German wine law and, 82, 262–67; quality designations on, 69–71; site names on, 265
Lage im Alleinbesitz, 23
Lake Constance area: of Baden, 166, 168–70, 262; of Franconia, 234; of Württemberg, 192, 199
Landesmuseum, 86–87
Langenlonsheim, 206
Latin loanwords, 96–101
Laubenheim (Nahe), 206
Laubenheim (Rheinhessen), 144
Lauda, 184
Laudenbach, 199
Laufen, 172
Lauffen, 195
Law (1971 German Wine Law), 251–68; blends and, 74–75; classification of wines, 253; fancy designations of proprietary blends, 140; Kabinett and, 218–19; labels and, 82; minimal "must" weights, 256; quality wine prerequisites, 253; sites and, 158, 257–62; testing, 254–56
Lees, 77, 78
Leinsweiler, 128
Leiselheim, 175
Leiste site, 230–31
Leiwen, 156
Lemberger, 47–48, 60
Lerchenhühl, 172
Leutesdorf, 241
Liebfraumilch, 138–40, 259
Lieser, 157
Lorch, 157
Lorsch, Benedictine Abbey of, 113–114
Ludwigsburg, 194
Luglienca bianca, 55
Lützelsachsen, 186

Madeleine angevine, 53–54, 56
Maikammer, 129
Maindreieck area, 262
Mainriesling, 52
Mainviereck area, 262
Mainz, 138, 144
Mainz basin, 137
Marcobrunn site, 210, 212
Mariensteiner, 59
Marienthal, 246
Markelsheim, 199
Markgräflerland area, 114, 115 118, 166, 170–73, 262

Martinsthal, 212
"Mash," grape, 68, 71
Maulbronn, 198
Maurus, Hrabanus, 58
Mayschoss, 246
Meddersheim, 203
Meersburg, 168–69, 170
Meerspinne site, 131, 259
Meisenheim, 203
Meraner Kurtraube, 46
Mertesdorf, 156
Merxheim, 203
Michelbach, 199, 223, 224
Microclimate and viticulture, 22–23
Middle Rhine region, 236–242; areas of, 262; climate of, 237; Lower Rheingau and, 207–8; Riesling of, 237; size of, 236; soils of, 238; wines of, 237
Mittelhaardt-Deutsche Weinstrasse, 262
Mittelheim, 213, 217
Mittelrhein. See Middle Rhine region
"Mixed setting," 106
Mockmühl, 199
Monasteries, 104, 106, 107, 109, 112–15
Monteneubel site, 101
Monzingen, 203
Morio-Muskat, 51, 128, 137
Moselblümchen, 153
"Mosella" (Fortunatus), 87–88
Moselle River, 18, 149
"Moselles," 18
Moselles, sparkling, 41
Moselle-Saar-Ruwer region, 149–164; areas of, 262; Lower Moselle, 41, 86, 150, 162–64; Middle Moselle, 29, 150, 156–162; Roman remains found in, 86–88; Ruwer valley, 149, 150, 155–56; Saar valley, 149, 150, 152, 153–55; size of, 149; soils of, 149–50, 162; Upper Moselle, 41, 149, 151, 153–56; wines of, 150–51, 152, 154
"Mülhauser Loch," 86
Müller, Hermann, 50
Müllerrebe, 43, 191
Müller-Thurgau, 27, 50–51, 128, 137, 150, 151; crossbreeds of, 53, 54, 55–56, 58
Müllheim, 172
Multaner, 57
Mundelsheim, 195
Münster am Stein, 204
Münster-Sarmsheim, 206
Museums, 88, 134–35, 145, 157, 213, 217–18, 230
Muskateller, 36–37, 128
Muskat Ottonel, 37
Mussbach, 131
"Must," 68, 71–72, 73, 75, 76; derivation of word, 97; minimal weights of, 256
Mutations, 49

Nackenheim, 143
Nacktarsch, 153, 160, 259
Nahe region, 201–206; areas of, 262; climate of, 202; lower area, 206; middle area, 203–6; size of, 201; upper area, 203; wines of, 202
Nahe River, 127
Names: proprietary brand, 139–40, 153, 267–68; site, 101, 158, 159, 257–62, 265
"Naturalness," 263–64
Neckarmühlbach, 185
Neckarsulm, 195–96
Neckar valley, 166–67, 183, 185, 190, 192–96
Neckarzimmern, 185
Neef, 161–62
Neipperg, 198
Neudenau, 185
Neuffen, 193
Neumagen, 87, 88, 157
Neumagen collections, 86–87, 157
Neustadt, 129–30
Neuweier, 181
Niederhausen-Schlossböckelheim, 203, 204
Niedernhall, 199
Niederwalluf, 212
Nierstein, 142–43, 257, 258, 260, 261, 262
Niesteiner Domtal, 139, 140
Nittel, 153
"Noble mold," 69, 142, 209, 211–12
Noblessa, 56
Nobling, 57
Nonnenhorn, 234
Nordheim, 228
Norheim, 204

Obberrotweil, 174
Oberdiebach, 238
Oberheimbach, 238
Oberkirch, 181
Obermosel area, 262
Oberstenfeld, 195
Oberwesel, 239–40
Öchsle "must" scale, 71–72, 256
Ockfen, 154
"Odenwald Wine Island," 249, 250
Oderheim, 203
Oestrich, 212
Offenburg, 178
Oidium, 107, 226
Oppenheim, 114, 141–42, 143, 260
Oppenheimer Krötenbrunnen, 140
Optima, 56
Originalabfüllung, 267
Ortega, 58
Ortenau area, 166, 177–83, 187, 262
Osiris, 59
Osthofen, 140–41

Palatinate. *See* Rhenish Palatinate
Patersberg, 240
Perle, 53, 223, 224, 226
Perlwein, 266
Peronospora mildew, 63, 107, 226
Pfälzer Weinstrasse, 126, 128–32
Pfalzgrafenstein, 239
Pfedelbach, 199
Pfinzgau-Enzgau area, 166, 183, 184
Phylloxera, 107–8, 226
Piesport, 157
Pinot blanc, 35–36
Pinot gris, 34, 35
Pinot meunier, 43
Pinot noir, 34, 35, 43, 44
Plantert site, 101
Plenetsch site, 101
Portugieser, 48–49, 59, 60, 128, 138
Precipitation, 21–22
"Pure setting," 106

Qualitätswein, 68–71, 80, 218, 253; labeling of, 265–66; prerequisites for, 253;
sugaring and, 256
Qualitätswein mit Prädikat, 218, 253, 262,
264; labeling of, 265–66; requirements
of, 256–57
Quality designations, 69–71
Quality signs, 81
Quality Wine. *See* Qualitätswein

Rabaner, 58
"Racking off," 78
Randersacker, 223, 229
Rauenthal, 210, 215
Räuschling, 40–42
Rech, 246
Red crossbreeds, 59–60
Red Mountain, 142
Red wine, 42–49; Blauer Spätburgunder,
43–46; crossbreeds, 59–60; Frühbur-
gunder, 46; Lemberger, 47–48; Por-
tugieser, 48–49; storage of, 82; Trol-
linger, 46–47
Regner, 55
Reichartshausen Castle, 211
Reichensteiner, 58
Remstal-Stuttgart area, 262
Rems valley, 192, 196–97
Restructuring viticultural acreage, 64–65
Retzbach, 231
Reutlingen, 193
Rheinbrohl, 241
Rheinburgengau, 262
Rheingau region, 207–219; areas of, 262;
climate of, 208; historical legends of,
102–3, 211–12; lower area, 207, 208,
214; Riesling of, 209–10; size of, 207;
soils of, 208; wines of, 209

Rheinhessen region, 136–48; areas of, 262;
climate of, 136–37; early viticulture in,
114; Roman remains in, 89; size of, 136;
soils of, 137; subregions of, 136; wines
of, 137–38
Rheinpfalz. *See* Rhenish Palatinate
Rheinriesling, 31
"Rheinweinlied" (Claudius), 117
Rhenish Palatinate region, 126–35; areas
of, 262; climate of, 126–27; Roman
remains found in, 89; Silvaner of, 128;
size of, 126; soils of, 127; wines of, 127–
28
Rhine Front area, 136, 140–44
Rhine valley, 15, 18; early viticulture in,
84, 86, 88, 93, 94, 95
Rhodt, 33–34, 129
Rhöndorf, 241
Rieslaner, 52–53, 59, 223–24, 226
Riesling (White Riesling), 28–30, 128,
132, 137, 223; blending of, 75;
crossbreeds of, 50, 52, 56, 57, 58, 59, 60;
of Moselle region, 150, 152; pseudo-
Rieslings, 30–32; of Rheingau region,
209–10, 217
Riparia, 56
Rödelsee, 227
Romans, early, 83–94, 96–97
Rosé, 45. *See also* Weissherbst
Roseewein, 266
Rossdorf, 250
Rosswag, 197
Rotberger, 60
Rotling, 266
Rott site, 250, 260
Rotwein, 266
Roxheim, 205
Rüdesheim (Nahe region), 205
Rüdesheim (Rheingau region), 211, 213
Rüdesheimer Berg, 214
Ruländer, 34–35, 52, 60, 128, 137
Rümmelsheim, 206
Ruppertsberg, 132
Ruwer valley, 149, 150, 155–56

Saale River, 232
Saarburg, 154
Saar-Ruwer area, 262
Saar valley, 149, 150, 152, 153–55
St. Boniface, 92, 112
St. Cyriacus, 117–18, 130
St. Gallus, 112, 114
St. Goar, 240
St. Goarshausen, 240
St. Killian, 112, 117
St. Laurent, 43, 186
St. Lawrence, 118
St. Martin, 118–19
St. Martin (village), 129

St. Nazarius, 113, 114-15
St. Nikolauswein, 70, 71
St. Rochus, 118
St. Urban, 116, 213
St. Vitus, 116-17
Samtrot, 43-44, 191, 196
Sasbach, 175
Sassbachwalden, 181
Sauser (young wine), 77
Scheu, Georg, 55
Scheurebe, 52, 137, 223
Schillerwein, 191, 266
Schliengen, 172
Schlossberg site in Achkarren, 175, 258
Schlossböckelheim, 204, 262
Schnait, 197
Schönberg, 249, 250
Schönburger, 58
Schoonmaker, Frank, 210
Schriesheim, 186
Schutterlindenberg site, 177
Schwabsburg, 143
Schwaigern, 198
Schwarze Katz, 153, 160
Schwarzriesling, 43
Schweinfurt, 227-28
Seals, quality, 81
Seeweine ("lake wines"), 168
Sekt, 41, 42, 155, 218
Selz River, 136, 145, 148
Septimer, 55
Serrig, 155
Siegerrebe, 53-54, 58
Silvaner, 27, 37-39, 128, 137; crossbreeds
  of, 50, 51, 52, 54, 56, 57, 59
Singen, 169-70
Sinzheim, 179, 182
Site(s): definition of, 23, 257; names of,
  101, 119, 158, 159, 257-62, 265; redivi-
  sion and reallocation of, 64-65; viticul-
  ture and, 22-23
Soil: of Germany, 17; humidity of, 21;
  loosening, 62-63; viticulture and, 23-26
Sommerach, 228
Sommerau, 156
Sommerhausen, 229
Spätburgunder, Blauer, 43-46, 49, 138,
  145, 214-15, 247; crossbreeds of, 58, 59,
  60
Spätlese, 70, 80, 218; meaning of, 68
Speyer, 93, 134; museum at, 88, 134-35
Starkenburg area, 262
State Domains, 49, 81, 107, 210-11; of
  Baden, 167-68, 169; of Franconia, 226-
  27, 230-31; of Rheingau, 210
Staufen, 172
Steeg, 239
Steigerwald, 227, 262
Steinbach, 182

Steinberg site in Eberbach, 216
Steinwein, 230
Sterilization of bottles and casks, 78-79
Stetten, 197, 232
Storage of wine: bottle, 79-80; cask, 79; at
  home, 82
Strausswirtschaften, 102
Strumpfelbach, 197
Stuttgart, 189, 194
Südliche Weinstrasse area, 262
Sugaring, 72-73, 256
Sulfurization, 68, 79, 263
Sulm valley, 195-96
Sulzfeld, 229
Swabians, 199-200
"Swabian wine route," 192-93
Sweetness of wine, 73
Sylvaner. See Silvaner

Table Wine, 75, 253, 264-65
Tauber valley, 184-85, 192, 199
Temperature: of air, for viticulture, 19-
  20; of wine, 82
Testing and quality control, 254-55, 268
Thüngersheim, 231
Traben, 160
Training vines, 61-62, 150, 238, 245
Traminer, 32-34, 128, 137
Trarbach, 160
Trier, 86, 87, 90, 95, 155
Trittenheim, 156
Trockenbeerenauslese, 69, 70, 80, 209,
  218, 253
Trollinger, 46-47, 48, 57, 60

Umlegung, 64
Umstadt, 262
Uugstein, 133
Unkel, 241
Upper Rhine valley, 29, 86, 105
Ürzig, 159

Vaihingen, 197
Valwig, 163
Varnhalt, 182
Varro, 84
Veitshöchheim, 231; State Viticultural
  Institute at, 52, 53, 58-59, 226-27
Verbessern, 72
Vine(s): bending, 62; blights, 107;
  crossbreeds, 49-60; derivation of word,
  98-99; flowering of, 65-66; fungus diseases, 63; grafted, 108; mildew, 107;
  protecting, 63, 66; pruning, 62; ranking
  of, 28; red wine varieties of, 42-49;
  spraying, 63-64; training, 61-62, 150;
  varieties of, in Germany, 27; white wine
  varieties of, 28-42
Vineyard, definition of. 23

Vintage years, 72, 266
Vintner, meaning of, 99
Vinum, 83–84, 97
Virgin Mary, 118, 123–24
Viticulture in Germany: climate and, 19–23; history of, 83–108; sites and, 22–23; soil and, 23–26
Volkach, 228
Vollrads Castle, 211, 217

Wachenheim, 133, 259
Wachstrum, 267
Waldböckelheim, 205–6
Waldrach, 156
Waldulm, 181
Walporzheim, 246, 257, 261
Wasenweiler, 175
Wasserlos, 223, 234
Wawern, 154
Wehlen, 159
Weikersheim, 199
Weinheim, 186
Weinsberg, 196; State Teaching and Research Institute, 43, 57, 60, 189, 196
Weinsheim, 205
Weinstrasse (Baden), 177–78
Weinstrasse (Rhenish Palatinate), 126, 128–32
Weissburgunder, 35–36, 51, 54, 75
Weissherbst, 45–46, 47, 49, 266
Weisswein, 266
Welschriesling, 30–31
Wertheim, 185, 232
Westhofen, 147–48
White Burgundy, 35–36
White Riesling, 28, 30. *See also* Riesling
White wine, 28–42; Auxerrois, 36; crossbreeds, 50–59; Elbling, 40–42;

Gutedel, 39–40; Muskateller, 36–37; Muskat Ottonel, 37; Räuschling, 40–42; Riesling, 28–30; Ruländer, 34–35; Silvaner, 37–39; storage of, 82; Traminer, 32–34; Weissburgunder, 35–36
Wiesloch, 183, 185
Wiltingen, 154
Windesheim, 206
"Wine Isle," 228
"Wine Loop," 228
Winepress, 75–76; Biblical references to, 111, 120–23; history of, 97–98
Winkel, 213
Winningen, 164
Wintrich, 99, 101, 157
Winzenheim, 205
Winzer, meaning of, 99–100
Wolfenweiler, 173
Wonnegau area, 136, 147–48, 262
Worms, 93, 138, 139–40
Württemberg region, 188–200; areas of, 262; Baden and, 165–66; climate of, 188; Lemberger of, 190; Müllerrebe of, 191; size of, 188; soils of, 188; subregions of, 192; Trollinger of, 190; wines of, 190–92
Württembergisches Unterland area, 262
Würzburg, 223, 225, 229–31; State Viticultural Institute at, 52, 53, 58–59, 226
Würzer, 55

Zabergäu, 192, 198–99
Zell, 160, 262
Zellertal, 127, 134
Zeltingen-Rachtig, 159
Zwingenberg, 249

Date Due